About the Authors

IAN MCDERMOTT is a leading trainer, consultant and author in the field of NLP and coaching. He is the Director of Training for International Teaching Seminars, the premier NLP training and coaching organisation in Europe, and has trained thousands of people over the last fifteen years using the NLP techniques outlined in this book. As a consultant, he works with many FTSE-100 and Fortune 500 companies, including Coca-Cola, Cable & Wireless and IBM, as well as organisations in the public sector and the BBC. He is the co-author of ten books on NLP, and his books have been translated into fifteen languages.

WENDY JAGO is a practising consultant, coach and therapist. She has a Diploma in Hypnosis and Psychotherapy and is a Master Practitioner of NLP. In addition to her busy private practice, she has been involved in a wide range of professional training courses, holding posts as Course Director for the UK College of Hypnotherapy and Counselling and, more recently, for the Tisserand Institute of Holistic Aromatherapy.

THE NLP COACH

THE

NLP

COACH

A COMPREHENSIVE GUIDE TO PERSONAL
WELL-BEING & PROFESSIONAL SUCCESS

IAN McDERMOTT
& WENDY JAGO

PIATKUS

Copyright © 2001 by Ian McDermott and Wendy Jago

First published in 2001 by
Piatkus Books Limited
5 Windmill Street
London W1T 2JA
e-mail: info@piatkus.co.uk

This paperback edition published in 2002

Reprinted in 2002 (twice), 2003 (twice), 2004, 2005, 2006 (twice)

The moral right of the authors has been asserted

A catalogue record for this book is available from the British Library

ISBN 0 7499 2186 2 (hbk)
ISBN 0 7499 2277 X (pbk)

Text design Paul Saunders
Edited by Barbara Kiser

This book has been printed on paper manufactured with respect for the environment using wood from managed sustainable resources

Data manipulation by
Action Publishing Technology Ltd, Gloucester
Printed and bound in Great Britain by
MPG Books, Bodmin, Cornwall

Dedication

To all those who have dared to dream,
Those who always knew there was more
And to those who just had the courage to start,
We want to say 'Go on!...Go on!'

And here are the tools to support you on your journey.

Contents

Acknowledgements

WE WOULD LIKE to acknowledge the originators of NLP, Richard Bandler and John Grinder and the community of developers who have contributed so much to the field which today is known worldwide as NLP. Equally we want to salute all those who have fostered the evolution of what today has become recognised as coaching. We wish to pay special tribute to Timothy Gallwey for his seminal contribution. Without Tim coaching would be a very different enterprise. Equally we want to acknowledge Laura Whitworth for her leadership and commitment to getting coaching out there – and for playing a Bigger Game.

Special thanks to our friend and colleague Jan Elfline with whom we have spent so many rewarding hours exploring and developing the relationship of NLP and coaching.

Thanks finally to Gill Bailey at Piatkus for pursuing this project and for her wise editorial feedback, and to all the editorial team who have so enhanced what you are about to read.

Introduction

THE NLP COACH is a practical book that you can use as an inspiration and step-by-step guide to achieving success in all areas of your life. It explains how the body of information and techniques known as Neuro-Linguistic Programming or NLP, along with the skills of coaching, can come together to give you clear and effective ways to achieve excellence in everything you do.

You may have specific goals in mind, or you may be looking to broaden your own repertoire of life skills. This book sets out to offer you support in achieving both through NLP. There are already many excellent books available on NLP itself, but this book is different because it links NLP for the first time to the skills of coaching, and shows you how dynamic this combination can be in your own life.

Though you could think of NLP as a body of tools, and coaching as the framework of support that leads you towards your chosen goals, in truth both NLP and coaching work because they offer you practical approaches which are focused on achievement and able to deliver it through specific techniques.

We first met each other on a professional workshop in the mid-1980s, when we were paired up to do a training exercise together. At that time Ian was setting up International Teaching Seminars (ITS), and Wendy was building up her practice as a therapist. By then we had both encountered NLP and recognised how much it could help people make sense of their lives and take them forward.

Since that first meeting, Ian has become internationally known as an NLP trainer, coach, consultant and author, and Wendy has helped hundreds of individuals through her work as a therapist, coach and trainer. When it came to taking her training in NLP, Wendy naturally turned to ITS, and our writing partnership grew from this renewed acquaintanceship some years later.

When we use the word 'we' in this book, we are mostly talking about ourselves as NLP coaches and as authors of this book. For clarity and directness, we will often use the word 'you', as in 'When you notice…' or 'When you want to…'. However, we want to emphasise that NLP is part of the fabric of our daily lives, and we've found the approaches and tools it offers invaluable.

▪ *What Can* The NLP Coach *Do for You?*

This is the first book to bring together the best of both NLP and coaching. It sets out to offer support in achieving your specific goals and in managing key aspects of your life far more effectively.

You may wonder whether reading a book can work as well as having a coach. We believe that using a book as a guide in this way can be a dynamic and interactive experience, and we hope that as you read through this one you will find yourself having productive internal conversations with yourself. Often, we will prompt these kinds of conversations by asking you questions that get you thinking, just as a coach would. Or we may suggest that you examine some incident from your own experience. As with person-to-person coaching, we periodically ask that you give yourself time to consider what your aims are right now, at this or that place in the book. When you know what you want, you can organise yourself – consciously and unconsciously – towards that end. So as you read, you'll be able to adapt what you find in the book to your situation, needs and aims.

The NLP Coach is divided into five parts. Part One explains about NLP and coaching in more detail. Part Two goes over the essential NLP tools you will need to help you achieve your goals. You'll find as you read that we frequently refer to these tools and show how you can use them for particular situations and outcomes, so you'll get more and more familiar with them as you go on. Part Three looks at what success and failure can mean – and how it can help you if you become curious about what you do rather than judging it in a black-and-white, good-and-bad way. Part Four looks at the five dimensions of success which are crucial to achieving your goals. Finally, Part Five concentrates on the key areas of your life and will help you to:

- Improve your self-esteem

- Build good relationships

- Maximise your brain power

- Achieve health, wealth and happiness

- Make work rewarding

- Become more spiritually alive.

Once you've mastered the NLP tools and coaching techniques, you can continue to apply them to all aspects of your life whenever you need them. We've found that as person-to-person coaching progresses, people begin to ask themselves the kinds of questions their coach would ask them – and find the answers. Coaching, in other words, can teach you how to coach yourself. And we believe that you'll find the same thing happening as you read this book. This is one reason why we sometimes leave an example 'hanging', or suggest a few NLP tools rather than making an exhaustive list. In our experience, the habit of asking 'and what else?' is one which grows through coaching, and it stretches you and continually demonstrates that there is even more to you than you'd previously believed. We hope and believe that as you read this book you'll come to enjoy being your own coach.

 **1**

Coaching and NLP

Introduction

THINKING, FEELING and behaving are all organised through your brain. NLP gives you the tools to understand, at a practical level, how you create your experience, and communicate with yourself and others.

As human beings, we are creatures of habit in what we think, what we feel and what we do. Some habits are really useful, while others can be ineffective, limiting or even undermining. With the help of NLP you can understand your own individual patterns, how they have been formed by your past history, how they affect you now, and how they can affect your future. More than this, NLP gives you the tools to change or fine-tune your patterns so that they dovetail with what's important to you and what you want.

Because it offers this kind of understanding, NLP has already proved itself a powerful tool for personal development and communication in all kinds of fields. It will enable you to build 'models' of excellence to enhance your own life. It will enable you to achieve your goals quickly and effectively. You can apply what you learn at work and at home. Understanding and using NLP will help you to become clear about what you really want; achieve your goals; find new ways to solve problems; acquire the skills you admire in others; use your time more effectively; develop your sense of purpose; be clear about your values and align your actions to them; discover how your beliefs can help – or limit – you, and make any changes you need; overcome the effects of negative experiences; and feel confident in whatever you attempt to do.

Where does coaching come into this process, though? Coaches work individually with their coachees, often on the telephone. A coach can help you formulate clear and achievable goals and work out what steps are needed to achieve them, identify internal and external resources that will help in the process, and keep on track and do what's necessary in order to make steady progress. Coaching gives you a clear and structured format, but it doesn't involve being told what to do or how to do it: it shows you that you actually have the answers to the questions what and how, even though you may have thought you didn't.

CHAPTER 1

What is NLP?

NEURO-LINGUISTIC PROGRAMMING is the study of human excellence, and it makes available a body of knowledge about *how* human beings go about making sense of their experience and interacting with others.

It all began back in the 1970s, when Richard Bandler, then a student of mathematics at the University of California, Santa Cruz (UCSC), began studying the work of the Gestalt therapist Fritz Perls. John Grinder, a professor of linguistics at UCSC, became fascinated by the linguistic patterns Bandler was replicating. Together, they started to question and then make explicit how several outstanding therapeutic communicators – first Fritz Perls, then Virginia Satir and Milton Erickson – succeeded in helping their clients make dramatic changes in their lives.

So began the pursuit of excellence that is the hallmark of NLP. From very early on Bandler and Grinder worked with an informal group of students and colleagues, some of whom became co-developers of NLP in their own right involved in the development of NLP. Among these were Robert Dilts, Judith DeLozier, Leslie Cameron-Bandler, David Gordon and Stephen Gillighan, all well-known names in the field of NLP and each a significant contributor and published author. The answers to their searching questions formed the basis of NLP. From the outset, their work was collaborative and hands-on, and NLP has remained this way ever since.

It's usual in many fields of endeavour to try to understand excellence by getting practitioners to talk about their theories: what the basis for their work is, why and how they think they achieve what they do. And depending on their individual experience and training – whether they are therapists or golfers – their answers often actually tell us more about their beliefs and theories than about what they actually do.

The developers of NLP asked different kinds of questions. They were interested in what actually took place when excellence was achieved – when therapy really worked and clients overcame their problems – both externally, in observable behaviour, and internally, in what and how the client thought and felt. They sought to get results, not just theorise. They wanted to know what actually worked. And they were led by their curiosity – 'fascination' might be a better word. Because the more they noticed and the more questions they asked, the more they began to understand what was actually happening, and the more evident it became that excellence (in this case, therapeutic effectiveness) had clear structures. As they began to elicit the structures, they began to teach them. Many of the early books on NLP published in the 1970s and 1980s convey the liveliness and excitement of these early beginnings. Published by Real People Press, their titles – *Frogs into Princes* (1979), *Transformations* (1981), *Reframing* (1982) – reflect their sense of wonder at the discovery of fundamental patterns in human thought and behaviour, and the excitement of being able to use this knowledge to develop powerful techniques to help people improve their lives.

But NLP is more than its specific techniques: it's also a body of knowledge and a way of looking at things, an attitude. It's based on how people actually think and behave, rather than theories about why they do what they do. So it's grounded in reality, not speculation. And because of this, the tools that NLP offers us are grounded in reality, too: they are based on what works, so they deliver what works.

From the beginning, NLP involved action: action between people and action within people. Coaching is the same: it's a process of joint engagement between coach and coachee, working together to achieve the coachee's goals. NLP and coaching both start from the belief that you can know what you want, and that it is possible – given the right way of going about it and the right resources – for you to achieve it. And it's the job of an NLP coach to help you find the resources you need and go about working towards your goals in a way that will give you the best chance of achieving them.

One of the guiding principles of NLP is that 'reality' is not something 'out there', but something that individual people actually, actively, personally construct in their own minds, and that it is shaped according to the way they process their experience. The same events literally mean different things to different people. Once we learn to see our own experience and that of other people in this way, it follows that we also know we have choices. And NLP in action offers each and every one of us more choice – be it to have better ways of relating, start a more suitable career or just live with more joy.

Can everyone really benefit from NLP? That is our experience. NLP is not the preserve of experts, offering its 'interpretations' and 'guidance' from a position of superiority. One of the delights of training and working with NLP is that it offers fresh insights, and fresh approaches, however much you know and however long you have worked with it. NLP is not a professional coat you put on when you are working, but a way of understanding and behaving that is integrated into thought and action precisely because it was derived from thought and action. That's what makes it easy to use.

▪ *Using NLP to Make Sense of the World*

The fact that we all make our own reality is one of the most fundamental discoveries made by the early developers of NLP. At one time or another, most of us have been surprised to find that our clear memory of an event was quite different from someone else's, that we had noticed different things, or reached different conclusions. Sometimes this can be amusing; sometimes we are lucky enough to gain a richer idea of the event through pooling our memories; sometimes, as in the case of arguments or court cases, the discrepancies can be disturbing. When we have been coaching couples or work colleagues, it has often seemed to us as if they are talking about quite different events! Evidently, each person has a 'truth' in which they confidently believe. How can this be?

NLP offers us some important clues to the process that underlies the formation of differing 'truths'. People have different ways of selecting and recording information that often operate quite unconsciously. The brain has ways of sorting and patterning information that differ markedly between individuals, and which can therefore easily lead to misunderstandings or mismatches.

For instance, our five senses deliver information to us about the external world (seeing, hearing, feeling, taste and smell), but we also use them to process that information. We literally re-present information to ourselves internally. For this reason in NLP we talk about Representational Systems. For reasons which are as yet little understood, individual people tend to favour some senses (usually one or two) more than the others in this internal re-presenting, though all of us can use all of the senses if we choose.

Anyone who really develops one representational system can seem pretty remarkable. This may even be a facet of genius. However, there are also some more immediate benefits. When you know what you do easily and well you can play to your strengths and get unexpected benefits. With representational systems, everyone has their favourites.

> Jeremy, one of our clients, was very adept auditorily. He loved music but he needed to learn to relax to bring down his high blood pressure. After some experimentation he found that listening to music in his head was one very effective way of creating an internal calm. With some practice, he found that he was not only able to 'play' whole stretches of music in his head, but that he could choose to follow either a particular conductor's recording of it or the part played by a single instrument. This did not strike him as particularly unusual – it was just something he could do 'naturally'. But this ability turned out to be very useful for him, because when he regularly played music to himself in his head he became more relaxed. After some weeks of regularly doing this, his blood pressure dropped to a normal level, which he was able to maintain provided he continued playing the music.

Once you know that the 'same' event is likely to be experienced through different sorting mechanisms with different sensory emphasis, you can more readily understand how people's realities differ.

> Mary and Rene went to the same team meeting at work. The meeting focused on plans for the coming year, and involved some heated debate over a particular set of proposals. Afterwards, Mary was really depressed. 'It was the same old issues, and the same old arguments,' she said. 'Another year has gone by and I can't see any differences. It's just the same as it ever was.' 'I didn't think that at all,' said Rene. 'I was quite encouraged, actually. I felt Sam had begun to shift ground, and that he was starting to take up a less intransigent position at last.' So

what was going on here? Clearly, Mary and Rene had both heard the same words. But the filters they were using internally were giving them quite opposite results. Mary was filtering visually ('see any differences'). In addition she was naturally tending to look for similarities between this meeting and past ones ('just the same as it ever was'). This is a particular meta programme. Rene, on the other hand, was filtering kinesthetically ('felt', 'begun to shift ground', 'less intransigent'). She was also running a different meta programme because she tended to look for differences between this meeting and past ones ('begun' and 'less intransigent position' at last). While both would need further evidence to determine whether their impression was going to be borne out in future, the filtering systems they were using in terms of their representational system and meta programme sorting gave them fundamentally different impressions of the same events.

In identifying these differences, NLP offers us not only a richer understanding of events, but also a greater potential range of ways of interacting, both with ourselves and others. This book will show you how you can literally learn to 'see things differently', 'get in touch with' someone else in a new way, 'hear' them properly for the first time, 'get a flavour of' a new experience or 'smell the sweet smell of success'.

You can also develop your ability to use the range of sensory processing to enrich and test out your imagined goals and make them more dynamic and compelling. NLP has demonstrated that people who achieve what they want tend to imagine their goals in very strong, vivid, lively ways, often using several representational systems. They may have clear, bright images of how it will be in their desired future; feel what it will be like then; hear words of praise – and so on. We'll show you how to use these and other NLP skills to load your future wishes for success. See page 33 for more on Compelling Futures.

Modelling

> **Once something can be described, it can be taught and learnt.**

The pioneers of NLP called this process of establishing exactly *how* someone did something **modelling.** The more we know about the person who demonstrates the kind of excellence we want to emulate, the easier it becomes to follow their way of working. In one sense, people have always known this: it's the basis of 'natural' and deliberate learning in the home, as children learn to imitate their parents, as well as of formal learning in later life – the detailed, highly structured breakdown of performance tasks involved in many nationally standardised skill-learning schemes.

NLP's contribution here is twofold: it gives us a way of understanding what is going on and how modelling contributes to learning; and, perhaps even more importantly, it shows you how you can incorporate others' effective interpersonal strategies into your own life.

Here's what we mean. It's fairly obvious that if you want to learn a physical skill – building a house, playing tennis, driving a car – you need to learn and practise the basic elements of that skill, and follow certain recognised steps in understanding and developing it. NLP coaching can offer valuable help in these areas – but the same principles apply to interpersonal skills such as building good personal or work relationships, or mental skills like enhancing memory or recovering from emotional setbacks. NLP shows us that it isn't simply an accident, or good luck, that some people can do these things while others may find it difficult or even impossible. If you want to improve your skill in a mental or emotional area, modelling an excellent practitioner is a wonderful NLP tool.

In order to model someone's skill, you have to know exactly how they go about it. This involves not just observing what they do and when, but also finding out about their attitude to what they do; what they believe about it; what they think as they are doing it; what they say to themselves before, during and after they do it – and how they cope with problems and mistakes. Modelling involves close observation and close questioning, and it also involves sieving all the information gained to find out what is most crucial – what NLP calls 'the difference that makes the difference'. See page 60 for more information on modelling. The models we need are available: either out there or inside ourselves.

We can usually find a model for practically all the skills we might need. If something can be done well, we can learn it, provided we get enough detailed information about how it is done and are prepared to practise it ourselves. Obviously, there are some constraints: our levels of capacity in different areas are affected by physical and mental ability, age and other circumstances. But that still leaves a quite realistic amount of scope for each of us to improve in the areas that matter to us.

NLP also shows us that we can model our own areas of excellence by closely analysing how we do the things we do really well. This can help ensure that we continue to excel in this field. If we model something at which we're less adept, we can begin to find out where we go wrong and what needs to change.

Some very exciting discoveries have come about through self-modelling. F.M. Alexander's detailed understanding of posture, movement and correcting postural problems – now known as the Alexander technique – arose from his grappling with major physical problems that nearly wrecked his career as a speaker. Moshe Feldenkrais also faced a personal health crisis, and through detailed observation of how he used his own body he found ways of identifying tensions and lack of symmetry in movement which he developed into a system of body work now known as the Feldenkrais method. The innovative American sports coach Timothy Gallwey, author of *The Inner Game of Tennis* and *The Inner Game of Golf*, reflected in detail on his own teaching style and discovered that his pupils achieved more when he asked them to pay attention to their own experience, and became more anxious and inhibited – and achieved less – when he 'taught' them more directly.

Feldenkrais and Alexander showed a marked ability to observe and reflect upon the meaning of their own experience – a highly effective blend of curiosity and non-judgemental awareness. Their discoveries, and Gallwey's, arose out of this attitude and way of working. Later in this book we show how you can develop your self-awareness, and learn to step outside the familiar framework of success/failure judgements, to find out exactly what needs changing in your life to make it more satisfying and to help you achieve your personal goals at work and at home.

We can, and should, all self-model. If you always get your reports done by the deadline, or maintain lifelong friendships, why not find out exactly how you do it? If your bank balance is always healthy and you have savings to spare, if you find learning easy and can remember what you learned, why not identify the skills that make this possible?

And there are added bonuses. In many cases, what works in one aspect of life can be transferred into other areas. For example, if you have developed strategies for getting a report done on time, you may also be able to use them, with some adjustments, to help you achieve a career path that meets your needs and ambitions in life. Both these skills demand the ability to relate current behaviour to a longer-term goal, and to pace what you do through a defined time period. Or you might have the ability to maintain relationships. If you can model how you do this, you could learn to help others do the same – or, less obviously, learn how to build a healthy relationship with money, as the section on becoming healthy, wealthy and wise (page 259) explores more fully. Once we focus on the process, it becomes easier to see possible applications which might previously have seemed unrelated.

Self-modelling the problems we find ourselves repeating can be as rewarding. This process allows us to find the critical variables and sequences which lead with seeming inevitability to another inadequacy, another crisis, another disaster. In Chapter 4 we show how failures tend to repeat – because they have a structure. It's not an accident that someone is almost always late for an appointment or never meets their deadlines; or, more seriously, has had several failed marriages. Any event that repeats must involve some repeated processes or sequences, and self-modelling can help unearth them. Once we ask, and find the specific answers to, the question 'Why did this happen again?' we provide ourselves with a recipe which we can modify or choose not to use. It's an exercise that can truly empower us.

> **NLP is concerned with structure rather than content, and is non-judgemental.**

When a friend describes some crisis they are going through, or a colleague tells us about some incident of office politics, the 'story' element catches our interest. Often, though, when we get hooked on the story we fail to notice the underlying structure. Your friend keeps having horrible relationships and tells you about how awful the most recent one was. Look a little deeper and you'll start to get curious about the structure of this process – there's a pattern here and it keeps repeating. No heroes, no villains, no judgement. Just a pattern that's not working.

Clearly, some processes just aren't working, or are working less well than people had hoped. But why? When you look at the processes, staying in a curiosity frame rather than a blame frame, you learn more, and you avoid contaminating the situation further by adding judgement.

Delivering More by Letting go of Judgement

We've already encountered Timothy Gallwey in this book. One of the most influential sports coaches ever, Gallwey came to some of the same conclusions as the pioneers of NLP, working at the same time as them yet quite independently. He recognised that *even praise can be detrimental* to the development of our full potential, because when people seek praise, or feel good because they have been praised, they want to continue to do well and often try too hard or become cautious and stop experimenting.

The readiness to experiment is a key factor in success, because this can lead you to discovering a range of successful behaviours, or solutions to problems, rather than just one. Similarly, the early developers of NLP found that in any situation, the person with the most flexible behaviour had the most influence. The amount of flexibility you have relates direct-ly to your ability and willingness to try different, perhaps novel or untested, responses and strategies.

NLP coaching offers you ways of learning, growing and changing that are skill-based and feel safer because when something doesn't work, you gain guidance for future action by looking at how it didn't work. NLP pre-supposes that failure is a form of feedback – and therefore can be valuable information. We explore this more fully in Chapters 4 and 5, when we show you how you can use the information your 'failures' give you as pre-cise recipes for turning things around. If you know exactly how something didn't work, you have also discovered important information about just what needs changing, whether it's a belief you hold, an old strategy you are still in the habit of using (though it's long past the time for updating), or a lack of flexibility in talking other people's language.

▪ *Summary*

NLP offers you a particular way of understanding how you and others function mentally and behaviourally, which means you can start to make easy and lasting change in your personal and professional life. Chapter 3 will show you how to use a number of important NLP techniques that have been proven to work with just about everybody. But before we go into the NLP tools in detail, we'll be taking a look at what coaching involves and how it can improve the quality and effectiveness of your life.

The NLP Way to Coach

DURING THE 1990S COACHING became a business buzzword. It started to emerge as a structured way of helping individuals take their lives forward. Coaching began to be seen as something distinct from teaching, training, counselling and therapy.

We all know about sports coaching. Here, passing on specific techniques and designing and overseeing the athlete's training schedule are what is usually emphasised. Much sports coaching is amateur, and can be a bewildering mixture of encouragement, exhortation and instructions. Nonetheless, the special quality of a personalised helping relationship is there. The British runner Sebastian Coe and his father even managed to maintain a coachee/coach relationship that was quite distinct from their roles as son and father. And we've seen how innovative Gallwey's approach was. Most important recent developments have occurred in executive coaching and life coaching rather than in the sports arena. And we'd say that the key features of any good coaching are that it is:

► **Personal** Coaching involves a relationship between you and your coach that's tailored to your needs and aims. (One outstanding coach often tells her coachees that they will need to teach *her* how to become the right coach for *them*.)

► **Goal-focused** You determine the goals of the coaching. The role of the coach is to help you formulate goals in such a way that they have every chance of being achieved, and to help you stay focused in working towards those goals.

▶ **Facilitative** The coach's role is a supportive one, helping you in the processes involved in working towards your goals.

By contrast, coaching is *not*:

▶ **Remedial or therapeutic in intent** Coaching is not primarily aimed at exploring past events or issues, or uncovering motivation or psychological processes, and the coach will not as a rule offer interpretations or seek to develop a transferential relationship as a psychotherapist might.

▶ **Instructional** A coach will not teach you specific skills or give you piles of information.

This book will coach you in how to use NLP techniques to improve your relationships, career, health and much more. This kind of coaching involves:

1. **A personal relationship between coach and coachee** Though we are not face to face with each other, you can still enjoy and benefit from a coaching relationship by reading this book. Indeed, much of our work as coaches is done on the telephone anyway, and on occasion via e-mail. The relationship between us, the authors, and you, the reader, as in all good NLP work, is collaborative. It is a working alliance aimed at helping *you* achieve what *you* want, so you can make it more personal by focusing on what matters to you.

2. **Being attentive** This means that you take yourself, your aims, your experience and your unconscious resourcefulness seriously. For some people this may mean setting aside regular slots of time; for others, it may mean that the time you do give yourself is quality time, in which you can give yourself your best attention without urgency or distraction. Being attentive for us means that we have thought carefully about what ideas, processes and strategies you might find helpful, and how to present them in a way that is readable and user-friendly.

3. **A facilitative way of working** We take seriously whatever it is that you want to achieve, even though we can't know what it is. Coaching helps you explore yourself, to find out how you go about things, to discover

your strengths and how to work on your limitations. NLP does exactly the same.

Here are some of the key characteristics which NLP and coaching share, and which come together in a collaborative NLP coaching relationship. Both are:

▶ **Outcome-focused** A very important question to ask yourself is 'What do you want?' Having identified that, your NLP coach – this book – will help you formulate your goals in ways that give you the best chance of achieving them.

▶ **Customised to your needs and your aims** Because NLP and coaching focus on the unique individual, the help they offer relates specifically to you: NLP tools and coaching strategies are all adaptable to your needs and your way of working.

▶ **Non-judgemental** This means it operates outside a blame/reward structure or a success/failure pattern (we go into this more fully in Part 3). Even when your way of thinking or behaving is less effective than you'd like, it isn't *wrong*. Virtually all mental and interpersonal strategies work in some situations – and less well in others. The art of NLP and coaching is to help you become more aware of what those are, so that you have more choice and can become effective more of the time.

▶ **Supportive** They encourage you rather than telling you what to do or how to do it. There are no 'oughts' in NLP or coaching, though there are plenty of skills and strategies. Experimenting with them, and monitoring what works for you, is a habit NLP coaches encourage, and one which develops your confidence and your independence in managing your life.

▶ **Based on the assumption that you have all the resources you need** We mean here the resources for achieving your goals. It's also vital that these can be accessed even though you may not yet know what they are or how to access them. NLP and coaching honour the individual. This isn't just a nice idea – it's based on modelling what works in practice. In many disciplines outstanding helpers respect the resourcefulness of those they work with and get far better results than others. Our experience as NLP coaches makes us pretty confident that as you use these tools and strategies, you'll surprise yourself with your own resourcefulness.

In addition, NLP and coaching both:

▶ **Keep you to your own agenda** This helps you keep your goals freshly in mind and draw your attention to wanderings or a loss of focus. You are in the driver's seat – and that means power and responsibility. NLP and coaching help keep you attentive to your own aims and ensure that you monitor how you are doing in relation to them. The aims, the agenda, and the pace of work in relation to them, are yours to determine.

▶ **Work in a curiosity frame** When we ask questions we get more information, and this gives us more to work with. The key questions to ask are ones which provide detail you can use. They provide a level of detail about internal and external events which allows you to find what needs to change – or stay the same – and where you can make the most effective interventions.

▶ **Help break down larger, longer-term goals into smaller, shorter-term achievable steps** Often, you can have a clear goal in your mind and not know how to begin working towards it; or you may be overwhelmed and even despondent at how far away the goal seems from where you are now. By breaking down the overall goal into its component steps, NLP coaching gives you practical, do-able ways of working towards it – and a series of successful experiences on the way that increase your motivation and sense of empowerment.

▶ **Increase your awareness of what is happening here-and-now** You'll also be more aware of how this contributes to the maintenance or change of ongoing patterns or the development of new ones. Greater awareness gives you access to more information that is potentially available to you, and that may be key to the structure of your difficulties or your successes.

▶ **Assume that change can be cumulative** This is a very important assumption, because it allows you to discover how big changes or achievements can actually be made through small actions, one step at a time. Yes, sometimes change can be big and dramatic, but often you may just want to make those changes bit by bit. NLP coaching helps you discover the specific ways that work for you.

▶ **Assume that everyone can engage in lifelong learning, provided they want to** The more you know about how you work, the more you can choose to do more of what works for you, and the more you learn about how to change what doesn't. Chapter 14 looks at learning more closely.

► **Work with processes and structure, not content** We respect the importance of your content to you, however. If you want to make changes, you need to do it at the level which drives the experience – and that's the level of process. If you want to succeed here you need to know the structures that hold these processes in place.

Why isn't it necessary for coaches to know more than, or even as much as, you about the area of content in which you are working? A coach has expertise in the process of defining and working toward goals, but not necessarily in the specific area of content you are concerned about. In fact, it can often help coaching to stay focused if we *don't* know too much. Where you need more information, it will become evident through the process of coaching itself, and you will be helped to identify what needs to be done to gain it. In this way, in contrast to the 'command and control' model of learning or support, the process of coaching also helps you become more resourceful and independent. It is our hope and our intention that this is how you will feel after reading this book.

There are two ways in which learning to coach yourself happens. The first, more obvious one is that we explain particular NLP coaching tools and ways in which they can be applied in specific areas of your life. But you'll also find that the more you engage with these processes as you read about them, the more familiar the approaches, questions and assumptions become – and so you learn them indirectly.

This is just how coaching works when it is face-to-face. A coach will ask you to look at certain processes or explore particular issues. This focuses your attention in certain ways and on certain areas. But over weeks and months, you find yourself starting to look at those processes or issues for yourself, and to ask yourself the kinds of questions a coach would ask you.

You become used to your coach being curious about you rather than making judgements about you – and begin to be curious rather than judgemental yourself. And it's our intention and our hope that as you read this book you will find the same things happening to you.

 **2**

NLP Coaching Tools

Introduction

WHETHER WE ARE COACHING ourselves or others, having the right tool for the job makes all the difference. As with any practical tool-kit, coaching works best if the coach can draw upon different tooks for different needs, and for each and every stage of the task in hand.

The same is true if you're coaching yourself. Once you've identified what it is you want to achieve, there are often many possible approaches. NLP suggests that in any situation the person with the most flexibility has the most influence, and that's true whether your task involves influencing someone else or helping yourself. Knowing what each tool is, and what it can do for you, is an excellent first step to becoming more effective. And a familiarity with your took-kit, above all, gives you *leverage*. It allows you to achieve most with least effort. There's a phrase that NLP and coaching have in common: *less is more*. This is why it's really useful to know your way around your tool-kit before you begin. You want to achieve the most you can in the most economical and effective way.

And that's where NLP comes in. NLP provides you with detailed descriptions of how people do what they do. It shows you how you make meaning out of your experience in your mind and then think of this as 'reality' – which for you, it is. It then gives you ways to understand more clearly the patterns that are involved in communicating with other people, so that you gain greater ability to work effectively with them. It's a great tool-kit for whatever you want to achieve.

CHAPTER 3

Tools for the Job

NLP CAN HELP YOU become more effective in many areas of your life. You might be excellent at your job, yet so anxious during interviews that you have avoided even applying for promotion. Or perhaps your partner or children complain that you 'just don't understand' them. Or maybe you have begun to realise that you have a pattern of weekend colds, or migraines when you have a deadline to meet. With NLP tools or techniques you can achieve specific results, and in this section we will describe the range of core NLP tools and how to apply them.

Think of this chapter as us showing you round the NLP workshop: the tour will give you a broad overview of NLP practice, along with simple introductions to many of the tools that we have found the most useful in our work as coaches. As you read through the rest of the book, you'll find suggestions of how particular tools can be used in specific situations. Then, if you want to know more, there's a Resources section at the end of the book which lists books and training courses that can help you explore further.

For each tool, we give the following information:

1. What it is.

2. What it does.

3. Some everyday examples of it in use.

4. Situations which could prompt you to use it.

5. How you can use it.

This selection is only a beginning, however. There are many other useful NLP tools and techniques. The ones we describe will enable you to start making changes, and as you do so you may well want to explore NLP further.

▪ *Anchors*

1. What is an anchor?

An anchor is any stimulus that changes your state. It can involve any kind of sensory input – visual, auditory, kinesthetic, olfactory or gustatory. Your state is created by your sensory experience, your thought processes and your physiology, so if an anchor is fired off that changes any one of these, your state will change. This anchor could be external: imagine, for instance, that you are driving along listening to the radio when a song comes on. Instantly it takes you back to a particular summer you spent with a special person, and all the feelings you had then come flooding back. Anchors can also be generated in the mind, for example a visual image that comes back to you and evokes particular feelings – whether happy or traumatic.

Your behaviour can be an anchor for others, triggering their responses. For example, suppose you're one of those people who pull away when you're feeling defensive. This may then trigger feelings of being neglected or ignored in the other person. They might then become irritated, or hurt. This then influences how they react to you – which influences how you are. And this is how a kind of chain of action and reaction begins to form.

NLP calls these chains *calibrated loops*. Loops such as these can be highly detrimental – or highly beneficial. Think of them as either vicious cycles or virtuous circles. If you want successful relationships, understanding calibrated loops is essential.

2. What does an anchor do?

Anchors 'fire' associations or memories, and can put you into resourceful or unresourceful states. Often you are unconscious of anchors and how they affect you.

3. Everyday examples of anchors

► Remembering a time when you were at your best makes you feel more empowered and ready to handle a new challenge.

► 'Our tune': favourite music will bring back feelings and experiences that you associated with it the first time you heard it.

► Just the smell of fresh coffee can perk you up and make you more mentally alert.

4. Think of anchors

► When you find yourself in an unwanted state all of a sudden. Has an anchor been fired in you?

► When you find yourself responding in a way that reminds you of events and feelings from the past.

► When you want to become more resourceful.

► When you anticipate being in a situation that may threaten you or put you under pressure.

5. How you can use anchors

Become curious about what anchors you into a resourceful and pleasurable state. One of our clients has only to put on a particular suit to feel what she calls 'ready for action'. Another realised that before any challenging situation he would remember the time when his father said to him: 'You've got what it takes, son.' Immediately he felt different and supported. So what are your positive anchors?

Notice any negative anchors you have. These will trigger unpleasant or unresourceful states in you. Sometimes it's enough just to have brought the anchor into awareness, since becoming aware of a state invariably alters it to some extent. But suppose it's not. Consider what you can do to lessen or remove it. For example, if you are thrown into a childlike feeling of inadequacy when someone at work uses a particular tone of voice, you might want to identify what old experiences this connects with and sort them out. There again, you could also make a change in the sub-modalities (see page **80**) involved and 'turn down the volume' in your mind, or superimpose some other sound over them.

Start noticing environmental anchors, like your home and your work-place. Do the layout, furnishings and decoration make you feel good and able to be your best? If not, are there some anchors you could change?

Recall some of your most resourceful states in the fullest way you can, and as you do so create your own kinesthetic anchor: for example, close your thumb and third finger together as you recall the state when you were at your best. Do this several times, so that you connect your chosen move-ment with the state you want to anchor. Practise in everyday situations until you know you can call up your resourceful state rapidly and unobtru-sively whenever you want. Then use it when you are under pressure, or as a means of breaking and changing an unpleasant or unresourceful state. To strengthen this anchor, keep building it with more peak moments as you experience them. How do you do this? As you are having a good experience, anchor it by pressing thumb and third finger together. The more good expe-riences you anchor thus, the more powerful the anchor.

▪ *Association and Dissociation*

1. What are association and dissociation?

There are two fundamental coding mechanisms that your brain uses with just about every experience you have. If you are associated at any given moment, you are associated *into* the experience and experiencing it in full. If you are dissociated at any given moment, you are dissociated *from* the experience, and experiencing it at one remove, possibly seeing your-self from a distance.

Being associated into an experience means you are 'all present' – when you are looking out through your own eyes, hearing it directly, and feel-ing it kinesthetically, you are associated into the experience. And because you're so closely engaged with the experience you'll also feel all the emo-tions that go with it. This is true whether it is happening right now, or whether you're remembering it, or imagining something that may hap-pen in the future.

Being dissociated means that your feelings are not activated. You may be noticing what is going on as if you were an observer. Again, this applies equally whether the experience is in the here-and-now, the past or an imagined future.

2. What do association and dissociation do?

They each give us a completely different take, even on the same experience. There are advantages and disadvantages to each. The vivid internal experience that you get when you're associated is great if you want to really feel alive right now and relive a positive experience, or design a scenario of the future that will be so compelling that you are drawn to making it happen in reality (see 'Compelling Futures', page **33**). But if you're associated into a traumatic or depressing internal experience, you are likely to dig yourself deeper into it and find it hard to devise ways around or out of it.

Similarly, there are times when dissociation will be very useful and others when it's a hindrance. It can be really helpful to dissociate for short periods of time to bear physical or emotional pain, say in an emergency. Your brain already knows how to do this, which is why people who've been involved in car accidents, for instance, will often describe how they seemed to suddenly be looking at themselves or the scene from outside their body. However, if you remain dissociated, you may simply leave a difficult experience parked somewhere in your mind rather than change its impact or learn from it.

It is useful to be able to step back and have a look at yourself and events from a neutral, dissociated position. This can be a valuable skill when people seek to be better strategic thinkers. On the other hand, we've found that when people dissociate for extended periods, they tend to feel somewhat remote – and not just from sad or bad experiences, but from life in general. It's as though their ability to feel at all has been turned down.

3. Everyday examples of association and dissociation

Association

► Telling someone about an event that was important to you, and finding that you're becoming tearful, excited or joyous just from thinking about it.

Dissociation

► Seeing yourself in an experience – you are observing yourself, maybe in order to see how you're coming across.

4. Think of association and dissociation

Association

▶ When you want to get more involved in something or help someone else do so.

Dissociation

▶ When you or another want to gain some mental or emotional distance from something in order to manage it more calmly or think about it strategically.

5. How you can use association and dissociation

It can be very important and helpful to ask yourself whether you and other people tend to go through life associated or dissociated. It may explain why you never really feel that involved in things, or why so-and-so seems such a cold fish. It may explain why you, or someone you know, is forever lurching from highs to lows, and may feel at the mercy of what happens next.

Overall, there are four possible ways of being associated or dissociated. It's for you to decide which is best in any particular context.

1. **Associating into both positive and negative experiences** You are very good at associating into the positive – so you feel great – and you are also very good at associating into the negative – so you feel utterly wretched at times. But you have not learnt to dissociate from anything, so it is difficult to get a perspective on anything.

2. **Dissociating from both positive and negative experiences** You are good at dissociating from negative things so that whatever happens, you can handle it by stepping back and looking at things from another point of view. However, you do this with everything. It's all going on at a distance, and never really touches or engages you – and this includes every positive experience in your life.

3. **Associating into the negative and dissociating from the positive** You are likely to be unhappy because you will be very good at associating into whatever unhappiness you have experienced. Because you

dissociate from the good times it means that you will not feel them. Also, you may not notice positive experiences a lot of the time because they never really touch you.

4. **Associating into the positive and dissociating from the negative**
   You are able to dissociate from negative experiences and associate into positive experiences. You are likely to experience your feelings but also to step back and see the positive aspects of what initially appears to be negative. In that way you will learn from them and you are more likely to achieve what you want.

Recognising patterns of association and dissociation in this way is an important step towards having more choice about how you experience your life. Each is powerful in shaping your *state*, and will have very different consequences. Here are some examples of how you can choose the kind of experiences you want.

Association

When you want to enjoy an experience more, 'step into' your body, be looking out through your eyes and make sure that all your senses are alive and engaged. If you find yourself thinking about mundane domestic chores or things you need to do at work next week, be aware that you have ceased to be present and so will be reducing your possible pleasure. Having acknowledged any concerns, bring yourself back to your here-and-now sensory experience by paying attention to what you are seeing, hearing, feeling, tasting and smelling.

Dissociation

When you want to gain some distance from what's going on, imagine you're a fly on the wall, and see yourself from outside and at some distance. You could become really curious about what's going on and why. You might want to see the scene from another vantage point entirely and notice any different information that comes to the fore. Then you can ask yourself what might help that person over there – you – who is having that experience.

▪ *Behavioural Flexibility*

1. What is behavioural flexibility?

Behavioural flexibility is about having a range of ways to respond or to do something. It's about choice in action. Behavioural flexibility can result from experience, knowledge, a willingness to consider how others will be affected by what you do, or a willingness to do something different.

2. What does behavioural flexibility do?

It gives you more options, and thus a greater possibility of influencing a situation. If you only have one way of responding or behaving, your possibilities of dovetailing your outcomes with other people's are limited, and so is your influence.

3. Everyday examples of behavioural flexibility

▶ Being able to change direction as you go along if the need arises. For instance, if your presentation isn't engaging your client, you switch and do something different.

▶ Finding ways to make your child's bath-time and story-time fun, so that going to bed doesn't become a confrontation.

▶ Deliberately changing your routine so you don't get stuck in the same old groove.

4. Think of using behavioural flexibility

▶ Whenever you are planning action. Run through a number of possible approaches first.

▶ When you get any feedback that tells you your approach to a situation may be running into difficulties, or there are factors you hadn't taken account of in advance.

▶ When you are in any situation that has been handled well by others. Consider doing what works even if what works is not your usual approach.

5. How you can use behavioural flexibility

Get into the habit of asking yourself: 'Is there something else I could do?'
Even when something goes well, it's a good idea to collect other options.
Observe how other people handle things, and model them so that you can
increase your repertoire of behaviours and reactions.

▪ *Chunking*

1. What is chunking?

Chunking is the process of grouping items of information into larger and
smaller units.

2. What does chunking do?

Chunking helps you organise your thinking and handle more information. Think of how we remember phone numbers. We cluster the digits
together into chunks. Just how useful this is to us becomes very obvious
when we're confronted with phone numbers from countries where they
group the numbers differently. We may have difficulty remembering the
number because we've got used to chunking differently.

Chunking also allows you to become more efficient at categorising
information. For example, you can classify things into groups, moving
from the specific to the general or vice versa. NLP calls this chunking up
or chunking down. Chunking is a form of information filtering: what gets
through depends on the chunk size you are using. For example:

Chunking up (specific to general)

fluid
↑
liquid
↑
drink
↑
alcohol

↑

white wine

↑

Chardonnay

↑

Carmen 1992

Chunking down (general to specific)

communication

↓

media

↓

book

↓

poetry

↓

Shakespeare

↓

Sonnet 23

↓

First line, 'Shall I compare thee to a summer's day?'

3. Everyday examples of chunking

▶ How we organise telephone numbers into groups of numbers.

▶ Enjoying a presentation because the amount of information was just right for you and it was presented in 'bite-sized chunks'.

▶ Any organising of material into sets or subsets. These could represent levels of difficulty and accomplishment that apply when learning an array of skills and subjects, like learning to play a musical instrument or skiing.

4. Think of chunking

▶ When you have a task in hand that seems daunting – chunk it down to find smaller, more manageable mini-tasks.

► When you feel overwhelmed by detail – chunk up to find overall purpose or meaning, or to help you 'get the big picture' or see 'the wood rather than the trees'.

► When you want to communicate more effectively.

► When you want to find ways of reaching agreement.

5. How you can use chunking

Get to know your chunking style and you'll know how best you can learn and take information in. Do you like to chunk down and go for detail? Or do you like to chunk up and get the big picture?

Get to know others' chunking preferences. Are you communicating effectively? If your boss likes large chunk processing, giving him loads of detail could be making him think you get lost in the detail, and drive him crazy.

Break tasks down into smaller chunks so that you have a sequence of achievable steps and mini-goals.

When negotiating at home or at work, chunk up to find a level of agreement. People who differ over issues of behaviour or environment may agree over aims or values. Once there is recognition that this is so, it becomes easier to negotiate compromises or changes over specifics.

▪ *Compelling Futures*

1. What is a compelling future?

It's a representation of a future state or experience which is so well realised and powerful that it has a compelling effect on you in the present. For example, many high achievers in sport or business have a really vivid idea in their minds of what it is they want to achieve: that moment of standing on the podium and wearing the medal; the moment when the deal is clinched and they shake hands on it. And when they are asked about this idea, it will usually be very clear and detailed. They already *know* what it will be like. This is a compelling future – in fact, it's so compelling it already exists here and now in their minds and their feelings! That's what focuses their minds and shapes their behaviour so that they are highly motivated to achieve it. The very vividness of it makes it irresistible.

2. What do compelling futures do?

They give you a taste of that future now and motivate you to do what it takes to make that future really happen. This compelling experience is likely to evoke more than one representational system. You might create your compelling future yourself, by imagining it or fantasising, or you might adopt one you encounter through advertising or a persuasive individual. Either way, you will process it internally through your own representational systems, so that you'll:

▶ *See* yourself doing what's involved, see the places and people involved.

▶ *Hear* the sounds, the words, the praise.

▶ *Feel* now how great you'll feel then, and experience the physical sensations involved – if you've climbed a mountain, you may be aching, sweating, out of breath, shaking and elated!

▶ If there are *tastes* and *smells* to be sensed, build them in too.

3. Everyday examples of compelling futures

▶ Getting the brochures and imagining your next vacation.

▶ Imagining how you will feel when you've mastered a new skill.

▶ Your sexual fantasy about how it's going to be this evening!

4. Think of Compelling Futures

▶ When you suspect you are being over-persuaded by someone else – that is, being 'sold' their compelling future! In that case, test out how compelling *their* future really is for you. If you do not want to buy into it, change the sub-modalities (see page **80**) of the representation to make it less attractive, or use internal dialogue to remind yourself that you can make up your own mind.

▶ When you need to motivate yourself or others.

5. How to use compelling futures

In motivating yourself to strive for something you want, use as many representational systems as possible. For example, if you want to lose weight, imagine how you will look and feel, how other people's compliments will sound to you, how good it will be to taste and smell foods that will nourish and satisfy you while at the same time allowing you to become thinner. If you are the kind of person who is usefully motivated by avoiding things you *don't* want (in NLP terms, someone who runs an 'away-from' meta programme, which is explained further in 'Meta Programmes', page **54**), it can be helpful to imagine how you will look, feel and so on if you *remain* overweight.

Or say you're a team leader. If you're going to be an effective team leader, you will need to be able to construct a future that others can buy into. This is very different from mindless optimism. It may involve pacing people by acknowledging that it won't be all easy at the outset, then leading them towards a vividly imagined achievement.

▪ *Contrastive Analysis*

1. What is contrastive analysis?

It's the process of comparing and contrasting two things which have some elements in common, but which have different outcomes. These could be a harmonious evening with your family as compared with one that ends in a row, or a task that you accomplished on time and one where you failed to meet the deadline.

2. What does contrastive analysis do?

By comparing and contrasting the two processes in detail, it becomes possible for you to discover what NLP calls 'the difference that makes the difference' – in other words, the key elements of success which, if you use them, enable you to consistently achieve more of what you want.

3. Everyday examples of contrastive analysis

► Some people find it easy to spell and others don't. Contrastive analysis of the exact mental and physical procedures these groups of people used allowed NLP to discover that good spellers naturally make pictures of how written words actually look, and then recall the picture in order to reproduce or check the correct spelling. People who process information more through kinesthetic sensation or hearing are likely to find spelling more difficult. But once they have learnt how to 'take pictures' of words and recall them, their spelling improves dramatically. For more information on how we process through different systems, see the discussion of representational systems on page **73**.

► Two cakes are made to the same recipe, but one rises and the other falls flat. What happened? You realise that with the fallen cake, you opened the oven door and created a sudden draught, or you needed to beat the mixture more thoroughly to incorporate more air into it.

► You gave a really good presentation last month. This month's wasn't so good. You want to make sure that next month you do really well, so you use contrastive analysis to find out the difference that's going to make the difference.

4. Think of contrastive analysis

► When you are aware of a contrast between two apparently similar things which have different results.

► When you want to get good at just about anything – learning, business, communications, personal relationships, interaction, strategic thinking or sports performance.

5. How you can use contrastive analysis

Compare and contrast internal states where you feel limited or unresourceful with ones where you feel competent or resourceful so that you can find out how you do each and what you might choose to change if you'd like to succeed in more spheres.

Compare interactions that work with ones that don't – for instance, a conversation that leads to arguments, and one that ends in accord. Look for differences not just in what's said, but in exactly how the people involved behaved non-verbally. Look for sequences – what happened in what order. These are often highly significant and very different.

Learn from your past experience by noticing what comes easily to you and what's more challenging. For example, you may have found it easy to remember some kinds of information, but keep on forgetting other kinds. You may find you can be decisive at work but not at home – or vice versa. You might be able to defend others but not yourself. How come? What's the difference that makes the difference in each case?

▪ *Criteria and Criterial Equivalences*

1. What are criteria and criterial equivalences?

A criterion is a standard we use for judgement. Our criteria indicate what's important to us. They are usually stated in abstract words such as honesty, trust, happiness, love, friendship, acceptance, genuineness. These words carry powerful meanings for each of us – but not necessarily the same meanings! Our experiences and our beliefs will all have coloured what any one of these criteria 'means' for us. As a result, we each will have specific behaviours which demonstrate to us that our criteria are being honoured or violated. Those behaviours are our evidence and are known in NLP as criterial equivalences. It is vital to understand that different people can have different equivalences for the same word – which can lead to serious misunderstandings.

2. What do criteria and criterial equivalences do?

Once you know that the same idea and word may mean different things to someone else, you can begin to find out more about what it means to them. For example, suppose the one you love says that one thing that's really important to them is that they feel you are there for them. You've got the criteria but not the evidence they use. So you might want to find out just what you would have to do or say to ensure that they knew you were there for them. This is the criterial equivalence. You can only guess what these specific behaviours are. Too often people assume that the behaviours will be the ones they would naturally use themselves. In fact, the behavioural proofs are often quite idiosyncratic and unpredictable. So ask!

3. Everyday examples of criterial equivalences

Here are some examples of different criterial equivalences for 'love':

▶ If he loved me he'd know what I wanted (that is, love means that he can read my mind).

▶ If she loved me I wouldn't have to ask her to... (that is, love means she'd anticipate my wishes).

▶ He knew his mother loved him because she was always there when he came home from school.

▶ Sending my mother a Mothers' Day card tells her I love her.

4. Think of criteria and criterial equivalences

▶ When someone uses an abstract word – so you can find out what it really means for them and what behaviours go with it.

▶ When you are involved in a misunderstanding or conflict about meaning or about what behaviour 'means'. Almost certainly there are conflicting criteria or criterial equivalences in play.

▶ When you want to institute change. Consider the meanings that may be assigned to your proposals. See your proposals as criterial equivalances in the eyes of others.

5. How you can use criterial equivalences

Train yourself to pay extra attention when you, or someone else, use a word that implies a criterion is involved. Ask yourself, or find out from them, what specific meaning this has. What actions or behaviours would demonstrate it? Criteria are abstract ideas: what would be the visible enactment of them – as far as you, or the other person, are concerned? Find out what would have to happen for you (or them) to know that this criterion was being met. What specifically would tell or show?

Aim to understand what alienates people or draws them closer to you.

You could begin by asking people what's important to them and then what would you or another be doing which would prove to them that they were having that criterion honoured.

Don't assume, when someone uses a word, that you know what it means. Check.

▪ *The Disney Creativity Strategy*

1. What is the Disney creativity strategy?

It's a strategy for developing your dreams and giving them the best possible chance of becoming reality. It's named after Walt Disney, who often took on three distinct roles when his team was developing an idea: the dreamer, the realist and the critic. Robert Dilts, an NLP pioneer, modelled and developed this strategy as an NLP tool.

2. What does the Disney creativity strategy do?

It separates out three vital roles – dreamer, realist and critic – involved in the process of translating creative ideas into reality so they can be explored separately for maximum clarity and effect.

3. Everyday examples of the Disney creativity strategy

Most commonly, people favour one or another of these roles:

► 'He's a killjoy' (critic).

► 'She's an ideas person' (dreamer).

► 'He's good at the nuts and bolts' (realist).

Sometimes work teams include a range of people who each 'specialise' in these different roles. Dilts developed the intentional use of Disney's three roles as a strategy and we have often used it in business consultancy and coaching work. Though it was identified in a business context, it's equally valuable in personal settings. You can also play the three roles yourself, switching deliberately between them, or get other people to play them for you. For example: 'Can you take a good look at this idea and spot any practical steps I might have missed?' (that is, 'Can you be my realist?').

Sometimes we have found that couples get stuck in one of the roles and need to start doing the others if they are to be happy. If one of you is always the dreamer – 'He's always got his head in the clouds' – and the other is too often the critic – 'All she does is bring me down' – both of you can end up very frustrated. Not least because the absence of a realist means nothing ever really seems to get done.

4. Think of the Disney creativity strategy

▶ When you want to promote creativity in yourself or a team.

▶ When you feel in conflict between dreaming and 'reality' or practicalities.

▶ When you want to test out how an idea, dream or goal might be realised.

▶ When you, or someone else, closes down exploration by saying things like 'That'll never work in practice.' Remind yourself that you (or they) are making a 'critic' judgement here, and that it is important to check out how things might seem from all three viewpoints before reaching that judgement. You might do this out loud, or just in your head. Too often people jump to the critic position before they've really done their dreaming and realising. All three perspectives are important for the development and realisation of ideas and visions.

5. How you can use the Disney creativity strategy

Allocate the three roles to different people (for example, in a team or family) to assess plans or tasks. Ask someone to act the dreamer role for a few moments, and tell you all about the possibilities of the idea. Ask someone else to examine exactly what would be involved in putting it into practice, and someone else to take a hard look at it and really evaluate its strengths and weaknesses. You may want to rotate the roles, to allow people to contribute from different perspectives (and so that no one gets limited by playing only one fixed role, either).

Break down a meeting or discussion into three stages, working on each role as a separate phase. Get everyone brainstorming and being creative first; then get them thinking about what would actually have to happen in practical terms; then get them critically evaluating the possibilities.

Make each stage explicit and clear. After all the stages have been explored, you will have plenty of valuable information on which to base a final decision.

▪ *Ecology Check*

1. What is an ecology check?

This is the process of considering what effects a course of action may have before you actually do it. These effects can relate to you or any systems of which you are a part.

NLP recognises that actions cause effects and reactions throughout the system in which they occur: feeling, thought, action, physiology all have an impact on each other; we affect our family and the organisational structures we belong to. Each of us is a system in ourselves, made up of smaller biological, mental and emotional systems; families are systems; offices and organisations are systems; societies are systems. Many systems interact with one another. So, just as ecology is the study of organisms' relations to each other and to their environment, an ecology check in NLP is a close look at how your proposed action or change will affect the many interrelationships and interlocking systems of your life.

To do an ecology check, you'll take a systematic look at what you do, and assess what the likely consequence of your actions will be throughout the systems that are involved. Ecology checks can involve analytic thought, gathering information from others, and creating and testing out the viability of future scenarios. Equally importantly, they involve paying attention to your gut feelings.

2. What does an ecology check do?

It gives you a means of evaluating the outcome of your actions to ensure that they have the impact you want, while checking for any undesirable consequences. It allows you to identify any obstacles and take them into account by reformulating strategies or behaviour *before* you act. It therefore makes change much easier and ensures it really lasts.

3. Everyday examples of ecology checks

► Paying attention to a 'gut feeling' that something's wrong, or that you are reluctant to do something, or noticing and responding to someone else's hesitation in voice or manner.

► Finding out what works well in present business practice before instituting a change programme. Considering the consequences of change.

► Checking your bank account before making a purchase!

4. Think of doing an ecology check

► When you are decision-making or planning.

► When you are aware of a conflict of goals or values, either within yourself or interpersonally.

5. How you can use an ecology check

When setting your outcome, ask yourself:

► What will the consequences of achieving my outcome be in the context of the wider social systems I'm involved in (family, friends, organisations, community)?

► Does my desired outcome fit in with what other people may want in their lives?

► Does it respect the integrity of the other people involved?

► Does it fit in with my beliefs, values and identity?

► Does it enhance my sense of self?

► Is it consistent with maintaining my health and wellbeing?

► Would there be any undesirable results?

► What would I have to give up, or take on, to achieve it?

► Do I have a good gut feeling about it?

If you find that what you want looks good given these criteria, go ahead.

If you find there are some question marks, just start considering how you might address them to everyone's satisfaction. Getting these sorted out before you begin will make your life much easier and less stressful.

▪ *Eye-accessing Cues*

1. What are eye-accessing cues?

The way we use our bodies can help or hinder us as we access information and process our experience. Hunching your shoulders, tightening your muscles and looking down long and hard will not help you imagine new possibilities! There are, however, some things we can do that will help us to be more effective and cue us to access our experience – and our potential. This is why we want you to know about eye-accessing cues.

The direction of people's unconscious eye movements when they are thinking has been found to correlate strongly with the particular representational system they are using. For the majority of right-handed people:

▶ Looking up and to *their* right indicates imagining something visually.

▶ Looking horizontally and to *their* right indicates imagining how something will sound.

▶ Looking down and to *their* right indicates getting in touch with feelings (physical or emotional).

▶ Looking up and to *their* left indicates remembering visually.

▶ Looking horizontally and to *their* left indicates remembering something heard.

▶ Looking down and to *their* left indicates talking to oneself internally, which NLP calls internal dialogue.

For left-handed people some of these may be laterally reversed. And in some people, these eye movements may not all conform to the representational system indicated. Even so, the overall generalisations listed above can be very useful, as we shall see.

2. What eye-accessing cues do

As we've seen, they indicate the representational system processing that the person is using at that moment. This makes it much easier for us to access a particular representational system deliberately, because we know where to look – literally. So you could actually teach yourself to become more visual, auditory or kinesthetic, if you wished. And this in turn makes it possible to learn new skills and ways of doing things very precisely, when we know which sequence of accessing cues produce success.

3. Everyday examples of eye-accessing

► Looking down when timid, embarrassed or fearful (reflects kinesthetic feeling).

► Looking up when trying to remember something.

► Looking rapidly from side to side when trying to locate something stored internally. The externally observable scanning movement of the eyes is matching internal scanning.

4. Think of eye-accessing cues

► When you want to develop brain power (see Chapter 14).

► When you want to improve or build rapport with someone by matching their 'language'. Once you have noticed their most frequent eye positioning, you are likely to have identified their 'lead system' – that is, the representational system they use to lead them to access their other representational systems – and can then tailor your language to fit with this. For example, you might use kinesthetic language if they tend to look down to their right a lot, or visual metaphors if they frequently look up right.

► When you see someone frequently looking down to their left. This suggests they are engaging in internal dialogue which may mean they are uncertain or discussing things with themselves.

► When you want to remember something you have heard (look horizontally to your left) or seen (look up to your left).

► When you want to escape from unpleasant feelings (stop looking down right for a while).

► When you want to imagine something – up right for visual, horizontal right for hearing, down right for 'finding out how it will feel'.

5. How you can use eye-accessing cues

You can train yourself to notice other people's eye-accessing cues, as a way of gathering more information about what is going on for them, or what their preferred representational systems may be. You can monitor your own eye-accessing. This gives you a number of useful options:

1. It allows you to cue into a particular representational system when this would be helpful.

2. It gives you a way of breaking out of patterns that may not be helpful and connecting with ones that will be more so: for example, if you can't remember something when you are taking an exam, your bad feelings about this are likely to be reflected – and reinforced! – by looking down right. If the information you want came to you visually (for example, through a book or television), you probably want to be looking up left to recall it.

▪ *Framing*

1. What is framing?

Have you noticed how, if you change its frame, a picture can suddenly look very different? The frame highlights certain qualities of the picture as it sets the boundaries of the image. The way we think can similarly frame our experience, highlighting particular aspects of it. Framing is the way we 'place' our experiences to give them meaning. Depending on the frame we use, we can experience the same event very differently.

NLP has identified a number of different frames which can be very powerful tools.

Problem Frame

If something unexpected happens, people often think of it as a problem. Problems have to be 'overcome' or 'dealt with'. Someone else having the same experience might frame it very differently: as 'an opportunity', 'a challenge' or 'something that puzzles me'. Each of these ways of framing the experience leads to other ways of thinking and feeling about it, and behaving in relation to it.

'Problems' require help, or solutions, as far as most people are concerned. Problems are what take people to the doctor and the lawyer and the counsellor. Framing an event as a problem is actually a judgement about it, which narrows the range of possible attitudes and actions. 'Something that puzzles me' is more neutral, as is 'something unexpected'. Both these phrases leave more possibilities open, in terms of both feeling and action.

There is a bias in politics, in business, in social work and in many individuals towards problem solving. At first glance, that may seem fine: all these problems getting solved presumably means that there are fewer and fewer remaining – if only!

Unfortunately, a problem frame means that we always notice what isn't working. Bear this in mind the next time you're watching the news, and ask yourself what is being framed as 'news'? Setting a problem frame may also entail looking for someone to blame. Individuals and institutions who use the problem frame habitually are less likely to model excellence – they just do not notice what *is* working.

Outcome Frame

An outcome frame is another way of looking at events: it points you in the direction of what you want. Just asking 'What do you want?' could be enough to set an outcome frame. Where 'Tell me about this problem' invites excursions into the present and explanations from the past, 'Tell me what you want' directs attention into the future. And since you cannot act in the past, the future you want is usually a better guide in helping you act in the present.

As-if Frame

This is a really good way of allowing yourself to 'try things on for size'. The as-if frame is about imagining a future scenario as if it were happening now, as if it could happen, as if it were real. And when the imagination is engaged, you create scenarios that seem very real, so you can assess how they look, sound and feel.

One time Ian was coaching a client who felt very stuck professionally. Ian said: 'I know right now you feel pretty stuck... but suppose for a minute you didn't. What would you be doing then?' The client paused, looked up, breathed more fully and began: 'Oh well, in that case I'd start looking around for a new direction. I'd talk to an old friend of mine in the recruitment business who I haven't seen for a couple of years and I'd see what new options there are these days.' A new course of action became possible just by stepping around the immediate obstacle.

Reframing

'I am open to reason,' 'You are impressionable,' 'He is gullible' – reframing is changing the meaning of an experience or an event by putting another frame around it. This causes you to see things differently: it's a new interpretation, with the result that you arrive at a different conclusion, evaluation or feeling. This is such an important form of framing that we have given it its own entry on page 72.

2. What does framing do?

Framing is the way we label experiences so that we 'know' what they mean. It 'colours' events or thoughts. If we change the frame, we change the meaning of the experience. When we change the meaning we often change our feelings about what is being framed.

3. Everyday examples of framing

▶ Problem frame: 'How long have you had this problem?'

▶ Outcome frame: Asking yourself what it is you really want in this situation.

▶ As-if frame: Imagine the year is 3001... Arthur C. Clarke's novel *3001:*

The Final Odyssey – like all fiction – takes us into an imaginary world where we can sample new possibilities.

4. Think of framing

▶ When you or other people feel stuck with a particular way of looking at something or reacting to something. Change the frame to get a new take.

▶ When you feel the way something is framed may be limiting you.

▶ When you want to consider other ways of experiencing or evaluating something.

5. How you can use framing

Framing comes into its own when you need to present an idea or a proposal in a way that gives your listener the best opportunity of taking it on board as you would like them to. Similarly, you can use it to set a context for a meeting or a discussion before it begins.

Train yourself to listen to the way others frame their ideas and proposals: is their frame one which sits well with you? Is the frame appropriate to what it contains? Start looking for people who are really good at framing in different contexts, from really clear public speakers to effective parents, and ask yourself just what it is they do and say that makes them so good.

▪ *Logical Levels*

1. What are logical levels?

Logical levels are a way of identifying underlying structures and patterns in thinking about ideas, events, relationships or organisations. They help us understand what's involved, or what's going on. The logical levels form a hierarchy.

People often distinguish between levels when referring to their experience. As one of our clients put it, 'On one level the house burning down was a disaster, but on another level it was what made me the man I am. Because I had to move away I had to start again and that's how I built my own business and I've never looked back.' One way of remembering the levels is that each of them gives us a different kind of information: it answers a particular kind of question. For clarity, we've put the key question for each level beside it in capitals.

► **Environment: WHERE? and WHEN?** This level involves issues or details of context. It may mean a physical context, as in a particular building, or a social context, for instance when with a certain group of people. It also includes the when of it all.

► **Behaviour: WHAT?** Behaviour is what you actually do – or don't do. Issues on this level relate to what is happening or being done.

► **Capability: HOW?** Capability is about the how-tos of life – the knowledge, skills and processes that make it possible for one person who has them to find doing something easy and for another who lacks them to find the same thing really difficult.

► **Beliefs and values: WHY?** Our beliefs and our values shape our understanding of why things are possible or impossible for us. They provide us with a rationale and drive our actions.

► **Identity: WHO?** Identity is to do with sense of self. This could be our personal identity or a corporate identity – in either case, who we are.

► **Beyond identity: FOR WHOM/FOR WHAT?** This is the level which relates to a bigger picture or larger system where questions about some larger purpose come into play. For us as individuals this often means the spiritual. It takes us into questions about our mission. This dimension of mission and vision can also apply to groups and organisations.

2. What do logical levels do?

Logical levels give you a way of understanding:

► What kind of information you are dealing with.

► Where a problem originates.

► On what level it is being experienced or manifested (these may not be the same).

► What the 'real' issue at stake is.

► What is the appropriate level for interaction or intervention.

If you are mindful of the key questions – who? why? how? what? where/when? – in any interaction with others, or in relation to your own thinking, you can usually identify the logical level involved. This in turn enables you to do other important things:

▶ You can find out where a difficulty is really coming from, as opposed to where it seems to originate (for example, problems about behaviour, or environment, often originate from issues about belief).

▶ You can find out where the points of leverage are to change the situation. Most people will find it easier to change a behaviour if they can be reassured that it doesn't involve them changing at a belief or identity level.

▶ You can find small interventions which will bring about larger effects: for example, providing a water-carrier, coffee-machine or kettle in an office (an environmental change) is likely to draw people to it (behaviour) which in turn may help them create or maintain a sense of belonging to a department or team (identity).

3. Everyday examples of logical levels

Let's take the example of going to see a film. Often tone and emphasis make it clear which logical level is important:

▶ 'I don't want to go to that movie.' This may be a statement about behaviour – in other words, I don't want to *do* that.

▶ '*I* don't want to go to that movie.' This may mean someone else may well want to but *I* don't – identity.

▶ 'I *don't want to* go to that movie.' This may indicate I have my reasons, though they are unstated – beliefs and values.

Other examples:

▶ How parents relate to their children: 'You're so lazy' (identity) vs ' Tidy your room' (behaviour).

▶ Culture change programmes that seek to win employees' hearts and minds (beliefs and identity).

4. Think of logical levels

▸ When you or others react to an apparently simple or trivial situation with more feeling than seems to be warranted. Almost certainly there's something going on at the level of beliefs or identity.

▸ When you are wanting to make changes in your life, or in an organisation. Consider at which logical level you are attempting to do this, and whether this is the appropriate level. Often organisations need to win hearts and minds – which means they need to operate at the level of beliefs and identity. Too often though they try a quick fix at the level of behaviour.

▸ When there seems to be more involved than is obvious on the surface.

▸ When offering criticism or praise. Criticism is most easily received if it is pitched at the level of environment or behaviour (and possibly capability), and least effective when delivered at an identity level because we feel a need to defend ourselves if our identity seems under attack. Praise is most effective when offered on higher levels, especially identity – for example, 'You're so efficient/thoughtful.'

5. How you can use logical levels

Use them to monitor situations and to identify what the real issues are. They can help you find the simplest or most effective point for leverage. Use them to help in rapport-building, by respecting what may be involved for yourself or others at an unconscious level. Logical levels can help you understand situations that seem puzzling: Just what is the issue here, and what logical level is it at?

Use them to help you assess 'fit' – between people and jobs, between people and environments, and between problems and proposed solutions.

▪ *The Meta Model*

1. What is the meta model?

The meta model shows how, in order to make sense of our experience and the information coming to us, we tend to simplify it in three ways:

1. Deletion – we leave information out.

2. Generalisation – we make broad or universal claims on the basis of limited evidence.

3. Distortion – we create meaning through concentrating on some kinds of information and ignoring others.

All three processes are quite natural. They can be helpful or they can limit us. For instance, imagine what it would be like if you didn't delete a lot of input that comes your way! Your head would be full of all sorts of unnecessary clutter – like every car number-plate you've ever seen. On the other hand, are you deleting important information? In an appraisal, do you delete all positive feedback and obsess about the one critical comment?

2. What does the meta model do?

It gives you a whole set of questions for retrieving what's missing, challenging unjustified generalisations and creating new meanings when things have got distorted.

3. Everyday examples of the meta model

Deletion

► **Negative** Not paying attention, being forgetful, ignoring warning signs that tell you you are overdoing it.

► **Positive** Not really noticing the drab surroundings because you're with the one you love.

Generalisation

► **Negative** Feeling everyone's against you (everyone? Every single person on the planet – including those you've never met?).

► **Positive** You've just done your first presentation and it went really well. You start thinking 'I can do presenting.' It gives you a new confidence.

Distortion

► **Negative** You see your boss talking with a colleague then laughing and you just 'know' they are laughing about you.

► **Positive** Your partner buys you a special surprise present and you just know they love you.

4. Think of the meta model

► Whenever you want to get clear about what you or others are really saying.

► Whenever you want to think more clearly.

► Every time you or someone else generalises.

► When your gut feelings tell you that someone is making a claim without really substantiating it.

► When someone is trying to sell you something or persuade you to do something.

► Whenever you are making claims or statements on paper, in discussion or in arguments.

5. How you can use the meta model

Deletion

Using the meta model, you can recover some of the missing information by asking certain kinds of questions:

► Where information is actually missing. If you say 'I feel fed up' you need to ask *'About what exactly?'*

► Where a hidden comparison is being made. If you say 'This is getting worse' you need to ask *'Worse than what?'*

► Where processes are being referred to as if they were fixed things. If you say 'Our relationship has gone downhill' you need to ask *'How exactly are we relating differently and how is that not as good as before?'*

► Where something is missing because you're not specifying who or what is involved. If you say 'People don't like me' you need to ask *'Which people in particular?'*

Generalisation

Using the meta model, you can differentiate between generalisations, and know how to challenge ones that keep you stuck.

▶ Universal statements – 'You never consider how I feel' *'Never? Never, ever?'*

▶ Musts, oughts and shoulds – 'I must get home on time' *'What would happen if you didn't? What would happen if you did?'*

▶ Can'ts – 'I can't do that' *'What stops you? What would happen if you could?'*

Distortion

Using the meta model, you can uncover how people are making meaning of their experience and challenge it if it's not working for you or for them:

▶ Complex equivalence – 'People who don't look you in the eye can't be trusted' *'How does looking you in the eye or not relate to being trustworthy?'*

▶ Cause and effect – 'Your remarks made me feel undermined' *'How exactly did what I said make you feel undermined?'*

▶ Mind reading – 'You're annoyed with me', *'How do you know that? What makes you think that?'*

▪ *Meta Programmes*

1. What are meta programmes?

Meta programmes are largely unconscious patterns of sorting information, which are hugely influential because they affect what you notice, how you form your internal representations, and how you organise your experience and make information from it. They are hugely influential because they are the means by which you organise your experience. Meta programmes are like filters – they enable you to filter out what is not significant to you and pay attention to what is. Without them we would be overwhelmed and would lack a way of distinguishing what's important for us from what's not. We're going to describe a handful of the key ones which will enable you to be far more effective in your career, your relationships, even your ability to be happy and healthy.

2. What do meta programmes do?

They provide automatic ways for you to sort and organise your experience, your thinking and your behaviour. Though you will share some of your meta programmes with other people, the combination used by any one person will be unique to them.

Meta programmes relate to various possible ways of behaving along an axis of possibilities: there are many positions on the scale. The opposite ends of the meta programme scale contrast strongly with each other, but people can be placed anywhere in between.

There is no 'right' way to process experience, and so no 'right' way to be with any specific meta programme. Rather, NLP stresses that each variant has its strengths and limitations *in particular circumstances.*

The art of managing yourself in relation to your meta programmes is to know how you function and to be able to assess this in relation to your desired outcomes.

The art of engaging and influencing others in relation to meta programmes is to know which ones those people respond to, and to use these when communicating with them.

3. Everyday examples of meta programmes

► Understanding people. One person just seems generally more optimistic than another – they tend to move towards possibilities and can find pleasure in the small details of life. Once you know about meta programmes, you can recognise the patterns that are contributing to making this person's life work.

► Being able to organise your time effectively because you can see how things fit into your schedule, versus opening your diary at the beginning of a new week and being horrified at how much somehow seems to have been jam-packed into it.

► Choosing a career that plays to the strengths of your meta programmes.

► Selecting staff, having got clear which meta programmes would best equip someone to hold the post you need to fill.

Common meta programmes

Moving away from – moving towards

You may be spurred to action by the need to avoid unpleasant stimuli or consequences, in which case you are moving away from them. Or perhaps you are motivated by things that attract you, in which case you are moving towards them. Knowing which is your predominant meta programme in a given context will enable you to motivate yourself in a way that really works for you. Similarly, there is no point in offering 'towards' incentives like promotion or better status if the people you are trying to motivate have a strong 'away from' meta programme. They will be galvanised into action by your making clear the unpleasant consequences that will ensue if they don't change – like loss of status. What gets one person going will not necessarily work well for another.

When people tell you about what they *don't* want, what they are about to get rid of or want to stay away from, you know they're moving away from things. When others tell you what they want and what they seek to accomplish or attain, you know they're moving towards things.

Necessity – possibility

If you are driven by what has to be done, or what ought to be done, necessity is paramount. If you are motivated by what could be, the new and the unknown, possibility is uppermost.

Necessity will frequently show up as a strong liking for procedure: 'This is the way it should be done.' When you hear people talking of having to do things that they ought to, or are required to, you're hearing the language of necessity. There doesn't seem to be a lot of choice here: there is a procedure and it must be followed. Possibility, on the other hand, will manifest as a liking for lots of options or alternatives. Choice is crucial and the language will be about wishes and hopes and what might be possible.

Focus of attention: self – others

You may focus on self – which does not mean you are selfish. It only means that you evaluate events and thoughts from your own perspective at first. However, this can result in your being 'inside' quite a lot of the time, and it may seem to others that at times you're oblivious to the outside world. If, on the other hand, you focus primarily on others and are initially concerned by how the same events affect other people, then your focus of attention is clearly others. You'll probably be perceived as externally orientated and attentive to the world around you. Either, if taken to an extreme, will be problematical: sorting by self ends up not just as selfish but narcissistic, whereas sorting by other ends up trying to please everyone at your own expense and being all things to all men.

Sorting for similarities – sorting for differences

A friend of Ian's is famous for saying, 'You know, this is just like...' His sorting for what's similar is so transparent that it's become a standing joke. People who think this way are matching things up: they see what things or people have in common and how the present is like the past. These connections are both pleasing and important to them.

So if you wanted to engage them you wouldn't be suggesting that a new course of action would be great because it was new and different. That's what would make sense to someone who sorts for difference. When sorting for difference you notice the exceptions, and what's missing.

Again, both are equally valid, and ideally we want to have the flexibility to do both. But we often tend to get stuck in one. Trying the other on is one of the fastest and most effective ways of freeing yourself up if you're stuck. Making sure that both styles are represented in any team is vital.

Preferred chunk size: small – large

We are all familiar with people who 'can't see the wood for the trees' or who, on the other hand, are so busy 'taking the global view' and seeing the big picture that they don't pay attention to the detail. These are extremes which illustrate how each of us tends to have a bias in one direction or the other.

If you tend to be really good at remembering and handling detail, but lack an overall framework to relate it to, you probably do a lot of small chunk processing. If you are great at vision and planning, but get impatient with the detail necessary to make your grand plan work, or overlook things that don't quite fit into an overall scheme, then you probably do a lot of large chunk processing.

Imagine what happens when you get two people together who embody these two different styles. They really can drive each other crazy; the small chunker's amount of detail feels overwhelming to the big chunker, while the big chunker's lack of detail seems vague to the small chunker and can trigger anxiety. Any good team leader will want both styles to be represented. It's essential if you are to cover all bases and have a balanced perspective and a fully integrated team.

Orientation in time: in-time – through-time

While many of the meta programmes may seem familiar, the notion that people can experience time differently is one that can feel quite strange. NLP explains that the way we relate to time can differ markedly from person to person. Everyone's experience is slightly different, but there are two main contrasting ways in which people organise their experience.

In-time

You may be really 'in the moment'. You live life to the full, and feel very present. You may find it hard to keep an eye on the time because you are so immersed in what is going on right now. Planning ahead can seem unreal – the further away, the more difficult it is to manage. You often think of the past as 'behind' you and the future as being 'ahead' or 'in front'.

NLP has shown just how spatial our awareness of time really is. If you ask someone who is in-time to point in the direction of yesterday, or tomorrow, they are likely to point over their shoulder for yesterday, and in front of them for tomorrow. Experiencing time like this may literally mean that the past is inaccessible because it's behind you, and the only bits of the future you can see clearly are those close-to. It's as if there is a line of time extending from the past into the future.

Through-time

Most people who experience time this way locate time on a left-right axis just in front of them. It's still a line of time. Usually, though not always, the past is to the left and the future to the right. As with a year planner, a glance in either direction allows you to see the sweep of time. Having this kind of spatial organisation for time means that it is easy to review and to plan, and through-time people are often good organisers and planners.

NLP describes the way we connect different times with one another and with our continuing experience as 'time-lines'. In-time people are usually on their time-line, whereas through-time people are mostly a little distance away from it. This can mean that if you are a through-time person you will find it easier to avoid being overwhelmed by here-and-now detail, but harder to 'get into things'.

Frame of reference: internal or external

If you decide what's right for you and don't like others telling you what's right, you're being internally referenced. Internally referenced people will be easy to engage with if you don't try and push them with talk about what everyone else thinks. Not only is this less important for them, it can become like a red rag to a bull as they rely on their own judgement first: 'I need to decide for myself.'

If you like to know what others say and how they're thinking, then to that extent you're being externally referenced. People who are predominantly like this will be likely to reach their conclusions by taking the views of others into account to a very high degree. 'People say... Well, the facts make it clear that that's the way it is.' Expressions like this make it clear that someone or something out there is being referred to as the source of authority.

As ever, neither is good or bad and both can be a liability in isolation.

These are some of the key meta programmes, though many more have been identified and described (and if you want to know more about these, see NLP Training Courses, page **353**, for details. We've chosen to highlight these particular ones because they give you a lot of leverage in understanding what drives you and what influences your choices. They also help you make sense of the pitfalls you may get into when communicating with others. And they can help you work out where your own particular talents will be most useful and effective.

The secret of managing all the meta programmes is to:

► Know what your natural preferences are.

► Know the strengths and weaknesses of each of your meta programmes.

► Find ways to extend your range of choices and behaviours.

4. Think of meta programmes

► If you want to play to your strengths.

► When considering job applications (yours and other people's).

► When seeking to understand problems in communication.

5. How you can use meta programmes

Build a personal profile of your own sorting preferences to understand why you do what you do. Then build a profile of the meta programmes of others you are close to or work with. Consider what the matches and mismatches between yours and theirs are. How might these be helping and hindering? Match others' meta programmes to help build rapport and influence them.

▪ *Modelling*

1. What is modelling?

Modelling is the basis of NLP, and arose from asking the question 'How do they *do* that?' It's the process of finding out specifically *how* people go about doing something, whether accomplishing a task, performing a skill, being in a certain state or living a fulfilled life. As a child you did a lot of unconscious modelling as you imitated certain people's mannerisms and even took on their beliefs. As an adult you have probably tried to consciously model people who excel at what you'd like to do better. So you can model consciously or unconsciously, and in very great detail, or more impressionistically.

The information we need for modelling is likely to be found in one or more of the following areas:

▶ Settings and environments.

▶ Behaviour.

▶ Skills and capabilities.

▶ Beliefs and questions of identity.

In NLP these are known collectively as logical levels (see above, page **48**). You can model others at any of these levels – and the more fully you model them, the closer and more effective your modelling gets. For example, if you want to become more effective in social situations, you could closely observe someone you know who's a brilliant conversationalist and skilled at making others feel at ease. But if you are not really as interested as they are in what makes other people tick, and how they feel and respond, your modelling will lack an important ingredient that is almost certainly present in the person you are modelling – their values and beliefs. In order to model them fully, and achieve their level of excellence in interaction, you will have to go beyond behaviour and skills and learn how they think about others as they interact with them.

Most people are very skilled at recognising, often unconsciously, the difference between surface behaviour and deeper attitudes, and this often unconscious distinction between what is genuine and what is surface will affect their responses significantly. So if you want to get really good, you won't just be going through the motions by aping someone's behaviour. You'll be getting under their skin and understanding what makes them want to do this thing in the first place.

2. What does modelling do?

Modelling makes the transfer of knowledge possible. It is the foundation of learning. NLP suggests that if we know how someone does something they do well, we can learn to do it too – provided we have information that's detailed enough.

3. Everyday examples of modelling

► Walking and talking like your parents.

► Learning a skill by observing someone performing it.

► Masterclasses – here a recognised master gives you not just instruction but an insight into how they think.

► Imitating a friend or colleague you admire.

► Following a recipe. You're being guided: 'Do this, then do this... and you will create a perfect meal.'

► Growing up as a member of your family's church or faith.

4. Think of modelling

► When you'd like to learn a skill or improve an existing one.

► When you come across anyone who's really good at something and you want to find out more about how they do that.

► When you want to emulate others.

► When you want to be able to repeat something effective you've done (self-modelling).

► When you want to change something you did that wasn't so effective – model what went wrong in order to know what to change next time.

5. How you can use modelling

Focus your attention on what you want to model, using as many of your senses as you can. You may want to model a specific skill, or a behaviour in a certain situation, or someone's whole approach or style. Modelling can be specific, which in NLP parlance is small-chunk, or more general and large-chunk (see above, page **31**).

Ask yourself: what are the key pieces? What is the difference that will make a difference and enable me to acquire this way of being or behaving? In the example we gave earlier, one key to becoming more effective in social situations is being interested in the people you encounter. But however fascinated you are, you will still need to talk about something. If you find it difficult to think of subjects to toss into a conversation, the key difference that may help you start to become more effective socially may be to prepare some questions that get other people talking.

Evaluate the information you get by asking yourself: When *doesn't* this happen? Negative examples often show up the key processes more clearly. Comparing two similar situations or results with one another and discovering what is similar and what is different between them is called contrastive analysis in NLP (see page **35**). For example, if one of your colleagues always makes you feel you have something to contribute, and another tends to leave you feeling small and inadequate, discovering exactly what are the key differences between them will enable you to identify what *you* can do to change this. You'll also know how to help other people feel *they* have something to contribute.

Gather information about how the person behaves and also about what is going on inside for them. Ask them how and what they are thinking, as well as what they actually do. It will be useful to discover what their preferred representational systems (see page **73**) and sub-modalities (see page **80**) are. Find out about their sequences and strategies. What do they think, or do, first? – and after that? – and then? Someone who is good at achieving their targets might, for example, keep a picture in their mind of the finished report, or object, they are working towards. They might talk to themselves encouragingly. They might forgive themselves when they make a mistake. There is established evidence, for example, that people who have had persistent weight problems are more likely to succeed eventually in becoming thinner if they forgive themselves for their lapses. People who criticise themselves when they snack or can't resist something on their 'naughty' list are more likely to feel bad as a result, and then to eat more for comfort or out of rebellion. Modelling people who succeed in as much detail as you can is more likely to provide you with your recipes for success.

If you are modelling someone you know, or can have personal contact with, establish and maintain rapport with them. Adopt an attitude of curiosity rather than judgement. You are asking them for their success recipe, after all. Even if something about it surprises you or strikes you as strange, it has worked for them. Ask yourself why that might be.

You don't have to know someone in order to model them. If you don't have personal access to them, you will need to rely on information from other sources – books, articles, TV programmes and so on. This makes it harder to model, but by no means impossible. If you are trawling sources like these, keep your eyes and ears open to make sure you don't miss any details which may turn out to be significant. The person who compiled the programme or the article may not be attaching the same emphasis as you are to the material they have collected, so something they think of as peripheral may be gold to you. Similarly, if you are reading your model's own account of what they do or have achieved, be attentive to small things they may not realise are significant in their own approach or behaviour.

▪ *Outcome Orientation: The Well-formedness Conditions*

NLP coaching is aimed at helping you achieve your goals, and it's effective. It shows you how to clarify and specify what you're going for so that it satisfies a number of conditions. In NLP these are called the well-formedness conditions because if you adhere to them you will be shaping or formulating your goals – forming them well, in short.

1. What are the well-formedness conditions?

State your goal in positive terms. The brain can't process negatives directly (you can see this if you try *not* to think of a blue tree). Saying what you *don't* want doesn't make it clear what you *do* want, and may just keep on reinforcing the negative. For instance, 'I must lose weight' will invariably cause the person saying it to focus yet again on what they don't want – their weight.

Imagine your goal in as much detail as possible, using all your senses. Be specific. When you've achieved it, what will it look like, sound like, feel like, even smell and taste like? By making it this specific, you make it vivid, and this is what makes a goal into an outcome. Until you get the vivid detail, all you've got is an idea. Give it oomph, drama, colour – and your brain will find it very compelling. So discover what will tell you that you have achieved your goal – what your sensory evidence will be.

Check that your outcome is under your control and that you can both initiate and maintain it. If you want something that involves other people, discover how achieving your desire might benefit them, too. (In NLP this is known as dovetailing outcomes.) People are much more likely to help you if they gain something out of it too, whether tangible, or intangible – such as feeling good because they have been able to help. You also need to be aware that some outcomes can't ever be within your control, so these can't be seen as well-formed in NLP terms.

Clarify the context – where and when and with whom do you want your outcome? It's equally important to consider where, when and with whom you don't want it.

Know the positive by-product of your present behaviour. In achieving your goal, will you lose, or significantly compromise, anything you're gaining by your current behaviour? If you will, this may make it difficult or impossible to achieve your goal. If getting promoted means lots more travel away from your family, you may unconsciously be limiting your ambitions. So we need to know if there are any advantages to the present way of doing things which ideally you would take with you when you achieve this outcome.

Consider the ecology of your goal. Ask yourself, is your desired outcome worth the cost (in every sense, not just monetary) and the time it will take, and is it in keeping with your sense of self? A well-formed outcome doesn't significantly interfere with anything that is important to you. Instead, it actually enhances your sense of self.

2. What do the well-formedness conditions do?

They help ensure that you frame your goals in a way that gives you the greatest possibility of achieving them. They also help you to get clear about whether you really do want something. Our clients frequently use this process, then decide on a different course of action. As one of them said: 'I think I've just saved myself 18 months of hard work to get somewhere which would have been wrong for me.'

3. Everyday examples of well-formedness conditions

Let's take one of our client's goals: 'I want to go round the world.' Then we can see how this matches up to the well-formedness conditions.

► It's stated positively.

► Is it sensory specific? Yes, if you know what this will involve for you. You might think, for example, 'I'll enjoy the travelling, I'll meet lots of interesting people, I'll see ancient places and different landscapes, I'll eat exotic foods, I'll be creating memories that last a lifetime.' Now it's beginning to be less generalised, but you'll make it much more vivid by specifying how you'll travel (by train, in Europe, plane across Asia and so on), just what those interesting people will be like, from which cultures, which particular ancient places and new landscapes you'll see and exactly which exotic foods. If you then add in the feel and colour of different climates, you'll make this outcome really live.

► Is it within your control to make arrangements and decisions? Yes, and you may need to collaborate with others.

► Contextualised: you know what your trip will involve. You know which countries you're stopping in, that you're going with your partner, that you're planning to visit your cousins, and that you're taking six months to do it, starting in June next year.

► Maintains positive by-products of your current state: it doesn't involve loss of income because you are currently between jobs, and it doesn't threaten your earning potential, as you're renting out your place while you're away.

► And what about the ecology? Consider the following factors:
  - Cost: You're between jobs anyway and you have enough saved.

- Time: Have you done the necessary planning? Is this the right time for you and are you okay with how long the overall trip will take?
- Sense of self: Are such new experiences, adventures and uncertainty all congruent with you?

An example of an outcome which is not well-formed is 'I want to win the lottery,' because this is not within your control. Equally, it wouldn't be a well-formed outcome to want to become an airline pilot if you have poor sight or can't do maths. But if you want to become a millionaire, this could become a well-formed outcome if you have a really good marketing idea, start-up capital, know your field, can see a niche and get clear about what it is *you* are going to do that can really make this happen.

4. Think of using the well-formedness conditions

▶ As a check whenever you want something.

▶ When planning career or life changes.

▶ When you're not achieving in the way you'd like to – it may be a sign that one of the conditions isn't being met.

5. How you can use the well-formedness conditions

When you have an idea, or a wish, take the time to run it through these conditions. Ensuring that your desired outcome is shaped in a way that meets these conditions will show you what may still need to be done, or where potential difficulties lie. When all the conditions are met, you will have given yourself the best chance you can of making your goal a reality, provided you take whatever actions are now necessary to follow it through.

▪ *Pacing and Leading*

1. What is pacing and leading?

Pacing literally means going at someone else's pace: fast if they are fast, slow if they are slow. In NLP, it also has a metaphoric meaning – acknowledging another by going at their pace in every way. In terms of behaviour, it may mean echoing their posture in the way you stand or sit; being as energised as they are; using similar metaphors or representational language to theirs; echoing their views. Pacing means you're going to be taking your lead from them.

Pacing is crucial in building rapport. Pacing someone gives them a powerful message that you respect them and are taking them seriously. It is likely to make them feel they are being heard or valued.

If you lead someone you give them direction. We do this when out for a walk and one person guides the other down this path rather than that. By analogy, leading is the process of attempting to influence someone else. This may be in obvious ways like telling them what to do, or in more subtle and indirect ways, such as offering a new choice which they find attractive at that particular moment. NLP modelling of people who are successful in influencing others shows that they first establish rapport through pacing the others involved, and only then do they attempt to lead. Too often people try to lead prematurely and merely trigger resistance.

Think of it as a dance. The sequence is pace, pace, pace, lead.

2. What do pacing and leading do?

They provide you with the essential basis for successful interaction with other people. They help you to build trust and cooperation, and make working together both a more pleasant and a more productive experience, whether at the office or at home.

3. Everyday examples of pacing and leading

► You decide you want a much better kind of job. When you start looking round you realise you need to get some qualifications. This feels a bit daunting so you decide to pace yourself by doing it one step at a time. In this way you build your confidence and lead yourself toward success.

► A friend is feeling down. Rather than trying to cheer them up too soon, you match their low energy level and only then do you start to lead them out of their state by gradually becoming more animated and suggesting you both go out for the evening.

4. Think of pacing and leading

It's vital to think of pacing and leading at all times, as it is the basis of all effective communication. More specifically, think of it:

► When you want to establish rapport and trust.

► When you want someone's help.

► When someone is frightened, anxious or hostile.

► When you wish to be more influential.

5. How you can use pacing and leading

Observe the other person closely. Look for posture, expression, stance, speed of breathing and speech. You can pace any and all of these. Listen to language that may indicate their favoured representational system(s) and incorporate some of this into your own speech. Pay attention to their meta programmes and incorporate them into what you're saying and doing.

Go at their pace, mirror their physical stance and movements in subtle ways (don't attempt to copy slavishly: this will be noticed and probably misinterpreted as mimicry). Continue to pace. Pace for even longer than you think you need to – until you begin to get signs that the other person is feeling at ease and that rapport is really established. Only then think about taking the lead.

▪ *Taking Different Perceptual Positions*

1. What are perceptual positions?

Your perception of any experience depends on the position from which you perceive it. There are three positions which experientially are particularly useful. They are known in NLP as first, second and third position.

► In **first position** you are in your own body, looking out through your own eyes, seeing things from your point of view.

► Being in **second position** means stepping into someone else's shoes, imagining what it's like to be them, looking at the world through their eyes.

► **Third position** entails taking a concerned observer's view of events in which you are involved, being a fly on the wall, and accessing the view or comments of your 'wiser self'.

2. What does taking different perceptual positions do?

Taking different perceptual positions enables you to step out of what you are currently experiencing. It allows you to see things from a different perspective and gather different information. You can also check out how your own behaviour may be impacting on other people, and how they may be feeling about you. In a similar way to three-dimensional computer graphics, it helps you to turn a situation around and experience it from different angles. Different positions can help you access information you already have unconsciously but which you are unaware of or ignoring because of the immediacy or strength of your first-position feelings.

3. Everyday examples of taking different perceptual positions

► Noticing what you feel, what you want, seeing from inside your own eyes (first position).

► Wondering what it's like to be someone else in the same situation (second position).

► Seeing yourself and others as if from an outside perspective, as a concerned observer (third position).

4. Think of taking a different perceptual position

► When there is a conflict at work or in a relationship.

► When planning a holiday or other project.

► When evaluating a situation, such as your colleagues' or partner's behaviour.

► When you feel stuck or over-emotional.

► When you are feeling overwhelmed by obligations or other people's needs and wishes so that you can reconnect with your own.

5. How you can use different perceptual positions

They are very useful in helping you improve rapport. They can enable you to check out the possible results of choices and actions before acting on them. Taking different perceptual positions can also help you understand where others are coming from in negotiations or disagreements. And they can help you reconnect with your own feelings and needs.

▪ *Rapport*

1. What is rapport?

Rapport comes from showing other people by your behaviour and by your words that you accept the validity of their experience *for them*. You are meeting them in their model of the world. By so doing you create the basis for cooperative communication – and that is rapport. Being in rapport is not the same as agreeing with them. You can disagree with someone but still have rapport with them.

2. What does rapport do?

Rapport creates the effective basis for communicating with others.

3. Everyday examples of rapport

► Caring enough to genuinely ask how someone else is.

► Building trust by being consistent.

► Acknowledging how it is for someone, perhaps by commenting non-judgementally on their current state.

► Remembering what's important to another.

► Choosing clothes that 'fit in with' a particular work or social occasion – this is creating rapport through matching them externally.

► Being able to join in the fun.

4. Think of rapport

▶ When you want to increase your influence in a way which is genuine and non-manipulative – be it in your marriage or at a job interview.

▶ When you disagree with someone's view but want to maintain a good relationship with them.

▶ When someone seems ill at ease or lacking in confidence.

▶ When you want to encourage someone to confide in you or 'open up' and say more.

5. How you can use rapport

Rapport is particularly important when you want to put others at ease or make them feel comfortable. It can help you to establish or promote a better relationship between yourself and others and to deepen liking and trust. Rapport can help your friends and colleagues know you are 'with' them before you start asking them to change in any way.

You can establish and maintain rapport through pacing and leading (see above, page **66**). You can pace people in many ways: by talking their kind of language; by mirroring their body positioning and gestures; by 'hearing them out' before you put in your penny's worth. Pacing someone is a powerful way of showing them respect. Once they experience this acknowledgement they are much more available. You could say it earns you the right in their eyes to begin to influence them. If you haven't established this rapport, why should they let you lead their thoughts in any direction? Put another way, pacing is a powerful way of connecting with someone; and only when we have made a connection can productive interaction begin to take place. Without pacing, all we are doing is telling people things, giving them orders or responding to information. We're not in a dialogue. With rapport established, we can move from pacing to leading.

▪ *Reframing*

1. What is reframing?

'I am open to reason, you are impressionable, he is gullible.' – reframing is changing the meaning of an experience or an event by putting another frame around it. Often reframing happens verbally, as in the above example. Sometimes a reframe can be a single word. For instance: in times of change you might want to ask yourself 'Is this change a problem or an opportunity?' It can also happen when a situation occurs that sheds a new light on something.

> One of our clients left school at sixteen and felt inferior because, though successful, he'd never been to university, and all his colleagues had. He was also happily married. When we asked him how he met his wife, he told us she had been a friend of someone he worked with in a particularly menial job he'd had about a year after leaving school. Then he paused. Suddenly he said: 'Thank God I didn't go to university. I'd never have met her, and she's the best thing that's ever happened to me.'

2. What does reframing do?

Reframing causes you to see things differently: it's a new interpretation, with the result tht you arrive at a different conclusion, evaluation or feeling. You can reframe experiences, single words, or even whole eras. For instance, you could think of the Industrial Revolution as the end of an era of 'natural' society and social relationships. Then again, you might think of it as the beginning of a way of life in which skill and merit were gradually freed from social class and location. Neither interpretation is the 'right' one – but as with every reframe you will think and feel very differently about the same set of events and their consequences depending on which perspective you take.

3. Everyday examples of reframing

► Realising that this problem actually creates a new opportunity for you.

► 'He failed his exam' vs 'He didn't pass this time.'

► 'Their marriage failed' vs 'She outgrew him.'

4. Think of reframing

▶ When you are faced with something which you or someone else finds unpleasant, threatening or difficult. Might there be another way of looking at it? For example, could it give you a chance to learn something new, or extend your skills in any way?

▶ When you need to get another perspective on anything. Put it in another setting and see how it looks then.

▶ When something seems too good to be true. Sometimes it can be a really good idea to test out whether it still seems as promising if you consider it from a different angle.

5. How you can use reframing

Train yourself to explore different ways of thinking about the same phenomena or set of events. Is having a cold a disastrous impediment to your work schedule – or a chance for a rest? Or something else entirely?

Train yourself to notice the subtle differences between words and the way they frame things and lead to different effects. For example: new, modern, inventive, original, radical, vs old, traditional, hidebound, stick-in-the-mud, well-tried and tested.

Notice how other people frame things, and how the media frame them. Are there other ways you could think of the same events – and how would it be different if you did? Where a reframe has an enabling or freeing effects, use it!

▪ *Representational Systems*

1. What are representational systems?

You get information about the world through your five senses, but you use much more than those same senses to represent the world to yourself internally. For example, while hearing is one of your five senses, hearing involves a great deal more than just picking up sound. You have to do a whole lot more neurologically to process, store and make sense of the sounds your ear takes in. The same is true for all of your senses.

Furthermore, you have the ability to make pictures inside your head, to replay or imagine speech and sound, to replay or imagine physical sensations, tastes and smells. NLP calls these complex forms of internal processing – and everything entailed in making them possible and understandable – representational systems because an entire system is involved in generating your experience. Sometimes they are also referred to as modalities, because each is a mode, or way, of operating internally upon the data we receive from the outside world.

Most people tend to rely more on one or two representational systems than the others, and often the language we use gives us and other people clues as to which representational system we're using at any given time. Often, common idioms give us a clue to what may be going on:

► I couldn't get on his wavelength (auditory).

► I just couldn't see it from his perspective (visual).

► I couldn't grasp the point he was trying to make (kinesthetic).

► We didn't see eye to eye (visual).

► It felt all wrong to me, though it was fine as far as he was concerned (kinesthetic).

► It sounded like Double Dutch to me (auditory).

Some turns of phrase have lost their freshness in everyday speech; so some may just be clichés. Nevertheless, if you pay attention to the words you and others are naturally using, you will get really valuable information as to what is going on inside.

2. What do representational systems do?

They create our world for us. Representational systems make the pictures in our minds, the feelings we sense, the words we hear in our heads, the way we talk to ourselves, the tastes and smells we experience and remember.

3. Everyday examples of representational systems

► Getting a *clear picture* of how you want your future.

► Getting a *feel* for a new job.

► Getting to *hear* what everyone is really *saying*.

► Enjoying the sweet *smell* of success.

► Experiencing something which really leaves a *nasty taste* in the mouth.

► Beginning to *feel* healthier.

► Getting a *handle* on running your business.

4. Think of representational systems

► When seeking to build rapport, so you can literally talk the same language as the other person.

► When trying to understand how someone else is experiencing something.

► When you want to experience things more fully or differently. By focusing on different sensory aspects of your experience, you begin to have a different internal experience – for example, you might switch your attention from how something or someone looks to how they sound.

5. How you can use representational systems

To understand which system(s) are most influential for you and to enrich your experience by:

► Paying attention to sensory information coming to you through your less favoured senses.

► By deliberately cultivating your less favoured senses in your internal processing. For example, if you are taking a walk in the country, you may naturally be noticing what you see. If you stop and shut your eyes for a moment, you will give yourself the opportunity to notice what you can hear, or feel or smell as well.

By becoming fluent in all of them you will be increasing your flexibility and you'll be able to get on with a much broader range of people – and to understand 'where other people are coming from'. Paying attention to the metaphors and phrases they use will tell you how they are thinking, and give you an opportunity of understanding the world as they are experiencing it.

People experience the world very differently and it's vital to be able to meet them in their map of their world if you want to build and maintain rapport and understand what's important for them. If you notice other people's language and begin to use metaphors and phrases drawn from the same sensory system(s) that they are using, you will be matching them in a natural and unobtrusive way; and matching is one useful way of creating rapport. The implicit message is 'I'm with you and I'm willing to speak your language.'

▪ *Sensory acuity*

1. What is sensory acuity?

Sensory acuity involves paying greater attention to the information you get through your senses. The more you pay attention, the greater your discriminating ability, the finer detail you can gather, and the more you can make comparisons between different sorts and degrees of information.

Sensory acuity is a process of refining your responses to the world around you – including your inner world. It's about making sharper distinctions and refining your awareness. For example, if you enjoy walking in the country, ask yourself exactly what it is that you enjoy so much. Perhaps it's seeing the fields and trees and wildlife, or enjoying the changes of the seasons. Perhaps it's the feeling of walking in the fresh air, the rhythm of striding along. Your pleasure may come from many things. Then next time you're out, notice even more detail within the range you know is important to you. If you delight in what you see, is it the colour, the shapes, the variety that pleases you? Is it the contrasts, the shades? Another time, you could pay attention to another of your senses. What can you hear? What about smells? Can you taste anything?

Information is potentially available to you through all five senses, but mostly you will be habituated to noticing only part of what is available. Widening the range of information helps enrich the experience. It will also help you wise up to what is going on. This enhanced sensory awareness is at least partly responsible for 'feminine intuition'. Many men miss a lot of the cues that would tell them what's happening and how others are responding, be it in a personal relationship or a business presentation. Developing your sensory acuity enables you to notice what's happening – and not least, what effect you're having.

2. What does sensory acuity do?

It gives you important information that can enrich the pleasure you take in life, enable you to learn faster and more accurately, become more informed about others and more influential in your dealings with them.

3. Everyday examples of sensory acuity

► Being able to read a change in the facial expressions of someone you know well.

► Appreciating the manoeuvres that lead up to a winning goal.

► Distinguishing between a table wine and a vintage wine.

► Noticing a disparity between what someone is saying – such as 'I agree' – and the flat, listless way in which they are saying it.

4. When to use sensory acuity

► When you want to find out the difference that makes the difference.

► When you want more information than words are giving you.

► Whenever you want to enjoy something more.

► When you are modelling someone.

► When you want to understand more about your own state or someone else's.

5. How you can use sensory acuity

Get into the habit of noticing more detail, and of asking yourself what kind of detail is important – the difference that makes a difference. If someone is well-dressed, just what is it about their clothing, or their choice of clothing, that tells you that? How does a ready-made lasagne differ from one that has been freshly cooked? Exactly how did you know that two people conversing on the train were friends and that they were gossiping? What are the micro-messages that you're picking up?

▪ *States*

1. What is a state?

A state is your way of being at any given moment. It involves:

▶ What's happening in your brain – your neurological activity.

▶ What's going on in your body and at what rate – your physical experience and level of energy.

▶ What you're doing and sensing – your general activity.

▶ What you're feeling – your emotions.

▶ What and how you're thinking – your mental activity.

You are always in some kind of a state, though often you are not conscious of the fact. You also change states as external or internal circumstances change. States often get labelled as though everyone experienced them similarly – for example, happy, sad, angry, worried. But you need to remember that because a state involves many elements, your experience of any one of them may well differ in some, or many, respects from that of someone else who apparently feels 'the same'.

Association and *dissociation* are two key states which shape our experience in profound ways. We discussed them in detail above, on page **26**.

The language you, or someone else, use will often give clues to whether you're associated or dissociated. Associated states are usually reflected in subjective language, with first person ('I') pronouns and active verbs, often using short sentences and words that involve the senses. Dissociated states are often indicated by phrases involving *it, they, that, there was* rather than 'I', passive speech constructions, longer and more complex sentence structure and a higher proportion of abstract words.

2. What do states do?

States profoundly affect how you feel and how you behave. They can be resourceful or unresourceful. They can make it difficult to achieve something or they may be just right for what you want to do. The everyday phrases 'getting in a state' and 'being in a fit state' reflect this. You will have a radically different experience of an event if you are *associated into* it from the one you'd have if you were *dissociated from* it.

3. Everyday examples of states

► Being anxious before a driving test or interview.

► Being calm (or panicky) before an important deadline.

► Being cheerful on a fine day.

► Reflecting on an experience after the event.

These examples also show how states can be linked with external circumstances and with the associations they have for us. You may look forward to performance situations such as interviews, for example, and you will therefore experience a different state from someone who dreads them.

4. Think of using states

► When you or someone else are 'in a state'. What is your current state? what would be a better state to be in? Remember you can change your states. There are many ways: anchoring, reframing, doing something different, exercising, to name but a few.

► When you want to be 'in a fit state' for something. What are the elements of that 'fit state', and how can you put them in place or trigger them?

► Whenever you want to increase your effectiveness, prepare your state beforehand if you can.

5. How you can use and change states

Get to know your states. Begin to notice how you experience some more frequently than others. When you are in a state that is unpleasant, or inappropriate to the situation, change your physiology: stand up, stretch, move faster or more slowly. Physiology is one of the most accessible aspects of a state to change. Even registering what state you are in will begin to change it. Ask yourself what triggered this particular state (see 'Anchors', page **24**).

When you notice a pleasant or resourceful state, ask yourself what triggered it. The section on Anchors will show you how you can recreate and even enhance this state whenever it is appropriate.

Think about activities that are important to you. Are you usually in an appropriate state for them? If you are in the right state only sometimes, or infrequently, identify the trigger – or anchor in NLP terms – that takes you into the right state, and practise using it so that you can recreate this state easily. Then you can ensure that you are in the right state for the situation or the task in hand.

▪ *Sub-modalities*

1. What are sub-modalities?

The five senses are sometimes known in NLP as modalities, because each is a mode or way of processing information. For ease of use, the initial letter of each modality is often given:

► Seeing involves visual processing (V).

► Hearing involves auditory processing (A).

► Feeling involves kinesthetic processing (K).

► Smell involves olfactory processing (O).

► Taste involves gustatory processing (G).

But these are broad categorisations. If we think about the different visual distinctions we can make, we could ask of any image:

► Is it in colour or black and white?

► Is it clear or fuzzy?

► How far away is it?

► Is the image moving or still?

► Is the image flat or three-dimensional? and so on.

NLP calls these distinctions sub-modalities, because each one of them is a particular way of describing or refining something that happens within the specific modality.

2. What do sub-modalities do

When you look at something out there, the impact it has on you will be affected by some of these sub-modalities, often without your being aware of it. Similarly, when you process images internally, their impact will depend on the particular way you have constructed the image for yourself. For example, brightly coloured images often have a more powerful effect: they may be more attractive – or more frightening. Moving images may seem more 'alive' – which can be wonderful or horrible. Particular sub-modalities will be especially influential. These are known as critical sub-modalities. Knowing which ones are more influential for you gives you an important key to structuring your experience. It helps you enormously if you want to enhance or change any internal representations.

Sub-modality Checklist
Here is a partial list of some interesting sub-modalities. These are what guide your experience of its particular quality – for good or ill.

Visual

Brightness	Contrast	Flat/3D
Size	Clarity	Associated/dissociated
Colour/black and white	Movie/still	Frame/panorama

Auditory

Pitch	Rhythm	Volume
Tonality	Distance	Clarity
Resonance		

Kinesthetic

Pressure	Location	Texture
Temperature	Movement	Duration
Intensity	Shape	

3. Everyday examples of sub-modalities

► Next year's *too far off* for me to *see it clearly* – it's *all a blur* at the moment.

► I love the *rhythm* of his speech and his *soft brogue*.

► When I'm anxious I feel like there's *a cold knot* in the *pit* of my stomach.

4. Think of sub-modalities

▶ When you want to get the most out of something. What representational system are you using? Which sub-modalities of that system work most strongly for you? Make sure that you build the strongest representation you can.

▶ When your current representation is unpleasant or limiting. Experiment with changing sub-modalities to find out which improve the effect of your representation. Are you remembering something horrid in vivid colour? Then make it black and white and put it further away in your mind's eye. Does this make a difference?

5. How to use sub-modalities

Use the checklist to find out which sub-modalities are most influential for you, and experiment to find the effects of changing any of them. If you make a change – for example, making a visual image colour instead of black and white – and this improves the effect, keep the image as you have altered it. But if the change doesn't improve things, alter it back to how you had it originally – or experiment with another kind of change.

Pay attention to clues other people give you about which sub-modalities are influential for them. This will enable you to match them more effectively – and to know where they are coming from.

These, then, are the NLP tools we'll be utilising in the rest of the book. In fact there are many others and a whole host of specialised techniques. However, we have found these ones particularly useful in coaching. But first we need to investigate how beliefs about success and failure can influence things for better or for worse.

PART 3

Success and Failure

Introduction

WHEN SOMEONE COMES to us for coaching, we like to begin by exploring with them not only what their goals are, but also what would count as success and as failure. We like to know what they believe about success and failure.

There are two reasons for this. First, unless you have a clear idea, in actual, observable (and sometimes measurable) terms, what would be success for you, your goal remains unclear and you have no clear way of measuring when you have achieved it. Second, what you believe has profound effects on how you go about something; and, in the case of beliefs about success and failure, if you're not careful this can load and predetermine your progress without your even being aware of it.

For example, if you apply for a job, and are told after the interview that someone else has been appointed, the way you understand what has gone on may be crucial for what happens next.

You may tell yourself you 'failed to get the job' and feel not only disappointed but inadequate. Perhaps you were foolish to even think of applying in the first place. Perhaps you should go for a job that offers less pay and asks for less responsibility next time. In short, framing the event as a 'failure' has made you feel bad. Feeling bad has had a knock-on effect on your self-esteem, and has made you lower your aspirations.

On the other hand, you may remind yourself that you don't know about the other candidates. Maybe one of them had just the combination of skills and personal qualities the employer was looking for. You tell yourself that that doesn't mean there's anything wrong with you – and in fact, if they preferred someone else it rather suggests the fit between you and the job wouldn't have been the best anyway. You run through what you remember of the interview and make some notes about a couple of questions where you thought you might have answered more clearly, or where you felt short on information. Next time you will be crisper, clearer, more authoritative as a result. By being curious about what happened, and by reminding yourself that there are many factors in a situation which are not known to you, you have stayed away from the trap of feeling bad, and have given yourself the best chance for next time.

Both these approaches depend on your beliefs about what was going on. Beliefs are theories, not facts – but they are theories which we treat as if they were facts, and because of this our actions tend to make them come true, as we shall see later. In our example, believing that you are inadequate is likely to make you underperform in future interviews, and 'fail' to get more jobs. But believing that your rejection was based on valid reasons that don't necessarily reflect badly on you – and at the same time taking steps to ensure you are even better prepared next time – is likely to give you a better chance of succeeding.

So one of the aims of this book is to help you establish what your measures of progress are. Part of our role as NLP coaches is to help you recognise what assumptions you may unconsciously be making, so that you can discover which are helpful and which are limiting. It's important to be able to identify these at the outset if you are to achieve your goals.

So often success and failure are in the eye of the beholder.

Two sisters, Jenny and Lisa, who were both divers, entered the same competition. While both achieved the same very respectable score, neither won. Jenny had set her heart on winning, so her performance was a 'failure' as far as she was concerned. Lisa had been experiencing problems with a particular dive, and had worked hard to overcome them. On the day, she was very satisfied that she had ironed out the basic difficulties and as a result her performance had improved significantly. For her, the very same mark was a 'success' – and a promise of greater success in the future.

Success or failure? So often it depends on who you ask. What about the elderly couple who had been married for many years? Some of their younger relatives thought that they were not really suited, and that they had only managed to 'rub along together' for so long largely because they had come from a generation in which divorce was rare. Yet the couple themselves valued many things about each other and their relationship, and considered it 'a success'.

Or take James, a man in his late eighties whose doctor diagnosed 'heart failure' – but who continued to live for eleven months, albeit with periods of weakness, and to carry out normal activities including driving his car, until two days before his death? What kind of failure was this?

Your beliefs – and language – are one significant way in which you can limit yourself and block your way forward by ceasing to look for new options or new ways of seeing the situation. The word 'failure' itself usually leads to such powerful feelings – sadness, despondency, loss of self-esteem – that what we do next is also imperilled.

One way to cut through this is to recognise that, stripped of emotion, 'success' means that you got what you wanted, or more; and 'failure' means that you didn't. Either events matched your hopes, expectations or aspirations, or they didn't. Holding on to this more factual way of describing what's happened can help you stay in a frame of mind where you can begin to ask the kind of questions that can take you forward: How did things come out that way? What do I need to adjust? What do I need to do next? What resources would help me do it?

▪ *Success and Failure: Three Guiding Principles*

As coaches, we have found three principles that can make a huge difference to what you are able to accomplish. If you know these at the outset, they can make your journey so much easier:

- First, failure is not an accident.
- Second, feedback is the foundation of success.
- Third, success has a structure.

In the rest of this section we're going to explore each of these principles more fully. Taken together, they can change old habits of thinking and your success hit rate. Once you have taken these three principles on board, you will find that instead of being downhearted or stuck and making no progress, you will have at hand a valuable source of information – and thus, effectively, a prescription for exactly the progress you desire. These three principles make it possible to turn what we used to think of as setbacks into success, get the feedback we need in order to know what to do next, and figure out the key factors we need to get right if we are to succeed.

CHAPTER 4

Failure is Not an Accident

FAILURE DOESN'T JUST happen – it has structure and sequence. Have you ever run a business that failed? Did you ever fail your driving test? Have you ever worked on a project or an experiment that failed? Have you ever been in a relationship that failed? In NLP, these 'failures' are taken as the results of interactions in a system.

Let us explain. NLP takes a systemic view of things. This means looking at the different elements in a situation as parts of a system which functions for good or ill. This system will involve people or events and a sequence of thoughts, feelings, actions and interactions. The outcome of events that we call 'failure' is the result of such interactions in the system. Once you understand how the system is working – for or against you – you have a means of structuring things differently in the future, and so can avoid 'failure' again.

People are creatures of pattern and habit. This goes for both the way our successes are achieved, and the way we unknowingly construct our 'failures'. In this chapter, we're going to look at how this kind of patterning leads predictably, not accidentally, to success and failure. And we're also going to show you how failure patterns can be turned around.

Our experience as coaches is that the labels 'success' and 'failure' can sometimes get in the way of useful understanding because they cause us to feel good and bad rather than curious. Even feeling good can, paradoxically, stop us investigating further what exactly has been contributing to our successes, so that we miss an opportunity of finding out more about how we achieved what we did. And as a result we're less able to repeat that success in the future.

But what about a business that's not making enough money to continue trading? Or someone who takes a driving test and is consequently refused a full licence? Or a farmer's crop which is adversely affected by bad weather conditions and makes only a fraction of its potential harvest? Surely these are simple, clear cases: 'His business failed', 'He failed his test', 'The farmer's crop failed.' The very language we use somehow implies that the 'failure' is a fact: that it is an external event with no possibility of other interpretation.

However, if we look a little closer, things can seem very different. Take the failing business.

> Bill had a little mail-order business. He sold small gadgets, so at first it was possible to manage the concern from his spare bedroom, with the goods and packaging in his garage. But because the product was the right thing at the right time, it became very successful, and the orders multiplied. Bill's wife and sister-in-law were drawn in to help. Space became a problem, but the turnover wasn't enough, Bill thought, to take the risk of renting premises. However, a neighbour had a spare room, so the packaging 'department' shifted there. Then the problems began. Orders got delayed and muddled, stock went missing and suddenly Bill found costs had risen more than he had anticipated. Before he knew it his customers were becoming dissatisfied and telling others, and his revenue started declining seriously.

Was this situation one of personal failure on Bill's part, or a failure of systems, structures and processes? It's an important difference. The idea of personal failure often implies that the person is inadequate in some way – that is, it's an issue which can be felt at identity level. But the idea of system, structure and process involves other logical levels (see page **48**) entirely: belief, capability, behaviour and environment become the places to begin looking for causes and cures. There wasn't anything wrong with Bill, but he certainly needed to put some new systems in place. That's when he decided to get some business coaching. Bill's coach helped him learn from his experience and rebuild his business on a sound footing this time.

And what about that failed driving test? Most of us would agree that the driving test is designed as a test of capability and behaviour – but somehow, failing the test often becomes an issue of identity! If you remember that the key thing to consider is structure, and look carefully at how you failed, you are in a better position to work towards a different outcome, and at the same time to avoid feeling so bad about yourself.

> One young driver who failed his test read carefully through the test sheet afterwards and realised that the failure-ticks all related to one major problem: he hadn't been seen to be taking enough care of other road users. He had glanced in his mirror without moving his head, so he wasn't clearly demonstrating his awareness of other traffic to the examiner; and when joining a bypass he had crept up the slip-lane so that cars behind him and cars on the bypass both had to slow down to accommodate him. Once he had worked out how his own actions had contributed to his failure, he also knew what he needed to do next time.

Finally, what about the farmer whose crop failed?

> The farmer was completely dependent on the yield from one kind of crop alone because he had invested heavily in it – so all his investment was affected. His neighbour had some milking cattle as well as fields of wheat, so he was able to offset a poor return in one area by a good one in the other. The first farmer gambled on the basis of previous good years, in which he had made a considerable profit from his sole crop. When he compared his experience with that of his neighbour, he decided that in future it would be wiser to spread his investment more widely.

In working with any of these people, an NLP coach would encourage them to accept that there was a clear relationship between their actions and the outcome they got – but also to recognise that blaming themselves will not promote success. To know how you messed up and what you could do differently from now on is really useful – but just feeling a mess isn't. If your choices have been limited or ineffective, a coach can help you:

- Retrieve useful learning from the experience.

- Look at other options that might have been possible.

- Clarify how you might behave differently in future.

This structured approach actually helps you move from a feeling of powerlessness after the event to a position of greater empowerment for the future.

• *The Structure of Failure Relates to the Individual*

As the young would-be driver realised, each failure has a structure. Things happen that cause other things to happen. There's a sequence. He already knew something of NLP, so by being curious instead of simply disappointed when he read his test comments he was able to identify the structure for failure which he had inadvertently been running, and to do something about it. He immediately made sure that every time he looked in the mirror he made a fractional head movement which would be visible to the examiner in their peripheral vision; and he decided to take some driving lessons with a specific focus on managing dual carriageways. He knew he had previously crept onto them in order to stay at a speed he could safely manage; but now it was time to learn to manage a higher speed so he could simply slot into the existing traffic pattern without impeding its flow.

We have all had experiences in life where we feel we have failed, or where some outside agency has made that judgement. It can also be true that a pattern that worked in some circumstances may come unstuck in others, as many people in Britain and the US found when they bought houses at the height of the housing market, then found themselves in negative equity when prices went down. The world outside does change, and we can all be affected when it does. But if we take a longer view, even these larger-scale events can be understood at a structural level. Nothing 'just fails' or 'just succeeds'.

Failure Relates to Our Personal Patterning

Human beings are creatures of habit. We learn skills, acquire knowledge and experience. Once these have been processed consciously, we store them at an unconscious level and they then become automatic. Hence, that reputation as 'creatures of habit'.

This process helps us in many ways by freeing our conscious awareness for new experience and decisions. But we are equally patterned about our mistakes and our so-called failures. We can all fail once at something – but what if we keep repeating the pattern, and failing again? Take a marriage that goes wrong: two people married young, then outgrew each other. She married again, but somehow chose the same type of man ... and after a while, that marriage went wrong too. Her ex-husband, on the other hand, stayed single for a while and went out with a number of different women, saying, 'I don't want to make the same mistake again.'

This man, like the young driver, was able to recognise that there might be a pattern to his failure, and started to examine his own behaviour carefully so that he could learn how to avoid a repeat.

▪ *Knowing Your Own Patterns*

As we've seen, NLP has a strong interest in the way human beings create and use patterns. The early NLP studies of outstanding but very different practitioners confirmed that excellent practice tends to involve many of the same patterns of thought and behaviour, whatever the theoretical orientation of the practitioner. You'll find the concept of patterning, which includes patterns shared by many people and patterns which are formed and repeated by single individuals, really valuable, whether you have a coach or are self-coaching.

We have also found there are some common failure patterns and we want you to have a chance to see if any of them apply to you. Once you become curious about the pattern of your mistakes, you are no longer a victim: you have begun to take charge of yourself and your life again.

Jane used to believe that she was bad at managing money: for years she had struggled to contain her spending, expending a great deal of energy in worrying and self-recrimination. But somehow her behaviour never changed. Then one day it occurred to her that somehow she never got seriously overdrawn either ... She started wondering about how she did that, and began to realise that in fact she was very skilful at managing to be consistently – but never seriously – out of pocket. Then she began to think that if she was skilful enough to do this, she must actually be quite good at managing money.

Her original belief about herself started to look rather silly. And her problem began to redefine itself: did she want to continue to manage in such a way as to be just over her financial limits, or would she rather put some of her skill into managing to be just within those limits?

She had stopped thinking about herself as a failure and started to think instead about her behaviour and how it could lead to very different consequences. Not only did she get a much better result, she felt differently about herself and she no longer believed she couldn't handle money.

When we notice how our failures are structured, we gain leverage to work on them. So let's see if any of these failure patterns are familiar to you.

▪ *Some Common Failure Patterns*

Staying Stuck

One common 'failure' is the failure to get going on something we need or want to do. Looked at from another perspective, it could be said there's an art to staying stuck. We each have our own favourite ways. The following is a very brief list of some common ones. You may find it useful to tick which ones apply to you and to add any others.

You can prevent or avoid change, even it you want it, by:

► Being afraid of the unknown.

► Spending a lot of time with people who just use a problem frame.

► Presuming change is hard work – and so discouraging yourself.

► Having unrealistic time frames for change.

► Believing what you want can't happen.

► Always doubting your own competence – worrying about the effect of the change on others and doing nothing.

► Taking 'No' for an answer.

► Becoming cynical.

► Keeping yourself under constant pressure.

► Not letting yourself dream.

Now look again at the ones you ticked. Do they form a pattern? Maybe they are all in some way connected with beliefs about yourself? Or perhaps you're worried about what others will think if you become more successful? Or are you afraid about what may happen if you stray outside the confines of what you know already? Or perhaps there is more than one cluster. Knowing the pattern is the first step to discovering how you can alter it.

▪ *Anti-success strategies*

There are also some insidious patterns people run that can produce a sense of failure over time. We call these anti-success strategies.

1. Belittling your achievements

Do you frequently achieve something but fail to acknowledge it to yourself? For example, when you receive a compliment do you brush it off – 'Oh, it was nothing', 'Oh, I just got it in a sale', 'Oh, well, if you stay at anything long enough you're bound to make some progress'? Even if you only think these responses rather than saying them out loud, the effect is the same. You wipe out not just the compliment but much of what it can do for you.

2. Moving the goal posts

After a bonus, a promotion or a success at any level, you instantly – and prematurely – focus on the next hurdle. So, while you feel it's good to have been made a team leader, you change the goal posts and say it but it would be so much better to become an area manager. It's fine to pass Grade Three, but really Grade Four is the one. If you use this anti-success strategy, even when you've got to the top of the formal ladder, you will still find new targets to obscure the successes you've actually achieved. There is nothing wrong with ambition or setting new goals, but never celebrating what you've achieved sends the message to your inner self that nothing is ever good enough.

3. Denial – not admitting your wants

Another, more insidious, self-limiter can be to pretend to yourself that you don't actually want something. Things are just fine as they are. This is often a form of self-protection – from risk, from being hurt, from disappointment. If you don't even allow yourself to think you want something, you'll never have the disappointment of discovering you couldn't achieve it. If, for instance, you don't admit that you really want a closer, more satisfying personal relationship, you don't have to deal with your present unhappiness. You can just have another drink or watch some more television instead.

▪ *Turning Failure into Success*

It is also really useful to question the label 'failure' itself. When James, the man in his eighties, was told he had 'heart failure', he just did not understand what that meant. How was it possible for him to be moving around if his heart had failed?

You will undoubtedly learn something from every 'failure'. The only question is, is it a good learning? Failures can be belief-forming because we draw conclusions from them, and these conclusions guide our future feelings and actions. If a failure leads to self-blame or a sense of worthlessness, it can restrict ambition, bring on depression and perhaps further damage our self-image. This can lead to anger and bitterness, cynicism, or a deviant and revengeful attitude to others, authority or even society in general.

Failure is a word very easily bandied about in education. Children 'fail' tests or exams. They 'fail' to get into the schools they or their parents want them to attend. They 'fail' to achieve their potential. Ian's own story reveals one response to such labelling.

Ian was a 'failure' at secondary school, so he left at 16, and went to what was then called a polytechnic – a college. It was so different from school. It had a wide mix of people from different backgrounds whose ages ranged from 16 to 35 and who were studying a huge range of subjects. The atmosphere was completely different: instead of work being compulsory, now it was up to him. No school uniforms and no detentions for not wearing your school cap; no lessons – just lectures. When you didn't have a lecture you were free to use your time as you saw fit. In short, there was an expectation that students were responsible for their own learning – and that they could be. By the time he left he was a 'star' student, even being cited as proof of the contribution such an institution could make as a safety net in the educational system. Under these circumstances he became a success and went to university.

So was it that his school had 'failed' him, and if so, does that mean that the polytechnic had 'succeeded' him? Or was it that the – as it seemed to him – petty and authoritarian regime of his school really hadn't worked for him, and the polytechnic had allowed him to prepare in his own way to achieve academic success while providing just the kind of support he needed?

When Ian looks back to that time he doesn't think in terms of 'failure'. Instead he knows the specific things which helped or hindered him and has been able to play to his strengths ever since.

We do not deny that you can experience events as failures. If you don't achieve a promotion, aren't granted a mortgage or find yourself getting divorced, you can feel that failure is indeed staring you in the face and this can affect what happens next. But you don't have to stop there. Step back from the situation and ask yourself: 'What is the learning in this for me?' Do this a number of times over a number of days if it's an important event. Also see the episode from the vantage point of an outsider who wished you well, and consider what learning you could get from the situation.

If Ian looks back on his days at school, it's clear that this 'failure' was the springboard to so many of the good things in his life now. For many years he has run a large NLP training organisation. In fact, it is one of the leading institutes world-wide. A large part of what makes it so successful is the way he and his fellow trainers work with people. They act on the belief that people are innately fantastic learners and just need to access their own potential again. So they make the learning direct, easy, experiential and fun. At the end of the day people go home stimulated, tired and happy.

Ian finds working in this way incredibly motivating, and he remembers the day he found out why. He was working with a big group and doing a question and answer session. One of the delegates said how they'd never been in a learning environment like this before, and how they felt really alive and like they were using all of their brain and even their body.

They wanted to know what made him do it this way. And before he'd really thought about it he heard himself saying, 'Ah, well, I am the teacher I never had.'

What beliefs did you form from your 'failures'? Is it time to identify and update beliefs that have limited you or made you unhappy? One way you can do this is by reframing, as we'll see now.

▪ *Reframing Failure*

You'll remember the NLP tool, reframing, from Chapter 3 (see page **72**). Basically, it's like taking a picture or photo out of one frame and putting it in a quite different one, so you can clearly see the difference the frame makes. Our thinking frames our experience. The idea of looking at failure for the learning in it is itself a reframe. So is the transformation of 'I was a failure at school' to 'The school didn't know how to cope with kids like me.' Here are more examples of reframing from people we've worked with.

> Jan was in her forties and had left school at the first opportunity with no formal qualifications. Later, when her children were teenagers, she helped them with their homework and began to get really interested in history. She wondered if it was too late to learn properly, but decided to attend an evening class anyway. Her first essay was muddled and rambling. When she read her tutor's comments at first she felt quite disheartened and thought maybe she just wasn't bright enough. When she talked to her tutor, however, he said that writing essays was just a skill – one which she had never really had the opportunity of learning. So she bought a book on study skills before she actually began writing her next essay, and showed her essay to a friend who had done well in history. She had reframed her initial belief – *I'm hopeless at writing essays* – to *I've got a lot to learn about writing essays, so I'll go and learn it.*

> John and his wife bought their first house. They hadn't much money, and soon after moving in found that the shower really needed replacing. They couldn't afford a plumber. But John was quite good with his hands, and though he had never done plumbing he realised that this job couldn't be too complex if only he knew how to go about it. He decided to buy a do-it-yourself manual which covered elementary

plumbing. John had reframed *I can't fix the shower* to *I don't know how to fix the shower – yet,* and was then able to make the next step: *I'll find out how to fix the shower.*

Rachel and Tessa were friends from school who had married and settled down in the same neighbourhood. They both liked cooking, and after helping out at a number of friends' parties and celebrations decided they'd like to set up a catering business together. Full of enthusiasm, they had some business cards printed and took advertising space in the local paper. Tessa was very sociable and loved negotiating with clients. Rachel was rather shy, and tended to get on with backroom activities. But after a while she began to realise that because Tessa was doing all the front-of-house work, she was also doing less and less of the actual cooking. Rachel's house was full of pots and pans, her family were getting fed up because all her efforts were going into the business, and she was feeling bored, lonely and hard-done-by. Suddenly this business wasn't working for her. So she decided that she and Tessa needed to sit down together and rethink how they were going to divide the work more fairly. Rachel reframed *Running a business together isn't working* into *It worked out differently from how I expected* and was then able to decide: *I'll find a way to make it work the way I want.*

Take some of your own ways of thinking about failure and explore how you can reframe them – and where that takes you.

Here are some examples to get you started.

- ► *I didn't do well enough* can be reframed as *I did the best I could – and now I could probably do better.*

- ► *I wasn't any good at spelling* can be reframed as *I never learnt a strategy for spelling well – but I could if I wanted to.*

- ► *I failed the job interview* can be reframed as *They appointed someone they liked better, or someone who had more experience or better qualifications – and there are things I can learn from that choice that'll improve the way I interview in future.*

- ► *I couldn't do it* can be reframed as *I didn't have enough skill or knowledge at the time – but I can learn and improve.*

NLP shows you how to become curious about your failures, and identify the patterns in them. This helps you gain not only understanding but a new control over your life. In the next chapter we're going to go into this more fully, by examining the meaning of feedback, and how it is an essential feature in helping you achieve what you want.

CHAPTER 5

Feedback is the Foundation of Success

MANY PEOPLE ASSUME that feedback is negative. It tells you what's not working. In this sense, it's like a kind of medicine: unpleasant but necessary if you're to get better. So far, we've been looking at how treating 'failure' as an important source of information can help you move away from the bad feelings which may result and towards more effective action. But it is equally important to do the same with good feedback – with success and praise as well as mistakes and blame. In contrast to people in the US, Britons tend to play down their successes, at least in public, and even if they are able to take delight in them in the privacy of their own heads, they often don't ask themselves exactly *how* they achieved what they did.

Yet asking the how, when, where and what questions about success is just as important as getting clear about exactly how you messed up. Think of feedback as the foundation upon which you're about to build your home. You need all of that feedback, to tell you what to avoid and to tell you what to do more of; to tell you how to, not just how not to. Architects do not begin by telling workmen 'Now, don't build a castle – or a bunga-low, and don't use inferior materials.' They first choose their builder carefully, and then specify what they do want rather than what they don't. You too need to know what you do well, and how, when building for your future.

Building a house can seem a slow business at first, and so can gathering feedback and learning from it. But both tasks gather speed as they go along. A small step, often repeated, can lead to massive change. A small change which leads to other options and other possibilities can lead to a massively different outcome.

▪ *Failure is Really Feedback*

Based on observations of how successful people themselves viewed any lack of success, NLP offers us a very important reframe for failure: failure is really only feedback. Once you start to become curious about your failures, you can learn from them. We want you to get curious about the how, what, when and where of your particular patterning. For example, let's say you've failed a test.

- ▪ How exactly did you do that?

- ▪ What exactly did you do that didn't work?

- ▪ When did you do this? Is timing important?

- ▪ Where did you do this? Is location significant here?

As we said earlier, why is often a much less useful question: if it is asked after a 'failure' has occurred, it tends to make us defensive (even if we ourselves are asking the question), and tends to direct our attention towards explanations, justifications and the whole success/failure framework again.

When you become curious about your 'failures', one of the most important results is that this almost always changes the nature of the problem. Starting to use feedback in this way moves you away from the global – 'I'm always late' – or issues that involve identity – 'I'm a poor manager' or 'I'm not thoughtful enough' – to ones which are much more specific, and much less threatening. Instead of lambasting yourself and repeating, 'What's the matter with me? Why can't I just do it right? There must be something wrong with me', you ask 'How do I manage to be late so often?' You may even start to realise that in an odd way, being late so consistently indicates that you have developed a certain skill in this area!

You can also start to make some very useful distinctions to help you get clear about what will really make a difference. 'What is it that I do – or don't do – that makes me believe I'm a poor manager?', 'Or is it the beliefs I have about what good managers should do that are the problem for me?', 'How would I begin to know that I was thoughtful enough – what would I have to do, what feedback from others would let me know?' and so on.

The language we use can tell us a lot. Identity statements, which usually contain phrases like *I am...*, *I never...*, *I always...*, *I'm just...*, imply that the thing we're describing is as much a part of us, and as unchangeable, as our genes. Once we become curious and really specific, the issues get brought down to details which in fact can usually be changed. The person who is always late might manage to be late by never allowing enough time between one thing and another. Or they might find that they tended to get so caught up in anything they were doing that they simply lost track of time. Such everyday phrases, once we learn to listen to our own speech with a curious ear, often tell us exactly what is happening.

Another way to explore these global statements is to check for any exceptions. Take being late. Are you really *always* late? Do you *always*, invariably, leave tasks until the last moment? With most of our clients the answer is 'No'. If this is true for you too, become very curious about the exceptions. When, in whose company, in what moods, for what kind of occasions, are you not late (or less late)? Which tasks do you do with some time to spare? Who assigned them to you? Did you assign them to yourself? How much investment – and what kind – do you have in getting the task done? Any of these questions may help you find out more about your own behaviour.

The twin arts of questioning and of observation can help us to discover information that we actually do have, even though we are not aware of it. Examining the way we say things, rather than taking surface meaning for granted, is an essential NLP tool.

The meta model, which we've already encountered (see page **51**), helps us to fill in the accidental gaps that feelings and beliefs can produce in the way we think and speak. Too often, terms like 'always' and 'never' lock us into believing we have only one choice, and we forget the times when we did something different. We need to restore the missing information to stop ourselves from oversimplifying.

Try this: write some statements that begin:

- I always...

- I never...

- I'm always...

- I'm never...

Then question each of these: Always? Never? Never ever? Find the exceptions and notice how it is for you to obtain this more balanced perspective.

▪ *Good Feedback Feeds Forward*

We've talked about 'gathering feedback' because you can actively seek it out. However, this doesn't have to involve any great effort because feedback is around you all the time if only you pay attention. Every response to any of your actions is potentially feedback that you can use. And when you use feedback, you can feed it forward to become a guide for your future actions. In this way feedback helps you do more of what works. It's hard to exaggerate just how important feedback is because the best feedback feeds *forward*; that is to say, it guides our behaviour in the future.

That said, it's important to distinguish between feedback and mindreading. Feedback is hard information: what actually happened, what was actually said. Mindreading, in this context, is what goes on in your head when you try to guess what something or someone might have meant. Mindreading often leads you way off track, because there's no reality check!

Feedback doesn't have to be written, or even spoken. It doesn't even have to be directed at you. Human beings spend their lives trying to make sense of their experience. We are all experts in interpreting expressions and at deducing relationships between what happens first and what happens next. For example, if you forgot a friend's birthday and he then didn't send you a Christmas card, you may think his feelings were hurt. Or maybe you are wondering if he thought you were cutting back on your greetings list because you hadn't seen each other in a while, and so he felt that gave him permission to prune your name off his list. Or did he just forget?

An event has occurred, but what it signifies is not clear, and that means you don't know what feedback you're getting. What's important is to know that you don't know. This too is feedback – the kind that's the signal to ask questions.

▪ *Kinds of Feedback*

External Feedback

A while ago we were coaching a young woman who was asked to investigate a problem that often occurred in the work of her department and write a report proposing some new ways to tackle it. She handed in her proposal, and was dismayed to find that no response was forthcoming from her boss. In fact, she told us that he had ignored her report. So she started imagining that her boss didn't like it. As days passed without any comment from her boss, she went from being puzzled to upset and anxious. Maybe he thought the proposal was really dreadful. Perhaps she might be demoted, or even lose her job? These thoughts were really just fantasies based on trying to mindread her boss. But they produced very real unpleasant feelings. She needed to do a reality check.

We worked with her to formulate some questions that would help her move on. These were:

1. Do I have any actual evidence that he doesn't like it?

2. How could I find out?

3. Why else might he not have responded to me?

4. What do I need to do next?

In this case, the first step was to check out whether in fact the boss didn't like the proposal, or whether there was some other reason for his lack of response. As it happened, he had had to attend an important meeting at the company's headquarters at short notice and had not had time to consider it. But by thinking of some questions, she had reclaimed some control of the situation, and she would have known what to ask if he really hadn't liked her proposal. She was indeed getting feedback, but it was about his feeling overwhelmed rather than her proposal.

Other useful reality-based questions to ask yourself about this kind of feedback might include:

► What is my immediate impression?

► What evidence is there to support my impression?

► Is there any way I can check it out independently?

▶ Are there any reasons why my impression might be coloured or biased?

▶ If I were looking at this situation from the other person's view, how might it seem different?

▶ If I were an objective observer, how might it seem to me?

Internal Feedback

Some of the most important feedback comes from within. When you're asked to do something and you don't feel quite right about it, that's a part of yourself giving you feedback. Equally important can be the physical feedback your body gives you, which you may not even notice.

> When we first met Paul, a middle-aged man, he described himself as having 'a history of horse-dust and hay-fever-like allergies'. So his description was a kind of explanation for his experience. For years he had accepted that his infrequent but long-lasting and debilitating 'attacks' of sneezing and watery eyes were caused by increases in the pollen count or cleaning his flat, or 'stress'. All we knew, though, was that sometimes he seemed to sneeze a lot. One day he had dinner with some friends, and on his way home began sneezing badly. The next day he was confined to bed with yet another attack. Thinking it over, and wondering what had caused it this time, he was able to eliminate the pollen count (wrong time of year), cleaning (he hadn't done any recently) and stress (work was going well, as was his personal life). What else could it be? Well, today was a Monday – and come to think of it his attacks often did occur on Mondays. Couldn't be about returning to work, because he enjoyed it and it was going well.
>
> So Paul started looking more closely. Perhaps it was a reaction to something that had happened at the weekend? Well, he had met some friends for a pizza on Saturday night, then gone out to dinner on Sunday. A food allergy perhaps? But the foods were all ones he often ate with no reaction. What else? Well, he had drunk about three glasses of wine on each night. Maybe, just maybe, it was that. He decided that as an experiment he would refrain from any alcohol for a month. He didn't want to do this, but anything would be better than going on getting these attacks. And, to his relief (and disappointment), he had no more of these attacks. So he decided it made sense to stop drinking

wine. Paul had found what NLP calls 'the difference that makes the difference'. He felt back in control of his life in a new way, and ultimately that proved more important than just stopping the sneezing.

• *The Difference that Makes the Difference*

In gathering information, it's often important to pay attention to detail. When you compare two situations or processes that seem very similar but have different outcomes, it's important to look for any differences between them, and then to find out which of those differences is the key to the different outcome. Often the difference that makes the difference can be quite small and easily overlooked, especially if it's part of our everyday life. When you know what makes the difference, you know what's going on and how to change things if you choose, both in your professional life and personally.

Contrastive analysis

We discussed contrastive analysis in detail on page **45**. This is the way to find the difference that makes a difference. Suppose a company has been successfully generating business by advertising in particular journals for some years. Then, suddenly, it doesn't go so well. Demand falls off and the interest just isn't there any more. What is the difference that has made such a difference this time? Or, to take a personal example, perhaps you have a number of friends whom you see often and whose company you enjoy. You begin to notice that though you have a general sense of give and take among the group, you are feeling a bit resentful about doing favours for one particular friend. What's the difference that makes the difference?

In contrastive analysis, which is the tool you'd use to answer these questions, you are contrasting similarities and differences between one situation and another, or between this friend and others, to find the difference that is significant. And when you find that crucial difference, it usually tells you where you need to take action.

▪ *How to Use Feedback Constructively*

You can make good use of feedback in a number of ways:

▶ **Take notice of feedback in all its forms** The fuller and richer the feedback you get, the more guidance you have. Put all feedback in a curiosity-frame: ask yourself how you can use it to avoid a recurrence of any unpleasant happenings, or to repeat successful ones.

▶ **If what you're doing isn't working, do something different** This is the time to be inventive. Something else might work in this situation. Be flexible.

▶ **If what you're doing is working,** get clear about what it is that is working so you can do more of it. Use your own behaviour as a recipe for future success. Find out the ingredients and the sequences, then repeat them.

▶ **Pay attention to detail** It won't be enough just to say 'Well, I just have faith in myself.' How do you do that? Is it by reminding yourself of past success – in which case, do you picture it, feel it, have a shorthand description of it in words or phrases? Is it by imagining how you will need and want to act in order to achieve what you want? Is it by reminding yourself of something encouraging someone once said? How do you do it?

▶ **Model yourself and others** The more exactly you find out how something is done, the more you have the ingredients and the processes you need to do it again, or to learn it from observing others. And the more small steps you break the process down into, the more chance you have of building it when you want to do it.

We started this part of the book by exploring how failure is something that is constructed through actions, assumptions and interactions that have knock-on effects within the person and/or within their interpersonal relationships – in other words, their personal and interpersonal systems. Now we're ready to do the same with success.

CHAPTER 6

Success has a Structure

▪ *What is Success in NLP Terms?*

In NLP terms, success acquires a wider meaning. It's not just externally observable achievements, though it includes them. NLP, as we've now seen abundantly, is much more interested in processes than events. Remember that NLP is based on the study of excellence – and excellence is what works, effectively, economically, often elegantly. Taken together, the NLP tools, which were identified through this study, form a handbook of effective ways of thinking, behaving and interacting with others. So in NLP terms, success goes beyond simply achieving your goal: it's about achieving your goal effectively, elegantly and as easily as possible.

In NLP coaching, we focus on:

1. Identifying your goal.

2. Checking your goal or outcome rigorously against a clear set of criteria – the well-formedness conditions described on page 63 – so that you ensure your outcome has the best chance of succeeding.

3. Identifying the appropriate resources, internal and external, which you need to achieve your goal.

4. Learning and using the most effective ways of representing your goal to yourself so that your thinking and feeling, as well as your actions, are all consistent with bringing it about.

5. Maintaining a consistent awareness of how progress towards your goals is going, through using feedback of all kinds and at all levels.

6. Being flexible and making any necessary adjustments.

7. Rewarding yourself at every stage for progress so that working towards your goals becomes enjoyable and satisfying in its own right.

We have emphasised throughout Part Three how important patterns are and how enabling it can be once you get to know your own. Having this intimate information about the way you do things puts you back in the driving seat of your life.

Modelling in this way helps you look for the structure of success in two ways: by finding out how you and other individuals do it, and by finding out what things all successful people have in common.

Most of the things we've said about finding out about your failures apply to finding out about your successes too. You need to:

▶ Find out what you are currently doing that works.

▶ Pay attention to detail.

▶ Use contrastive analysis to find the difference that makes the difference.

▶ Notice the importance of certain sequences because they work really well.

▶ Be alert to what is going on outside – observable behaviour – and inside – your internal representations of seeing, hearing and feeling, and your internal dialogue.

▶ Break down your goals into small and achievable steps.

These are things that successful individuals often do unconsciously. We have three other key recommendations for building success, which all come from building yourself:

1. Ensure that success is a reward in itself

Celebrate success, don't just look at it as a step on the way to somewhere else. Celebration may involve treats, special events or sharing with others. But the heart of true celebration is allowing yourself to enjoy the fact that you have done something well and to relish it. For many people, this doesn't come easily, and it may need practice.

You are reading these words. Do you remember having learnt to read, and how that felt? Did you have a chance to celebrate that then? Just how many of your achievements never really got celebrated and then became commonplace? What about other skills you have? Other projects you have accomplished? What about subtler things – your personal qualities? Some people have an amazing capacity to delete this kind of information about themselves. This was true of one woman Wendy was coaching, so she decided to write down on Post-it notes every compliment she could ever remember having been paid, and to stick them randomly all round the house. She kept them there for a month. This way she kept coming across them: each time was a reminder.

2. Turn specific compliments into something you can truly own

That means turning compliments into part of your identity. Wendy asked her client to make sure that when she read a compliment that began 'You did such-and-such' or 'You are such and such', she took a moment to translate it in her head and really notice how different it was to hear, or say, '*I* did such-and-such' or '*I* am such-and-such.' It made a huge difference to how she felt about herself.

You could try saying or thinking to yourself, 'I am the kind of person who...' or 'I'm an... kind of person.' This is where a generalisation can be really helpful: just as negative generalisations have power, so a positive generalisation can magnify the effects of positive feedback. By using the words 'kind of person' we are telling ourselves that this particular incident, behaviour or quality is true of us generally: it's the sort of thing we do.

Imagine yourself going into some daily situation, or into a special or taxing one, with that sense of who you are: that person who had those compliments, owning them, having them as an internal part of you, as much a part of you as the shape of your ears or the colour of your eyes. For example, as you travel to work you could be reminding yourself of the way you handled that difficult customer yesterday, and how by the end of the conversation they were calmer and more accommodating. You could be saying to yourself: 'That was my doing. I'm the sort of person who helps people feel they matter.' You might replay in your head fragments of the conversation, noticing how the customer's voice tone changed from hasty, strident and abrupt to reasoned, slower and more approachable. You could generalise this sense of yourself as someone helpful and good at relating to others by taking a moment to bring that awareness into your mind and body at the beginning of every day, so that it informs whatever follows. And the more you practise this approach, the more natural it becomes.

3. Ask yourself 'Why not?'

What makes one particular market trader a millionaire? What makes one particular guy with a bright idea into a successful inventor? What makes the old lady a famous author? Many things, and a good measure of luck; but one thing they all have in common is that they dared to dream, and to wonder about what it would take to achieve that dream. Of course, it can take effort, and time, to make your dreams into realities; but success is based on allowing yourself to entertain the idea that what you want might conceivably be possible.

Too many people stop themselves before they've really begun. One way to prevent yourself closing down when you have a bright idea, or think of something you'd like to do or be, is to ask yourself, 'Why not?'

Sometimes the question may bring up things that need to happen first: if there are any, you'll certainly need to know about them. If there are obstacles, you'll need ways round them. But sometimes the question reveals to you that there is no real obstacle other than your fear of your own ambition – and that's what needs to be tackled.

As coaches, we find that people have the resources they need to achieve their goals. From experience, we know that NLP provides one of the most effective, elegant and user-friendly bases for helping people to help themselves. Each and every one of the NLP tools you might first come across with a coach, or in a book like this, is something you can learn to use for yourself. So when the coach is not around, and the book is back on the shelf, these tools can be yours and you can really master success.

Why not?

PART 4

Your Five Dimensions of Success

Introduction

IN THIS SECTION we will show you how to use NLP to examine the raw material available to you – namely, yourself and your life. We shall also be coaching you on the five dimensions – your potential, style, personal balance, world and, of course, yourself – that in our experience are most crucial for achieving your goals. We're going to explain here what these dimensions mean, and just why you'll find it helpful to consider them in the light of NLP.

What prompts many people to want to make changes in their lives is some evidence that the way they currently go about things isn't working. In NLP terms, this is an away-from motivation. Nothing wrong with that: as we explained earlier, negative feedback is still feedback, and therefore potentially useful. But the limitation is that negative feedback frequently brings bad or sad feelings with it; and these may mean that we are not in a good state for learning. When confidence is eroded, readiness to experiment is restricted: we want to play safe. We've just had a bad experience, better not risk another. An important presupposition in NLP is that if what you're doing isn't working, do something different. This may appear to call for courage – or for confidence. So the very thing that can be eroded when things aren't working is just the thing that is needed. The problem seems circular.

As we've seen, though, once you have learnt to look on failure as feedback, you are in a position to take any apparent setback as really useful, really precise information about exactly what you now need to do in order to take things forward. If you recognise that every setback is potentially a source of information, you don't have to feel so bad about it, or stay feeling bad for so long.

However, we want to go beyond this now, and focus your attention on the resources that you already have. These resources will make you more empowered. In our experience, people have all the resources they need to achieve what they want – but they frequently don't believe this is so, don't know what those resources might be or don't know how to access them.

▪ *Your Potential*

We'd like to draw your attention to two key success factors: faith in your potential and a readiness to learn. So the first of our dimensions of success has to be your potential. What are you capable of? How might you know? What would you wish to be capable of? People often talk as if potential is something fixed, like the genetically determined possibility of growing to a certain height. Many NLP practitioners and coaches in a variety of different fields have found that, far from being a fixed quantity, potential is something that grows as it is nourished. One of the key roles of this book is to nurture your potential and help you learn how to do that nurturing for yourself.

▪ *Your Style*

You will get tremendous benefits from becoming more aware of yourself and your characteristic ways of operating. Not surprisingly, NLP has found that there are many successful ways of operating, both internally and externally: no one way is effective in all circumstances – every pattern works better for some things than others and for some people better than others. Once you recognise what your characteristic patterns are, then you are in a position to play to your strengths and take the pressure off your weaknesses. You are also more able to identify areas in which you could benefit from further learning. This is what we have chosen to call your style.

▪ *Your Personal Balance*

Another valuable way of taking control of your life is to ask yourself what kind of experiences does it consist of? Increasingly, people talk about achieving 'balance' in life, but what does this mean? Is it about balanced time allocation – you spend your time living and loving, working and resting and not endlessly doing too much of just one activity? Or is it about having a balance of interests? Or both?

As NLP coaches we have learnt that two key processes are very important in this context. First, whether or not we stop to think about it, the repeated pattern of our daily activities has cumulative effects. Becoming aware of this and taking the time to examine these patterns is the first process. The second is to ask ourselves the question: is this what I want? Is it what I want now? And is this pattern, and these consequences, what I want to have shaping my future? So the third dimension of success is your personal balance.

▪ *Your World*

NLP offers us many useful skills for becoming more aware of events outside ourselves and how we relate to them. So the fourth dimension of success we shall look at is your world and how effectively you interact with it. We might say that this involves exploring all the other dimensions in a wider field of action. NLP draws our attention to the fact that people do not think and function in isolation: they are part of wider systems – partnerships, families, groups and cultures. But, equally, each person consists of interacting physical, emotional and mental processes: internally, we are a system too. NLP gives us ways of understanding and learning how to work effectively with both internal and external systems.

▪ *Yourself*

The fifth dimension is yourself. What kind of a relationship do you have with yourself? We all know from experience how much difference a good teacher can make to someone's learning, whether that person is called a teacher, a manager, a parent or a friend. All these good teachers build an effective, supportive relationship with their 'pupils', explain things clearly, break learning targets down into manageable chunks, offer encouragement and recognise progress.

Do you have this kind of relationship with yourself? Many people do not – or they lack it in specific areas of their lives. How much hectoring, self-blaming, undermining, putting down, minimising of achievements goes on in the privacy of your head? Gallwey called this 'Self 1'. Freud called it the 'Super-ego'. Both men are labelling our ability to impose judgements and rules upon ourselves. This skill can sometimes be very useful, but when it becomes an habitual voice in your internal dialogue it can have very damaging effects and seriously interfere with the achievement of your potential. So how you are with yourself is going to have a very significant impact on the quality of your life and what you can achieve. NLP coaching can help make sure that your relationship with yourself is really working.

Taken together, an understanding of these five dimensions and what they involve as far as you are concerned will help you identify both what you want to change and what resources you have to help you do it. As you engage with us in these investigations, you are also likely to recognise how some of the NLP tools will be useful for your specific needs. If you find note-keeping a helpful aid, you might want to find a notebook for your personal work-in-progress, and jot down observations as they occur to you.

CHAPTER 7

Your Potential

POTENTIAL ISN'T A fixed quantity. The word is derived from the Latin *potentia*, meaning power or ability – itself derived from the verb 'to be able'. Potential, then, is the capacity to learn and develop which is inherent in everyone.

Admittedly, there are perhaps a few ways in which our potential is limited: we mentioned height as being genetically determined, for example. And clearly people have natural aptitudes for certain things. But one of the crucial discoveries of NLP has been that where something that is done well can be described, it can be taught to other people. This doesn't necessarily mean we can all be Olympic athletes, business tycoons or world champion chess players. But it does mean that we can all radically improve our athletic ability, business acumen or play a much better game of chess – *if* we want to.

A number of things can help you develop your potential:

1. Wanting something enough to make it a goal.

2. Gaining enough information, in accessible and usable chunks, about how people who are excellent at this particular thing go about doing it, both internally and externally.

3. Breaking down the goal into a sequence of stages which will bridge the gap between the current state of affairs and the state you desire.

4. Keeping on track in progressing towards your goal, either through

external support and coaching or through self-encouragement and self-coaching.

5. Finding ways to make each stage of the process enjoyable and rewarding in itself. People who are really excellent at what they do often do it easily, without apparent effort. As Gallwey tells us in *The Inner Game of Work*, 'It was only when I was enjoying myself that I did my best work and could make my best contribution to others.'

In his coaching for sports performance in the 1970s, Gallwey discovered how crucial thought and feeling were in helping or inhibiting his coachees' learning and achievement. He found that minimising comments, whether from others or as internal monologues from the coachees themselves, and encouraging potential, improved the coachees' performance. We really don't know how much we are capable of – but we do know that if the right conditions are provided we can develop significantly.

When you think about what you want, two things are likely to hold you back: one is that you may flip between being unrealistically ambitious (dreaming about winning the lottery, for example, or envisaging a wonderful marriage on a first date) or equally unrealistically depressed ('I'll never be able to…'). An important step forward is to do a reality check. Ask yourself:

- What would need to happen for me to do this?

- What makes me think that I couldn't do this?

These questions help eliminate unreasonable fantasies on the one hand, and unnecessary and self-limiting caution on the other.

Sarah worked in a design studio after qualifying at art college. She had dreams of becoming a famous designer and running her own studio. Often, these sustained her through a day of work on some design project she actually found boring and beneath her talents. She had not dreamed, while at college, that she would earn her living designing new labels for tins of tomatoes. So she would fantasise about having her own studio, with exciting projects and famous clients, about products that would be 'worthwhile' and carry a logo she had designed all over the world. All too often, however, something would bring her back to the 'reality' of her situation, and she would slide into the despair of realising how far her daily activities, and daily achievements, were from the magical career she had dreamed about. Whether she was fantasising or depressed, nothing changed.

Eventually, she realised that she needed help, and that's how Ian met her. When he asked her whether her 'famous designer' goal was realistic, she really didn't know. She could only say she had done well at college, and been chosen for her job from a large number of applicants. Nor did she have any clear idea what opportunities she might have for advancement in the company. She had several times been reprimanded for failure to meet deadlines.

During Sarah's coaching, an important step was when she decided to ask for a meeting with her studio manager to assess her performance. Another was when she decided to continue to do her own independent work in her free time, to allow herself to explore what she might really be capable of.

The meeting with her manager helped her get a clearer idea of what she needed to do to advance within the company; and she was able to work in a more focused way and achieve her manager's targets. At the same time, she realised through her coaching that she really wanted to work on more worthwhile projects. She began to think that she would like to specialise in book design. A friend introduced her to a publisher, who looked at her portfolio and then asked her to do some sample layouts for book jackets.

Finding out what she really wanted to do was an important step for Sarah. It helped her become much more realistic. She realised that making a career in publishing would involve effort and risk, and decided that she would continue with her existing job while she built up contacts and began to get work in the new field. But now she knew where she was going.

Sarah swung between fantasy and despair. Another common way to limit yourself is by thinking too small. It's easy to confine your dreams to those which are small and achievable, and to limit your potential in the same way. If the next goal is a bigger, more prestigious car, or a promotion from assistant to assistant manager, you may well achieve those goals, while at the same time failing to realise that you could have achieved something bigger, better and more satisfying. The new car may disguise from you that what you really want is a more spacious and satisfying lifestyle. If you are lucky, a faint sense of disappointment after the initial excitement has worn off may help you realise that more is at stake. But again, the habit of thinking small may still limit your potential: perhaps what you need next is a conservatory... a week's skiing to liven up the winter blues...

It's clear that because of the powerful ways we represent things to ourselves internally, we do have the power to align our actions with our dreams, and make our dreams come true. This means that if the dreams themselves are limited, we will end up limiting what we can achieve. We will be limiting our potential.

There are useful ways out of this dilemma. You'll need to tease out the real aspirations that may underlie your immediate wants and goals. Sometimes wanting a new car may be just that: but sometimes the desired item stands for a lot more, and it's often quite easy to find out what.

Paul came to see Wendy for coaching, because he was being pressured by his girlfriend to 'settle down'. He had qualified as an electrician, but had moved jobs a number of times and had failed to stay in any one place for very long. He said he was always on the lookout for new challenges: once he could do a job he felt it was time to move on. He loved the excitement of change.

Now he wanted to move to Australia. A new continent, a new hemisphere: that would really be something! Though his girlfriend was willing to go with him, she was concerned that after a few months he would want to uproot again. She wanted a stable base, a chance to make a career for herself, and eventually marriage and children.

Wendy asked him what moving on did for him. 'Well, it gives me variety.'

'And what does variety do for you?'

'It means I've got a new challenge – something else to try my skills on.'

'And what does that do for you?'

'It shows me I've got what it takes.'

'And "having what it takes" – what does that do for you?'

'It proves my dad was wrong when he said I was a lazy layabout who'd never manage anything.'

Paul was really surprised by what he had just said. While the answers had just 'popped out' they had led him rapidly from the wish to move to Australia to an important issue about his identity. This new plan, like so many of its predecessors, had been another attempt to prove his own worth in the face of his father's low opinion.

Through continued coaching he was able to separate out what he needed to do to re-establish his self-esteem from what he actually wanted in terms of a career and a relationship. In addition, he began to find ways to relate more assertively to his father.

EXERCISE: Unpacking Your Dreams

1. Take a wish that you have and ask yourself: What would having [x] do for me? Repeat the question with each answer that comes until you find no more answers coming: almost certainly, you will have reached some purpose which is very important to you.

2. Now look again at the item you wanted: is this the only way of achieving your deeper purpose? How else might you achieve it? Knowing what the deeper purpose is, do you still want this in its own right?

Unpacking your wish list in this way allows you to find out what you really want – and why. You may still choose to look for the bigger house, the better car, the promotion; but if any of these represented deeper wants you now know about them, and can incorporate these into your future plans. A clear purpose is a more achievable purpose. You can refer to the well-formedness conditions on page **63** to ensure that your desired outcome has the best chance of becoming a reality.

▪ *Go for More*

One of our themes in this section has been the importance of your recognising what you truly want, and not limiting yourself. One useful way to test out whether you are limiting yourself is to go for more. By enlarging the scope of your ambition, you can test out whether you truly want the dream you thought you did, or whether in fact you want more still – and you can learn a lot about what may have been unconsciously restraining you.

But what does 'more' mean? Well, it may mean more in terms of quantity. Do you want to earn another thousand a year – or would you really prefer to earn far more? One thousand might be 'enough', adding a few more comforts, making things just a little easier at the end of the month.

Five, ten, twenty or a hundred thousand might allow you to branch out and live a quite different life. What do you really want? If you really, truly only want another thousand a year, it will quickly become clear to you. If, on the other hand, you have been unconsciously censoring your real wishes, it's important to know.

'More' may also mean 'better' in terms of quality. 'I want more time to spend with my family' doesn't usually just mean more hours in front of the television or sharing chores. Recognising this may mean that, even if more hours are not forthcoming, you are able to take decisions that result in redistributing and reallocating those you do have. One couple we knew who wished to 'have more time together' realised that, of the time they did have, a whole evening a week was spent on housework. For them it was worthwhile to employ a cleaner so that they could claim back those precious hours and convert them into quality time together.

More may mean that instead of making either/or choices, we find a way to make both/and choices. Talking over the issue of wanting more time together and realising they were sacrificing it to having a clean house resulted in that couple having a clean house and more time together.

Finally, there's another way to check if you are limiting yourself. When you find yourself stuck, or in some way failing to fulfil your potential, there are two really useful NLP questions we want you to remember:

1. What stops you (from achieving your goal)?

2. What would happen if you did (achieve your goal)?

In our experience, people usually know what is holding them back, but may well be overlooking the reason or even disguising it from themselves. These two questions offer us powerful levers for moving things forward.

What stops you?

Sometimes the block is practical. This is more easily recognised. Let's take two people who have very different dreams.

- I can't go to Rome.

- What stops you?

- I haven't got the money.

- I can't go ahead with developing my invention.

- What stops you?

- I haven't got financial backing.

Even in these cases, making the block explicit allows you to begin to move forward.

I can't go to Rome because I haven't got enough money – yet. If you really want to go, you can start planning ways to save the money you need, and a timescale in which you will save it. The addition of the simple word 'yet' opens up the avenue that has been blocked and allows you to explore how you might move forward.

I can't develop my invention because I haven't got financial backing – yet. What would you have to do to get it? Where might you go? Who might you ask? Do you know someone who might know?

Both these issues have been 'opened up' by looking beyond the immediate block to a state in which it has been solved. Assuming you do go to Rome, how will you have got enough money? Assuming you do develop your invention, how will you have obtained the backing you need?

As you think about the issue in this way, you may even find yourself asking more daring questions.

- Is there a way in which I can go to Rome without money?

- Is there a way I can develop my invention without financial backing?

Even if the answer turns out to be 'No', you will have taken a close look at your assumptions (visits to Rome necessitate money; developing inventions requires backers). Perhaps you could be paid or find an exchange programme? Perhaps you could form a consortium with other inventors? Perhaps you could share or exchange skills with others?

Asking 'What stops me?' can also help you uncover a different kind of blockage, the kind that we can all unconsciously create at times to protect ourselves from some unpleasant consequence.

- I can't go to Rome.

- What stops you?

- I'm frightened my elderly mother, who is ill, might die when I'm away, and I'd never forgive myself.

Or it might be:

- I can't go to Rome.

- What stops you?

- If I spend all my savings on this, I won't have anything in reserve for emergencies and that makes me feel afraid.

What would happen if you did?

This is a good question to ask yourself when even you can't see why on earth you don't do something that is 'obviously' to your advantage. Perhaps your relationship is not going well, and for ages your friends have been saying, 'Why don't you split up, then?' Or you know you should lose weight, and you've bought the diet books and joined a slimming club, but somehow you put off really making a start. Nothing is actually stopping you – you tried asking that question. But of course something is, because you haven't begun. So maybe what is stopping you is something you anticipate happening when you have achieved your aim.

- I think we should split up but I don't do it.

- So what would happen if you did split up?

It may be that though your relationship isn't fully satisfying, you are afraid of being on your own again, of the uncertainties of being single, of not finding anyone else and ending up on your own. If you are to make the decision, you will need to anticipate and find ways to manage these possibilities. Asking yourself the question helps you elicit the information you need so that you can protect yourself while still moving forward.

- I want to lose weight but I seem to be putting it off.

- So what would happen if you did lose weight?

Losing weight will improve your looks and your health – but perhaps it will also make you vulnerable to some of those predatory lads at work. Or it might make your sisters – or your partner – jealous. Or perhaps you grew up in a family where food was a major means of reward, and so it's one of your ways of rewarding yourself too. Or it's hard to resist the business lunches and the drinks.

If you take away 'treat' food, do you have another set of treats ready to give yourself? Asking the question helps give you the information you need to find other ways around the problem.

These questions can open up a range of important ways in which we constrain our own potential: our assumptions, our learning from past experiences, the consequences we anticipate and fear, our anxieties about failure. In our experience, NLP gives people some very useful ways of discovering what is really involved – and of nurturing their own potential beyond their wildest dreams.

EXERCISE: Going for Your Goal

1. Take a goal of yours which you are making little or no progress on. Ask yourself:
    ► What stops me from achieving this goal?
    ► What would happen if I did achieve this goal?

2. Make a list of both practical and emotional issues that may be preventing you achieving your goal.

3. Now list how you would feel and the results you would expect if you did achieve it.

CHAPTER 8

Your Style

IN DISCOVERING YOUR personal style and assessing its effectiveness and limitations, you can draw upon three key NLP tools. These are modelling, meta programmes and sensory acuity.

▪ *Using Modelling*

As we saw in Chapter 3, modelling lies at the heart of NLP, both in terms of its historical origins and the leverage it gives. The key modelling question is 'How do I/you/they do that?' So in coming to an understanding of your own style, you need to model yourself, becoming both an observer and a describer of the way you yourself go about things. You are seeking to build up a profile of your unique style – for each of us is unique in our own way of operating, both internally and externally.

EXERCISE: Your Unique Style

Make some notes about yourself. The list below offers some ideas to get you started.

- ▪ I'm really good at...

- ▪ I find it easy to...

- When I have a task to do the way I approach it is...

- I find it difficult to...

- I like...

- I hate...

- I worry about...

- I'm not very good at...

- I have been praised for...

As you begin to build this profile you'll be encountering things which you think of as your strengths and your weaknesses. But put those judgements to one side, as they often get in your way.

Some of the information you are looking for to build your self-profile can be discovered or amplified by referring to Chapter 3. For example,

- What are your preferred representational systems?

- Which sub-modalities are most influential for you?

- Where do you naturally come on the various meta programme axes?

Successful people know their style: they play to their strengths and avoid putting pressure on their weaknesses. Really successful people also seek to work on their areas of weakness, often reframing weakness as a signal to undertake new learning.

We've sometimes speculated that one of the legacies of the Puritan ethic for many people is an attitude that it's somehow wrong to trade on your strengths and avoid your areas of weakness: it's as though there's a kind of moral responsibility to try, try, try again at things you find difficult rather than just putting your energies somewhere else. This seems to go along with downplaying what you're good at or find easy – as though it was somehow worth less. However, in studying people who excel at what they do, we have found that excellence is often apparently effortless, and may actually be experienced as easy by those who possess it – even if they have worked hard to achieve it.

Becoming aware of what you are good at, and exactly how you go about it, is really useful. Becoming aware of what you are less good at – provided you stay away from the blame-frame – can give you information which you can choose to use to strengthen and enrich your personal style, if that's what you want. But you are not morally obliged to.

Let's look at some examples.

One of our friends is a solicitor. He is careful, meticulous, orderly. He is a good solicitor, charming and rather self-effacing. One of his main hobbies is archaeology, which requires care, meticulousness and order-liness. At weekends he enjoys using these natural gifts of his in an off-duty setting, working on local digs. His hobby trades on and allows him a different kind of expression for his strengths. Why not?

By contrast, a woman in her forties came to us for coaching, seeking help in finding a new direction in life. Ever since she started work, she had been helping other people in a variety of contexts: as an untrained care-worker, then, after training, as a social worker. At the time she began her coaching sessions, she was managing a team of workers in a residential hostel. She related well to the young homeless clients, but found it very stressful to manage the team. She was dreading the forth-coming team-building weekend.

We helped her to build up a profile of her style; and she became aware that the thing she most enjoyed was working one-to-one – with both clients and staff members – to encourage their development. She had never really wanted to be a manager, though she had been a 'nat-ural' selection because she was efficient and clear-headed and people seemed to get on with her.

When Ian asked her to talk about how she felt when challenged, she said that it made her 'shrivel up inside, like when my mother told me I was no good'. As far back as she could remember, her mother had never praised her, but had always criticised her and pointed out the things she couldn't do. She realised as an adult that her mother had been an unhappy and probably quite disturbed person, but somehow this didn't help. And in her own career she had taken a number of dif-ficult 'frontline' jobs, culminating in the current one. She said she felt she ought to overcome her diffidence and learn to take conflict and criticism.

For this client, one outcome of coaching was that she began to accept that it was okay to take herself out of this frontline situation: she didn't have to continue being exposed to challenge, criticism and feeling undervalued in this way any more. She built a stronger sense of what she was really good at, and decided that she would begin to look for another job which would allow her to work at her strengths rather than putting pressure on her vulnerabilities.

The most important thing she learnt from this was that your style and how you use it is not a moral issue: you have a choice. Could she have changed how she felt in these team situations? Using NLP techniques, the answer is undoubtedly 'Yes'. But in this instance, it was more liberating for her to decide that she didn't have to keep testing herself. Later she returned much happier in her new role as a personal consultant, and said that now she was ready to deal with her past.

▪ *Using Meta Programmes*

However, there are times for each of us when we recognise that our style gets in the way of what we do want. Any style has its limitations, and the other key to success is to identify how your style limits you, and recognise that what you might need to do to is to free yourself from those limitations.

Wendy's father used to say: 'We all have the weaknesses of our strengths.' In NLP terms, he was talking about meta programmes, which we introduced in Chapter 3. An approach or skill which is really useful in one situation may be quite inappropriate in another. The engineer who is really good at working with fine detail may find it harder to take the larger view. He naturally feels at home working with small chunks, in meta programme terms. In some circumstances, this may limit him. Many helpers may habitually put others first and overlook their own needs. Often this results in overload and exhaustion – sometimes in buried resentment and indirect forms of self-reward and nurturing, such as overeating. The very degree of what in meta programme terms is called sorting by other, which makes them good at what they do, may also wear them out – and end up eroding their skills in the long term. If you look at these and other common meta programmes as described in Chapter 3, you'll be able to see the strengths and weaknesses each involves. Ask yourself what your governing meta programme preferences are: what are your strengths – and weaknesses – as a result?

Once you have begun to identify the limitations of your strengths, you are in a position to consider what you might want to change and to learn. In order to tackle these limitations, you need to become more aware of what is currently going on, to take account of feedback and to experiment. Meta programmes may be habitual, but they're not irrevocably fixed. Becoming aware of how you naturally function is the first step to having more choices, and more flexibility.

For example, if you are someone who tends to sort by other (see page 57), you might experiment with one of a number of possible strategies for change:

▶ Ask whether you are more able to remember your own needs and rights in certain circumstances rather than those of others.

▶ Consider whether there are any specific triggers that lead you to be self-effacing – for example, the way a request or instruction is worded, the tone of voice in which you are asked to do something, the way you yourself imagine or assume things might turn out if you said 'No'.

▶ Re-run some scenarios from the past, imagining how things might have gone differently if you had taken your own needs more into consideration.

▶ In re-running past scenarios, find out at what points you might have been able to make a more self-caring choice, and imagine different ways of doing this.

▶ Identify some situations which are likely to occur in the near future and run various possible scenarios with a range of different responses, which build in a greater degree of self-consideration.

▪ *Using Sensory Acuity*

One of the recurrent themes in NLP is the importance of noticing what is actually going on inside and around us. NLP calls this sensory acuity. It's important because only with precise, detailed information, grounded in actual experience, are you in a position to act in a targeted, effective way. Once you have this kind of detailed information, it becomes much easier to make any changes you need.

We can develop the acuity of our senses in response to both external and internal events. We are all accustomed to making judgements about ourselves and others rapidly and accurately, often on the basis of unconsciously processed information. A shift in the angle of someone's head, a fraction of a change in facial expression or colour, the tempo of someone's walk, the set of their shoulders, the inflection of their voice – all are potent sources of information.

One way of developing a skill is to heighten conscious awareness – to bring your attention to bear on the information you currently have and to begin to deliberately seek more. So it is with your style. Noticing how you currently do things, whether in your head or in the outside world, gives you essential information that helps you do more of what you do effectively – and even improve it. It will also help you change what you do less well by identifying the smallest and easiest changes that will start improvement.

One of the great discoveries of NLP is that change can be easy. NLP does not subscribe to the 'no pain, no gain' theory. Change takes application, but like shifting a heavy stone with a lever of just the right length, the process can often be surprisingly easy. Once you stop thinking of yourself, your potential and your ways of operating as fixed and begin to treat them as processes, change becomes just another adjustment you can make. The more aware you are of the fine detail of your current style, the easier it becomes to fine-tune it.

CHAPTER 9

Your Personal Balance

▪ *The Wheel of Life*

IF YOU WEIGH UP the balance of activities in your life in the present, you can begin to assess both whether it is how you want it now and how it is likely to stack up cumulatively over time.

In NLP coaching we often use an exercise we call the Wheel of Life. It's a great way of enabling you to take stock and consider how satisfied you are with different areas of your life. You could use many categories but we find the following ones give a pretty accurate readout on how things are for you right now. Here's how you can do your own now.

EXERCISE: Free Wheeling

If the centre of the wheel is 0 and the outer edge is 10, just draw a line across each category area that reflects your level of satisfaction with this area of your life right now.

Inventory – Wheel of Life

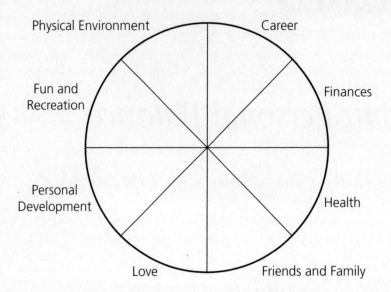

In a perfect world, balance and fullness would perhaps go together, and you would no doubt have 10s all round the wheel. The reality is probably rather different. Remember, this is not what you would like to be the case: it's a graphic representation of what the reality for you is at this moment in your life.

Here's what one client's wheel of life looked like:

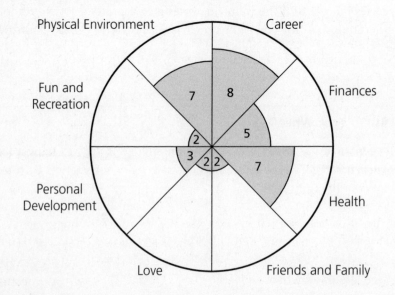

Other people saw him as very successful but he didn't feel happy with his life. And once the wheel was drawn it wasn't too hard to see why. Immediately he could see what he needed to do. As soon as he and his coach started to give some attention to his personal life, he began to feel much better very quickly. To be out of balance is to be at odds with one-self. So moving from, say, a 2 to a 4 in any area invariably produces a disproportionate increase in overall satisfaction ratings, and a general sense of well-being.

▪ *Making Changes to Your Life Balance*

This is surprisingly straightforward. It all hinges on asking yourself some simple questions and then committing yourself to living the answers.

1. Ask yourself 'What do I want?'

2. Now doublecheck: ask yourself 'Is that what I *really* want?' Often, the answer will differ – perhaps a little, perhaps a lot. One person might first of all answer: 'I want a promotion.' Asking themselves what they really want, however, they might answer: 'Actually, what I really want is to get out of the rut I feel in, and have a more interesting job.' Being promoted is not the only way to achieve this, so you may find you have more choices than you thought.

3. Ask yourself 'What am I not paying attention to in my life right now? What am I not honouring as much as I could?' If the answer to this question affects your answer about what you want, take time to make any adjustments, or to modify the goal you started with. For instance, if you say you want more free time but you have a longstanding habit of taking on new projects because you get excited by the possibilities they offer, it could be said you're not paying attention to the consequences of this behaviour. You keep stopping yourself having what you say you want. That's interesting. How come?

4. Ask yourself 'What is the easiest step I can take now, today, or this week in the direction of what I want?' Having identified it, make an agree-ment with yourself that you will do it. If you have a diary, put it in. If you work on lists, put it on your to-do list. If you like to quietly imagine ahead, imagine when and how you will take that step. If you find yourself coming up with reasons why not, check what your objections are seeking to achieve for you. You need that information in order to distinguish the goal from possible routes you might take towards it. If there's a problem with the first route you thought of, be flexible and invent another route to get to the same goal.

If it's a step that needs repeating, imagine the next few times you will take it, and how it will feel as you begin to recognise that it is becoming habitual and its effects cumulative. How will you feel a week from now? a month from now? a year from now? five years from now with this step just effortlessly part of how you do what you do? And imagine how at the end of a week, a month, and six months – or five years – you will feel as you appreciate the differences you have made.

5. Make an agreement with yourself to review your personal balance from time to time, whether or not there is any feedback that suggests you need to. Perhaps you might want to do it every month or every six months, or annually on a particular date (your birthday? New Year's Day?). Making regular reviews of how things are going is part of form-ing the good habit of regularly checking in with yourself. And the more ready you are to check in, the more information you will have access to. It's another habit that builds and becomes more effective the more you repeat it.

▪ *Patterns Over Time*

One important fact that is often overlooked is that your actions accumu-late over time. This is a really useful principle to bear in mind.

Some years ago a man died. He had worked in the Scottish Highlands for many years, walking a number of miles each day to and from work. As a young man he had become interested in trees, and began collect-ing and planting seedlings. Each day he planted one as he crossed a bare hillside on his way to work. By the time he died he had planted a forest.

A young lad started smoking when his friends offered him a cigarette behind the bike-sheds at school. It felt very grown-up, even though at first he didn't like the taste. Gradually he got used to it, and his smoking increased from an occasional cigarette when he was with his friends to a few every day. Over the years his consumption increased: a packet a day; two packets a day – more if he was stressed. By the time he was in his fifties he was up to three packets a day, and experiencing symptoms which he feared might indicate lung cancer. How had this happened?

Any pattern consists of the repetition, perhaps many hundreds or even thousands of times, of a particular behaviour or sequence of behaviours. Any change in that pattern can become a pattern itself, provided it too is repeated. What is repeated one day at a time, over many days becomes a habit. Good habits can be created one day at a time.

▪ *Stocktake of Your Patterns*

Events repeated over time build into results that are greater than any one of those events in itself. This is equally true of events that don't happen. Some people put off treats and pleasures for later – when they will have time, a larger income, when the kids have grown up, or when they retire. What they may not be recognising is that they are building a habit of not giving themselves treats and pleasures. So when they pass a landmark in their lives, they may simply not notice and may just carry on. After a while maybe they don't really know how to celebrate any longer.

To maintain balance in your life, you need both to review the current balance of activities and also to look at the long-term consequences that this will create if you don't change it.

CHAPTER 10

Your World

ONE OF THE REASONS NLP works so effectively is that it recognises things don't happen in isolation. Every thought has effects – on feelings, on other thoughts, on bodily processes, on actions in the external world and maybe on others. Every person is a grouping of interrelated systems; and every person is part of many systems in the outside world: family, work, friendship networks, cultures and subcultures, nationalities and so on. That's why we're going to look at different aspects of your world from this more systemic perspective.

▪ *You and the World Inside*

Simon is a student and sprains his ankle playing squash – nothing serious, but his doctor tells him to rest it and keep it up as much as he can for a few days so that he'll be ready to enjoy his vacation in Spain next week. This frustrates him, but he manages to do what the doctor said, more or less, for a day or two. Then the weekend comes. He has been invited to a 21st birthday party. Of course he can't miss this...

Helped partly by the general excitement and partly by alcohol, Simon hardly notices his ankle at all – in fact, he even dances on it a bit – and the party goes on most of the night. The next day, he wakes up with the expected hangover – but also with a really painful and swollen ankle. This time, resting it doesn't seem to help, and soon he is back at the doctor's again. Now he finds it takes months to really heal and his vacation in Spain proves to be a very limp affair – literally.

Why did his ankle get so much worse? The body does much of its repair work overnight. While you sleep your immune system is in top gear. (This is why it's good to sleep when you're ill.) Simon made things worse by putting weight on his ankle and making even more demands on his body with activity and alcohol while at the same time denying it the conditions it needed to carry out the repairs.

Tara had taken up running, and had joined her local club. While she regarded herself as very much an amateur, she was surprised by how well she kept up with the more dedicated club runners she trained with, and let them persuade her to become part of the club's second team at a local competition. She stepped up her practice, but on the day, she felt stiff and wooden and had nothing left for the final sprint.

What had previously just been 'a bit of fun' had become serious: as part of the club team, she felt she owed it to her companions to perform well, and ended up becoming anxious and trying too hard. Tara's change of attitude meant she was relating differently to other team members and unwittingly undermining herself. Fortunately, the team had a good coach. He worked with her to restore her confidence. He helped her develop her natural ability through a proper training programme, but first he made sure she stopped feeling she had to live up to the others.

Both Simon and Tara made life harder for themselves than it needed to be because they failed to see their behaviour as part of a larger system. In Simon's case, he just carried on as if nothing had happened till the morning after the party, when he found that his immediate world had become seriously different. Tara too put pressure on herself by changing the way she was interacting inside her head with her new local club. When she changed how she was in herself in this new world, her performance improved dramatically.

▪ *You and the World Outside*

Understanding how we create our world and the systems comprising it can be very empowering. We begin to recognise how we can have much more influence than previously.

> Two colleagues who worked in the same office became friends, introducing each other to their partners and developing a regular pattern of meeting socially. As they grew older, each couple had children, swapping baby-sitting and sharing family outings. Each couple thought of the other as among their closest friends. After a number of years, the firm opened up a new office several hundred miles away. One of the men was offered a major promotion if he moved there, and after some heart-searching accepted. When he and his family relocated, the two couples agreed that they would keep in touch through phone calls and weekend visits. Yet somehow, though things started off that way, contact became less and less frequent, and eventually was reduced to Christmas and birthday cards. What had happened to that important friendship?

Again, the answer was systemic. Neither couple realised that their friendship had been largely created and maintained by circumstances rather than by a deep level of intimacy. Work, partners, shared social events, then families, all maintained a commonality of interests. But when regular contact through work and through living close to each other came to an end, each couple found themselves turning for friendships to people who were physically closer. This didn't mean that the friendship had been a fake, only that it had rested on something none of them had recognised.

Once that element in the system changed, other things changed with it. Understanding how they had drifted apart, and realising that this was the result of changed circumstances rather than changed feelings, led one couple to take the initiative to re-establish contact again. They decided to have a joint weekend in London twice a year so that they could enjoy doing things together away from the kids. So began a new chapter in their friendship.

> By contrast, Garry, a young man who had spent a year after graduation working in a large insurance company, seems to have intuitively understood how to remain connected to a system even while physical-

ly at a distance. Garry decided that if he was to travel and see the world he should do it now. He had relatives in Australia, and spent six months visiting them and exploring the country before spending a further six months gradually working his way round the world. However, he also thought it would be sensible to make some provision for work on his return, and that the best way to do this was to keep in touch with his work contacts. So while he was away he made a point of e-mailing them, and he also did some temporary work in various insurance offices while in Australia to keep his hand in. Knowing that he was about to return, his old manager told him that a vacancy was coming up, and he was able to apply, and be accepted on the strength of his record and experience while abroad.

Garry understood that during his first year of work he had become part of a system at work, and anticipated the need to keep connected to that system if he wanted to be able to return to his old workplace, even for a while. While he chose to keep his contacts there alive in a largely informal way, he made sure that he also acquired some new and relevant experience which would make him a good proposition for re-employment.

EXERCISE: How You've Been Creating Your World

1. Take an example of something in the past which didn't turn out as you wanted, or as you expected.

2. Consider what happened, but from the point of view of the different systems involved, both external like your immediate family, friends and colleagues and internal like your health and state of mind.

3. How did these different systems interact and affect each other? Given the interactions, how might you approach the situation differently if it were to occur again in the future?

▪ *Learning to Pay Attention*

Becoming more aware of what's happening both internally and externally will make you much more effective. Many people have learnt to override internally generated information, yet it is one of the most crucial and accurate sources of information available to us. The 'feeling' that something is slightly different in a familiar situation, or that you aren't quite comfortable with someone you have just met, or the vague reluctance you have in saying 'Yes' to some request or proposal – these you ignore at your peril.

The golden rule is, pay attention. Once you get in the habit of doing this, you will begin to find that the reasons for your feelings become apparent more and more readily. To start with, you may need to buy yourself time before responding so that your feelings can be 'translated' into language your conscious mind can understand. And it's much easier to communicate a decision to someone else on the basis of something you can put words to!

As we get used to 'tuning in' to our own responses, we become aware of just how rich a source of information is there. In developing your skills, you will find it useful to pay attention to the ways in which you characteristically operate. To get you started we have three questions for you:

1. Do you tend to 'see pictures in your head', 'feel what it's like' or 'hear it how it is'? Do you tend to favour the same representational system for everything – or do you, for example, hear yourself being told off or put down but picture yourself doing something well? There are no right answers – but if you want to restore your confidence after someone has put you down it will be helpful to know the way that is most effective for you. You may need to experiment, for example, to discover whether in this case it's more effective to make changes in the criticism you're hearing in your head, or to strengthen the success pictures you run in your mind's eye. Or you may need a combination of both: a video with a supportive soundtrack.

2. What kinds of processes and sequences result in good feelings, or in bad feelings, for you? NLP has shown that the order of internal and external sequencing can be very influential. For example, if you make a mistake and then immediately tell yourself off and then feel bad (action→internal dialogue→unpleasant kinesthetic feeling), you could make an

immediate difference if you either a) encouraged yourself in your internal dialogue or b) added in a picture of yourself correcting the mistake, both of which would change the sequencing and achieve a different feeling.

4. What do you know about your internal dialogue? Internal dialogue is often very influential. It can be helpful to catch these internal remarks and comments that go on in your head and ask yourself where the internal 'voices' come from:
   ▶ How are you with this voice?
   ▶ Which other people's voices play a part in your dialogues?
   ▶ Are the comments a replay of what has actually been said in the past?
   ▶ Are they your fantasy about what a person might say if they were here with you now?
   ▶ Are there any changes you might want to make?

The information you gather from this kind of personal investigation, taken together with the appropriate NLP tools, gives you an enormous range of material to work with. This is your personal foundation for making your transformations – for bringing about what you really want.

CHAPTER 11

Yourself

THE MOST CRITICAL variable for your success in achieving what you want is you. It is easy to assume that external circumstances have to be just right for you to make the breakthrough you want, but in fact, even if the circumstances are favourable, you will only be able to take advantage of them if you are in the right frame of mind.

Harry had worked as a civil servant since he left school, making modest progress up the lower rungs of his career ladder. He wasn't particularly keen on his job, but it provided a reasonable income which paid the bills and supported his family. His wife also worked part-time. His hobby was woodwork and he loved making cabinets and chairs.

When Harry was forty-five his manager told him that his department was moving to a new location out of town. Harry had the choice of keeping his job and moving, or of taking a modest leaving package. What should he do? He and his wife talked things over. They felt anxious about the future, fearing that Harry might not get another full-time job and that the lump sum would not last all that long. He had never had to promote himself, and wasn't at all confident that he would be able to develop the independent business he wanted as a furniture restorer. He was sufficiently torn between cautiousness and wanting a new career that he decided to seek help, and made an appointment to see a coach.

With his coach's help, Harry was able to realise that he did in fact have many of the qualities he would need. He was deft with his hands and had plenty of experience working with furniture. People trusted him and got on with him. He could budget and manage money. He decided that he would find out about courses that might help him with starting up in business. With some qualms, but more confident now that he had taken stock of his personal assets and knew that he had his family's support, he decided to take the risk. And though his new business grew slowly, it did grow. Word began to spread as his clients recommended him to their friends. Some years later he knew without a doubt that he had taken the right decision – but his wife reminded him that the decision was only right because he had been right in himself about it.

▪ *Investing in Yourself*

Harry had literally invested in himself. And this is probably the single most important thing we can do, at every level. Many people have learnt to put other people and their needs first, and keep only the remainder of their attention for themselves. In our experience as coaches and trainers it needs to be the other way about. Only if we nurture ourselves adequately will we have enough resources available to nurture others. You can't make a journey if the petrol tank is empty – and if you start off when petrol is low you may run out.

Investment can happen in many ways and at many levels. Consider how much you invest in yourself in the following ways:

- Time on your own

- Relaxation

- New stimuli

- Presents and treats

- Fun

- Off-duty activities

- Doing things you like

- Being with people who make you feel good

- Praising yourself

- Appreciating your uniqueness

- Spending money on yourself in ways that enhance your life, your skills, your opportunities

- Honouring your needs.

Having a coach is another way of investing in yourself. But we'd like you also to be able to coach yourself. So how good a coach are you towards yourself?

Let's recap some of the things coaching involves:

- Collaborative endeavour

- Clear outcomes

- Regular effort, regularly monitored to ensure that you are on target with agreed goals

- Regular meetings (be they face to face, by phone or on-line)

- Absence of good/bad or success/fail judgement

- An attitude characterised by curiosity and awareness.

The more your attitude towards yourself, and the way you treat yourself, fits with this coaching profile, the better a coach you will be to yourself or anyone else.

Self-coaching

To be a more effective coach to yourself, consider these points:
- ▶ What are you best at doing for yourself? How do you do that?
- ▶ What are you least practised in doing?
- ▶ What might be a first step to help you become more practised?
- ▶ What is the first improvement you can make then in coaching yourself?
- ▶ What might you do next?

▪ *Building Rapport with Yourself*

Most people don't think about needing to build rapport with themselves, only with other people. When there is rapport, then you have more influence, and suggestions can be offered, and are more likely to be accepted. This is true with other people, but it's also true for you. So you need to establish this approach with yourself if you are to help yourself most effectively.

Building rapport with yourself is just like building rapport with someone else. It takes careful attention, and a genuine respect at a deep level. Often people act in ways which will undermine their respect for themselves. Sometimes, for instance, instead of just being critical of a specific behaviour they jump to having a bad opinion of themselves as a whole.

When one person builds rapport with another, NLP has shown that they need to start from 'where the other person is'. That's how it occurs naturally; and that's how it can be done deliberately. This means acknowledging the other person's position and what's important to them, and showing that acceptance verbally and non-verbally. It means accepting how you are at this moment, rather than leaping in with judgements or suggestions for change.

Exactly the same applies if you want to establish rapport with yourself. Start from where you are – warts and all. You certainly don't have to pretend that everything about yourself is wonderful, great or marvellous. Rapport founders just as much on unrealistic praise as on unrestrained criticism or unleashed oughts and shoulds. We know we aren't perfect: but we need to be reminded that we've been doing the best we can.

NLP makes clear that the really effective helpers are those who act on this respectful assumption that we are doing the best we can. Equally, this is what works when we coach ourselves. That best can probably be improved, once we know how. Even when things are going well it's important that you maintain this respectful, purposeful, supportive relationship with yourself.

▪ *Honouring Different Parts of Yourself*

Do you sometimes use the phrase 'a part of me wants this and another part of me wants something else'? This is a very common experience and may indicate some lack of internal rapport. In its more extreme forms, it can reveal a conflict between different values, goals or interests you may have.

Ultimately, we all need to find ways to create harmony within ourselves. We can utilise the ability we have to interact with ourselves internally to enquire, respectfully, what each part wants, to track those wants back to their deepest intent and to help each part of ourselves recognise that it is valued for its attempts to achieve something important for us. If you actually do this, you'll be surprised at how much information you get, sometimes in words, sometimes in images or sensations.

One of these well-intentioned parts is what Gallwey called Self 2, which he, like the developers of NLP, recognised as playing a highly significant role in our internal dialogue. This internal voice tells us how we should be doing and what we ought not to be doing; it exhorts and sometimes bullies us; it frequently criticises, reminds and belittles us. But it is also, in its own way, trying to do its best for us. We need to establish rapport with that moralistic, judgemental voice just as much as with any other part of ourselves: we need to enquire what it is trying to achieve. Often it is to save us trouble, embarrassment, failure or pain; but we don't have to stop at that. Sometimes we need to take issue with that voice and continue the dialogue rather than meekly giving in; sometimes we need to explore other ways of achieving the same aims; sometimes we just need to refocus our awareness on what is actually going on, because it may be rather different from what that part fears or foresees. Dealing with that voice is an important part of developing an effective coaching role with ourselves.

Next time you notice, by tuning in to your internal dialogue, that you're giving yourself a hard time, pay attention to what is being said and then step back and evaluate it. Is it reasonable, useful and credible? What effect does the tone in which it is being said have on you? Frequently, simply changing the tone and volume of such internal dialogue enables people to benefit from the content of what's being said without feeling bad any more. You can make as many sub-modality adjustments to the way the voice sounds as you wish, until you feel more at peace with yourself (see page 80). As one client put it: 'What was an enemy has become my ally.'

PART 5

Success Secrets

Introduction

NLP DIRECTS US to what works, and how it works. In this part of the book we're going to look at how NLP can help you in some of the key areas of your life: self-esteem, relationships, brain-power, health, wealth and happiness, work and being spiritually alive. Each chapter outlines four key 'how-tos'. Modelling people with high self-esteem, for example, shows us that they consistently do four things: have a strong sense of self, like themselves, manage their states, and have a sense of purpose. Our chapter on self-esteem therefore looks at what this means in practice, and shows you ways in which you can use your understanding of NLP and its specific tools to help you.

We take the same approach in each of the other key areas of life. Whether you want to make improvements in just one area, or take an overview of your whole wheel of life, you'll find many ways in which NLP can help you make changes for the better – as well as revealing your existing recipes for success so that you can be sure of using them again.

CHAPTER 12

Self-esteem

S ELF-ESTEEM MATTERS. It's more than just self-confidence. The very word esteem tells us why it's important: etymologically, it comes from the Latin word *aestimare*, 'to put a value on'. And it shares the same root as the word 'estimate'. So self-esteem is, quite literally, the value we put on ourselves.

So what are the key ingredients of self-esteem? People with high self-esteem have a strong sense of self; they like themselves; they can recognise and manage their internal state; and they have a clear sense of purpose. These things are not magically allotted at birth. We use the phrase 'how-to' below to emphasise one of the basic presuppositions of NLP: what others can do, you can learn. That's what this section is about: showing what people with high self-esteem do, and breaking it down into distinct and manageable chunks so that you can begin to learn how to do this too.

Taken together, the four how-tos we're going to explore will enable anyone to enhance their self-esteem.

How to Strengthen Your Sense of Self

Some people who seek coaching say that they lack self-confidence. As we've seen, self-esteem is how we value ourselves, but self-confidence relates to actions. The word 'self-confidence' means to trust in ourselves, so at its root it implies some kind of challenge or task. More specifically, confidence usually relates to some kind of competency. We are confident *in* our ability to do something, to behave in a certain way in a certain situation, to rise to a certain challenge.

In our experience, it is difficult to have self-confidence without self-esteem.

Jo was a schoolteacher whose ability had quickly been recognised by her head of department. She was bright, able and hardworking. She got on well with the kids, and presented her lessons clearly and in an interesting way. All in all, a real asset to the department. After a year, her head of department recommended her for a promotion, and she was given some special areas of responsibility, together with a modest increase in salary. After a few years a head of department post became vacant at a neighbouring school, and Jo's own HOD urged her to apply. He told her he would certainly be reluctant to lose her, but he felt that she deserved an advancement in her career and had the ability to handle the job. But Jo was shocked at the suggestion, and felt she wasn't good enough even to think of applying. She always managed to find reasons for dismissing praise, telling herself she really didn't deserve it, anyone could have done as well, one day someone would realise she wasn't that special really... and so on. So she didn't apply.

Many people are like Jo: they have low self-esteem and aren't able to generalise from the good results they keep getting, or the acknowledgement they receive. In a way, they don't really 'hear' the praise at all. Because of this, Jo lacked the confidence to apply for the promotion; and many people with low self-esteem consistently underachieve in their lives. They may spend years, or even a whole lifetime, underestimating themselves and feeling unworthy.

We want to explore how people who do have self-esteem actually think and behave. That fundamental NLP question has popped up again: 'How do they do that?'

> Liz liked being who she was. She had done reasonably well at school, had lots of friends and found herself in an enjoyable first job in a busy office without too much effort. Her firm was expanding and taking on larger office premises, and Liz helped her manager with preparations for the move, which involved quite complex arrangements to shift equipment and furniture in a short time-frame with as little disruption as possible to customers. Liz didn't see being asked to help with this as anything special, though her boss chose her specifically because she was efficient and calm even under pressure. Two days before the actual move, Liz's manager went down with a stomach virus. The regional manager asked Liz if she would oversee the move, since she had been involved in all the planning. Liz took a deep breath and agreed: after all, she did know most of the arrangements that had been made, and if she really had to, she could phone her manager at home.

It wasn't just that Liz had a more easygoing temperament than Jo. When it came to it, she was more comfortable with herself, and this meant that she could in turn take the leap of confidence *in herself* needed to assume the last-minute responsibility.

Both young women were able, but whereas Jo had a low sense of self-worth, Liz believed in herself. And you?

Here are some questions to ask yourself:

► Can I take a compliment straight, without verbally deflecting it and without blocking or qualifying it in my head?

► Am I afraid that one day someone will find me out?

► Can I list five things I like about myself without hesitating?

► How do I react (inside and outside) when asked to try something I haven't done before?

► What am I telling myself when I'm about to do something difficult or challenging?

Do your answers suggest that you like yourself, that you think well of yourself, or that you are less than happy being who you are, feeling critical about yourself and your abilities? You might find it useful to write these answers down, so that later on you will have a benchmark for the changes you have made.

Let's go back to those questions again, and explore some NLP ways to begin changing things.

Compliments

The simplest and most effective way to take a compliment is by just saying 'Thank you.' Remember a compliment someone paid you: hear it in your head, or say it out loud to yourself, and say 'Thank you.' You may need to experiment with different tones of voice, and different facial expressions, to find a way that's comfortable for you, and that seems natural. Practise in front of the mirror, if that helps, until it comes naturally. When someone next pays you a compliment, don't be disheartened if your old dismissive response gets in first: simply catch yourself at it, smile and then add 'Thank you' anyway.

Being found out

Ask yourself honestly: what is it I don't want other people to know? Probably, you don't want them to think as badly of yourself and your capabilities as you yourself do. This kind of fear almost always has to do with what you anticipate, not with reality. So this is the time for a reality check. The vast majority of people who feel unworthy (for example, about their capabilities at work or their personal attractiveness) are underestimating themselves. You have only to take a good hard look at other people at work who seem quite contented with themselves so see that contentment and ability aren't correlated! Equally, you have only to look at couples in any public place to realise that beauty is in the eye of the beholder. It may also help to use two other good NLP questions to discover other possible reasons for your fears.

- What stops me (feeling good about myself)?

- What would happen if I did (feel good about myself)?

Liking yourself

Take a piece of paper and list anything you can think of that you like about yourself. It might be the shape of your fingernails. Or the crinkle at the corner of your eyes. Or the fact that you can add up quickly. Or that you try to tell the truth. Keep on collecting items, however small, over the next week. As you explore these aspects of yourself, check against the logical evels (see page **48**). Think of your beliefs and values, your capabilities, your behaviour, your environment. It may be easier to find items on these levels than on the level of identity; but of course, your characteristics on each level do contribute to your unique identity.

Trying new things

If you respond with anxiety and fear, spell out the worst-case scenarios you have in your mind. Sometimes this is enough in itself to make you realise how unlikely these fears are. But if your worst-case scenario could happen, think about how it could be managed. Think of someone you know who could manage it – how would they go about it? Instead of burying the fear, take it on and find a strategy for dealing with it. Usually, one or other of these approaches will defuse the anxiety. If it doesn't, your instinct may be correct: don't do it!

What you tell yourself

NLP has shown how influential our internal dialogue can be. If you are telling yourself not to make a fool of yourself, or reminding yourself of how things went wrong last time, or pointing out how useless you are, that little voice inside may well be contributing to your problem. What would you say to someone else in the same situation if you wanted to encourage them? Work out how you would try to help them. Write the words down, if it helps. Then say them – as convincingly as you can – to yourself. How does it feel to hear this kind of voice instead? Monitoring and changing your internal dialogue can be a really powerful way of improving how you feel about yourself. And because we engage in it so much, every time you make your internal dialogue more self-supportive you make a real difference to your self-esteem and self-confidence.

How can you tell if someone has self-esteem?

Is self-esteem observable from outside? Well, yes, it often is. One of the surest indicators is that people with self-esteem *don't need to prove themselves*. This means that they usually don't:

- Boast

- Put others down

- Show off

- Name-drop

- Hog the conversation

- Tell you all about their achievements.

People who do these things often have quite low self-esteem.

Some years ago, Wendy was speaking to a national women's organisation at their AGM. Over 600 members were gathered together to listen to a panel of speakers. One of the speakers was nationally known, and seemed very much at ease in the conversation before they all went onto the platform, telling various anecdotes about recent experiences and showing no signs of anxiety about speaking to such a large audience. But Wendy noticed that this famous person never asked questions of any of the other speakers, or showed any real interest in them as individuals. Instead, she kept up an apparently relaxed, light-hearted monologue, focusing all the time on herself. It was all one-way. Wendy suspected that it wasn't all that comfortable being this famous person after all. This was confirmed in a conversation after the speeches, when the celebrity discovered Wendy was a coach, and asked her to give her the name of a coach she could work with.

People with true self-esteem, however famous they are, usually exhibit very different behaviours:

► They have a quiet confidence.

► They don't fish for compliments – but they do accept them: they know what they are worth.

► They may be quite humble.

► They recognise and are often interested in other people and their achievements.

► They may not be bothered about receiving external recognition.

Their body language usually speaks for them: they are often relaxed, upright, calm and measured in movement, decisive and without hesitation. And they make good eye contact.

In our experience, there are many, many people out there who, despite their apparent competence and confidence, actually doubt themselves and their abilities. (You may be one of them.) These people may be able to stand up for others, but not for themselves. They may be sensitive and sympathetic – but not about their own limitations. Bear in mind that when you meet other people, whether they are strident and dominating or just quietly efficient, they may still suffer from a lack of self-esteem.

As usual, modelling can be a real help. Think about people you know who seem to have a strong sense of self: how do they behave? How do they seem to think? What is important to them, what do they believe? What tells you that they are genuinely comfortable with themselves? Make use of your best sensory observation, and your gut feelings, here.

Imagine you were watching yourself from outside. How could you begin to incorporate what you have learnt from your self-valuing models into your own repertoire?

▪ *Improving Self-esteem*

There are many ways of improving self-esteem. We're going to look at some simple and really useful ways that NLP has identified. They are:

▪ Behaving as-if

▪ Emphasising what works

▪ Positive stocktaking

▪ Accepting yourself as you are

▪ Building co-operation between conflicting internal parts.

Behaving as-if

If you look again at the description of how people with self-esteem actually present themselves, you'll find a kind of recipe for external behaviour:

- Stand or sit upright

- Move in a measured, deliberate, purposeful way

- Make eye contact with people.

As trainers and coaches, we often meet new people, and with practice we've learnt to tell a good deal about them simply from details such as these. But the strange thing NLP has demonstrated is that *if you do the things a confident person does, as they would do them, you will actually feel more confident yourself.*

NLP calls this 'behaving as-if'. You can try it at home, or in the pub, or going to the office. Walk up to the bar *as-if* you expected to be served immediately. Talk to the person serving you in the shop or the bank *as-if* you expected them to respect your situation and your needs. Stand tall, relax your shoulders and bring them back, so that you correct any defensive hunching, before you say anything. Look at them as you speak. Speak more slowly than usual, if nervousness usually makes you rush, or more distinctly, if you are usually quiet and hesitant.

Behaving *as-if* may be deliberate, but it is not fraudulent. You will find that as you make these changes you do feel more confident; and as you feel more confident the changed behaviour will feel more natural. All you have done is to stop the old cycle of self-effacement and turn it around. But it's you who have done it, no one else.

Emphasising what works

Feelings and behaviour affect each other. Behaviour reveals our feelings, and also affects them. Usually, we assume that to change behaviour we need to feel differently first; but often, it's easier to begin the other way around.

Someone with poor self-esteem will focus their attention on what hasn't worked, on the critical comment rather than the praise; on what there is still to do rather than what they've done already. In exactly the same situation, someone with high self-esteem will look for what did work, repeat the praise to themselves, and remind themselves of what they have achieved. This doesn't necessarily mean they are unrealistic:

they may well be aware of what remains to be done, or could be done differently – it's just they are using the 'good' information as fuel to provide energy and motivation.

Positive stocktaking

Think back over today. We want you to:

▶ Take time to relish something that went well. Giving yourself time to appreciate what has been successful is one way to make yourself feel better – and to notice the patterns of feeling, thought and behaviour that were involved. That way, you can learn from them and use them again.

▶ Go through it again in your head. Repeating something helps to ingrain it in your mind.

▶ Praise yourself. Praise is nourishment and reward in one. Even if no one else is there, even if no one knows what you did but you, you can nourish and reward yourself. Each time, you build your self-esteem.

▶ Encourage yourself. Encouragement builds your resources for the challenges and difficulties you may have to face. Think of what you'd say to someone else – then say it to yourself.

▶ Comfort yourself when something didn't go as you wanted or hoped. Wounds need to heal before we can stress the area again. Emotional wounds are no different in this respect. Taking time to comfort yourself is a way of pacing yourself before you try to lead yourself on again. (For the important relationship between pacing and leading, see page **66**.)

▶ Think of anything that went well in the past, such as a work project. This is not just a way of escaping from something unpleasant in the here-and-now. It's an important way of preventing yourself from making negative generalisations ('I never get it right', 'I'm hopeless...'). As our discussion of the meta model (page **51**) shows, generalisation is one of the ways in which we can lose track of reality. Making negative generalisations about yourself can lead you seriously astray.

▶ Remind yourself of a happy moment or a good feeling. This too is a way of eroding negative generalisations. But it's also a way of helping you change state, because whenever you imagine something vividly (as, in this case, recalling something that made you feel good), you inevitably make changes in your state and your neurophysiology.

If you did none of these things, are you blaming yourself right now? Take the information as feedback, and make yourself a promise that you will explore at least one of them today, and others this week.

Accepting yourself as you are

One of the cornerstones of self-esteem is self-acceptance. This means accepting yourself as you are. By this we don't mean an unrealistic blanking out of things that give you difficulty, or pretending to yourself that you're perfect. We mean exactly what the words say: accepting yourself *as you are*. There is a lot of evidence from different schools of therapy that once people can accept themselves honestly and without blame, recognising but not condemning their limitations and weaknesses, they begin to be able to grow and change. The therapist Carl Rogers said: 'I find that when I stop trying to change myself, then it happens.' We believe that this is generally true, because trying to change yourself suggests some sort of effort on your part which may well entail overcoming some internal resistance. When you stop trying, you stop the resistance. That doesn't mean you don't want to change, but it does mean you achieve it differently.

Too often we assume willpower will do it. We'll just force ourselves to make the change. However, in our experience willpower is far more effective when all of you is behind the change you want to make. Trying to force ourselves is really only an attempt by one part of ourselves to overcome another part.

Building cooperation between conflicting internal parts

In such situations, NLP assumes that *both* parts of ourselves have a valid role to play, and that each is trying to achieve something for us. In fact, NLP finds it useful to presuppose that *all* behaviour has a positive intent. And great things can be achieved when we stop trying to overrule one part or another and seek to discover what each part actually wants for us. The same goes for the conflict between willpower and the part that is resisting. When someone tries to achieve an outcome through willpower they are often really trying to impose something they want at one level on some other part that has another outcome in mind. Mostly, willpower is what the conscious mind wants or thinks it should do, whereas the objections are coming from other parts of you.

> Alex had tried many times to give up smoking, but failed every time. Using NLP, he decided to get clear about the positive by-products of smoking for him. He realised that among other things it was a reward, a distraction when under pressure, it gave him time to think, a sense of being adult, provided something to do with his hands when he was with people, and gave him a great sense of cameraderie with his band of fellow smokers, who would huddle together outside the office. Every time he tried to stop, these needs got in the way. With his coach, Alex found alternative ways to meet these needs. He still liked the thought of having a cigarette, but in fact his smoking just dwindled and then stopped.

Even responses which seem quite negative have a powerful positive intent.

> Mary, for instance, was afraid of heights. She and her boyfriend were interested in history, and loved exploring ancient buildings – but Mary couldn't climb towers or walk along narrow bridges and battlements. She knew she was perfectly safe – but she just couldn't do it, however hard she tried. Things got worse because her boyfriend couldn't understand why she had the problem at all, and told her to 'stop being silly'. It was only after they had had a great row one day, leaving Mary frozen with terror half-way up a narrow staircase until eventually she had to be carried down with her eyes shut, that she remembered how as a child she had nearly fallen off a ladder. She hadn't fallen – but every time she was up in the air and looking down all the feelings flooded back: her brain was trying to protect her by reminding her in the most vivid way it could of the possible danger she was in.
>
> Knowing that her fear was valid in terms of her experience made Mary feel much better about herself, and she was then able to get help from an NLP therapist to deal with what she felt was now an outdated response.
>
> The NLP therapist used a rapid and very effective NLP technique called the Fast Phobia Cure, which has helped many people rapidly and permanently overcome long-standing and debilitating phobias. Mary realised that though it was appropriate in the original circum-

stances, her fear had become generalised so that any situation that seemed even slightly similar triggered it. Through the Fast Phobia Cure she was able to change that response. The following weekend she was up on the battlements with her boyfriend, much to his astonishment, and she didn't feel stupid anymore.

One important key to these changes is accepting that the unwanted behaviour or feelings have validity, rather than disliking and attempting to fight them. Think of someone you know and love. They are probably not perfect. In fact, if you think about it, they may have qualities that irritate you at times. But you would probably not want them to change all that much: their irritating qualities may in fact just be the 'other side of the coin' of a quality or behaviour that is helpful, useful or admirable. Can you develop the same overall tolerance, or acceptance, of yourself, with your linked good and bad qualities, helpful and unhelpful behaviours?

Sometimes it can be helpful to ask yourself: if someone else behaved like this, would I be able to accept it as just a part of their unique self? Even if I wanted them to change this behaviour in some way, would I still accept them as a whole? If you find you answer 'Yes' to these questions, while condemning the same quality or behaviour in yourself, you are working with a different, harsher standard for yourself than for the rest of the world. And this is quite common. So ask yourself, when you think about this quality or behaviour in someone else, just *how* do you go about finding it acceptable, understandable, forgivable? Do you, for example, just see it as an eccentricity? Or do you remind yourself of other things they do which you like? Are you aware that it doesn't happen very often, that it's not bad enough to outweigh all the good things about them...? What happens if you treat yourself and your limitations in the same way? Try it.

▪ *Tips for Building Self-esteem*

1. **Start treating yourself as though you mattered** If you consistently treat yourself with impatience, or as if you lack importance and worth, what message are you sending yourself? For instance, imagine being ignored or dismissed by someone else, and how that feels. Then think of how it feels to be ignored or dismissed by *yourself*.

By contrast, giving yourself the message that you matter will make you feel more valid and worthwhile. So how might you do this? What would be tangible evidence? Would it be caring for yourself, listening to your inner voice, paying attention to your needs, or what?

2. Find a time at the beginning of every day to 'tune in' to yourself
Ask yourself:

▶ How do I feel today? Make use of your sensory acuity (see page **76**) to monitor yourself from day to day and to notice those slight changes in physiology and state during the day.

▶ What is important to me today?

▶ What could I do for myself today?

▶ What do I need to do for myself today?

▶ What will tell me I've achieved something today? Answering this question helps to ensure that your aims for the day meet one of the well-formedness criteria (see page **63**) because it gets you to identify what sensory evidence will tell you of your achievement. What will you be seeing, hearing and feeling that tells you you've achieved something? When we construct a sensory profile of achievement like this, we ensure that we really feel the achievement when it happens. And that builds self-esteem.

3. Ensure that as the day goes along, you keep these things in mind and do something about them If you find difficulty in looking after yourself in these ways, become really curious about what stops you, and exactly how you manage to avoid, or defer, the things you wanted or promised. The information you get will be really useful, because it will show you just *how* you currently don't build your self-esteem.

When you achieve something, however small, take a moment to appreciate what you've done. Relish the sight of the tidy desk, the pile of screwed-up done-it Post-its in the wastebin. Look at the pile of smooth ironing before you slap it in the cupboard and get on with the next chore. Reinforce yourself.

If something goes wrong, use your internal dialogue positively to remind yourself of something that went right – yesterday if not today – as well as trying to set it right. Remind yourself that your behaviour is not the same as your identity. If you made a mistake, it doesn't mean that there's something fundamentally wrong with *you*. Separating out behaviour and capability from identity means you can learn from and correct the mistake without feeling it's about who you are at an identity level.

4. At the end of the day, find a private moment It may be taking the dog for its last walk, a soak in the bath, or thinking for a few minutes after you put the light out. Ask yourself:

- ► What have I done today to be proud of?
- ► What tells me so? Find the details, remember the moment, the feelings, the sights, sounds, words and gestures. Rerun those moments in your head.
- ► If anyone paid you a compliment, go over it again in your head. Replay the event, listen to the words again. Maybe even remind yourself: 'That's me!'
- ► Think forward to tomorrow. What do you want for tomorrow? Run a movie of it in your head – it only takes seconds.

What if something goes really wrong?

How do people with high self-esteem deal with real disasters? There are times when we do make serious mistakes, or get into horrible rows with people we really love, or meet hostility at work. NLP modelling of people with high self-esteem shows that there are a number of ways they manage the situation and still retain their self-esteem. You can use some of their effective strategies.

Separate your behaviour from your identity. Recognise that though you are responsible for your actions, your behaviour is just an attempt to achieve certain goals you have. It may not be the best means and it may need to change. Even so, it's not who you are. You are much more than this.

Ask yourself what was the positive intention behind the behaviour – yours or others'. NLP suggests that all human behaviour is purposeful, even that which we think stinks. For example, failing to meet a deadline when we know we need to, perhaps even want to, may be our way of asserting ourselves in a really basic, childlike way. It's like a six-year-old saying 'Shan't', even if that means they suffer for it.

Recognise the positive intent of your actions; this achieves two things:

1. It gives you information about something you really need or want or that's really important to you, which you probably weren't aware of in this situation.

2. Once you know what it is you really want, you can usually find more constructive ways to go about getting it.

Wondering what others may be trying to achieve by their strange or obnoxious behaviour is a way of getting at this same information. Often you can get a change in others when you're able to give them other means for achieving that same end. Get clear about what it is in your power to do now. Regroup so you know what your choices are and then decide on a course of action. Pace yourself – if you need recovery time, figure that in to any plan. This may mean simply taking time out and not just screaming back at your partner, or choosing to sleep on things before deciding what to do.

Tips for building and maintaining self-esteem in the longer term

1. **Look out for distortion, deletion and generalisation** when you think about yourself and find 'evidence' for your beliefs. Our discussion of the meta model (see page **51**) explains more fully how these three processes can skew our impressions of ourselves and the world around us. As a general principle, you will help yourself most if you:
   - ▶ Acknowledge and accept everything that you are.
   - ▶ Pay attention to all of your experience. Don't dismiss or overlook things. Small difficulties may give you pointers to changes you can make. Small goodies can be relished on a bad day. Honour yourself. Be as respectful of yourself and your experience as you would of someone who is very important and very precious to you, or someone very vulnerable. You are all these things. You need your respectful attention.
   - ▶ Get into the NLP habit of assuming that even the most bizarre or apparently self-destructive behaviour is purposeful: check out what that behaviour might be trying to do for you.

2. **Trust your intuition** 'Gut feelings' are a really important source of unconsciously processed information, and we ignore them at our peril. The unconscious works much faster than the conscious mind, and our bodies reflect it. This means that a 'sinking feeling' is often the first sign that we are unsure, or unhappy, about a situation. Don't override this: note it, and if you can, buy yourself time to investigate further before reacting or making decisions. There will always be useful information in that sensation about how you really feel and what you really want. You can still choose to override a reluctance, but if you override it auto-

matically because you think you 'ought' or because you can't think why the feeling is there, you are likely later to regret it. What begins as a 'gut feeling' takes time to translate itself into something your conscious mind can understand: give yourself that time if you possibly can.

3. **Be clear about what you really want** You can modify your goals, settle for less or do without, if there are good reasons. But you need to know what you want first. And, perhaps more importantly, asking yourself 'What do I want?' encourages you to build a habit of self-consulting – and that in turn builds your self-esteem. If you imagine how someone else would feel if you never asked them how they felt or what they wanted, it's easy to see how they could come to feel unwanted, unimportant or worthless. The same applies to the way you treat yourself. Treating yourself as though you matter is the quickest way to help you feel that you do matter. This in turn leads you to behave as though you matter in your interaction with others in the world outside. And when people act as if they matter, other people tend to respond accordingly. So by first treating yourself as though you matter, you are creating a ripple of positivity which spreads wider and wider.

4. **Filter feedback positively** If your boss at work says 'You have a lot to learn', make sure that you hear the positive implications as well as the negative ones. You 'have a lot to learn' *before you are in a position to...* become an efficient secretary, take a senior post... Don't just stop at the point where you have translated this into 'What he means is that I don't know much at all', even if you are pretty sure that is what he might mean. NLP stresses that what we believe is a construction in our own head, and that it's based on our understanding of 'reality'. If the 'reality' we experience is actually something we construct, it makes sense to construct a reality that's useful rather than limiting. This does not mean you have to be unrealistic. If your boss thinks you have a lot to learn, note it – don't pretend he thinks you are marvellous. But remind yourself that things can be learnt. Ask him, perhaps, exactly what it is that he thinks you need to learn in order to... And be clear with yourself that even if his tone was a put-down, to say you have a lot to learn is somewhere to presuppose that you can. So go ahead, be an effective learner even if it's just for your own satisfaction. That way, you have got something really useful out of the exchange, and maintained your self-esteem at the same time.

5. **Build a strong first position** (see the section on taking different per-

ceptual positions on page **68**.) Some people tend to put the needs of others first. Perhaps this began in childhood, perhaps it's a feature of their job. Carers of all kinds learn to minimise their wishes and feelings in order to take care of their clients or patients. Hospital doctors working impossibly long hours, secretaries to high-profile bosses, mothers to young children, head teachers and managers of large companies – all tend to drive themselves through tiredness, depression, even illness because of their beliefs about what their role entails and a habit of putting the needs of the company or the client first. There can come a point where they don't even notice how they are feeling.

This is potentially dangerous. It can produce self-defeating attempts to take care of self in indirect and short-term ways – such as by smoking, overeating or drinking alcohol – rather than in direct and long-term ones. It's as if you are giving yourself a quick treat, but in a way that progressively erodes your self-esteem as you find you can't do without it, yet still don't feel good much of the time.

Eventually, some last straw breaks the camel's back. The teacher leaves the profession and becomes a driving instructor; the boss takes early retirement; the nurse goes off sick for months with a damaged back; the doctor decides to work in a private clinic with regular hours and pleasant surroundings. All of these may be valid decisions – but they are not, in these cases, decisions of deliberate choice: a forced decision does nothing for our sense of self.

It's our experience that putting oneself first actually means that we are in a better position to look after others. If we are fit and well and feel good about ourselves, we have plenty to spare for others. We can give generously, without begrudging it. Putting time and energy into building your self-esteem is one of the best investments you can make.

How to Like Yourself More

What makes us like people? Think of someone you like: why do you like them? You might find yourself answering 'Well, I just do' – but whether you are consciously aware of them or not, there will be some particular reasons. You could probably come up with a list of qualities which you find likeable in others. Liking involves engaging with another and finding qualities you appreciate and enjoy. This is why we can like people who we'll probably never meet but who are in the public eye. You could respect someone but not necessarily like them. To like is to enjoy the other.

Much the same applies to liking ourselves. As we said in the last section, we don't have to be perfect. Self-esteem rests on self-acceptance, whatever we are like. Liking comes after self-acceptance. Your liking for yourself will increase once you know more about how you function and learn to accept yourself as you are, warts and all.

Think about popular public figures. Frequently, one of the key things that draws people to them is not their accomplishments but the fact that they have foibles and frailties. This is what chat magazines are based on – showing the off-duty behaviour and problems of famous people. Their message is *Actually, they're just like us*. What people remember about King Alfred is that he burnt the cakes, not that he was a learned man who tried to improve the standard of education in Britain. He got distracted, just like the rest of us. Princess Diana was loved for her humanity, and sympathised with for her marital and eating problems. Both showed themselves to be human.

If this process of being drawn to what is individual, quirky or fallible works between people (interpersonally), it can also work inside ourselves (intrapsychically). Actually, it can be a relief to allow ourselves to accept our limitations and idiosyncracies – to become quite fond of them, even, provided they don't hamper us much or interfere too severely with our lives.

▪ *Building a Profile of Yourself and Your Way of Being*

Acceptance allows us to investigate more closely, to begin a detailed self-profiling which is both fascinating and enabling. For a start, use the information on meta programmes to find out your habitual ways of sorting information and reacting to things. See our discussions of representational systems (page **73**) and sub-modalities (page **80**) to help you discover just how you construct your reality from the information your senses bring you – and how that affects your thinking, your feelings and your behaviour. Self-profiling not only allows you to get to know yourself better, it also allows you to understand just how you do the things you do effectively, as well as how you are limited by your characteristic ways of functioning. Moreover, it offers some clear recipes for change, if change is indicated.

Jenny was 45 and had an important and successful job in training. She was well-liked and respected by her colleagues. Inside she recognised and thought well of her own abilities. But she didn't like herself all that much, because she had always felt she was plain. She *knew* that looks didn't have to be that important – but somehow she *felt* they were. Even though she *knew* men found her attractive, when she looked in the mirror she always *felt* disappointed in herself. It was as though she had somehow let herself down. She valued herself; at times she even admired her abilities; but she didn't really *like* herself. And for her, looks were the deciding factor.

She never told anyone about this, until one day it somehow popped out in conversation with Jill, a close friend. Jill was astonished, and said without thinking: 'But you've never seen your face moving – it's so expressive, and that's what men have found so attractive.' This unexpected comment completely turned things around – it reframed both the way she saw herself and the way she thought about herself. Soon after she saw herself on the video of a friend's wedding reception. And she began to like herself. She also felt a sadness and a sympathy for this poor self whom she really hadn't enjoyed that much for so many years.

EXERCISE: What Is It You Like About Your Friends?

Think about two or three people whom you like. What tells you that you like them? What do you like about them? Do they have characteristics in common? When you think about them, do you see them in your mind's eye, hear the tone of their voice, feel warm or comfortable, excited or relaxed, remember their touch...? Make a list of the following:

► What characteristics you like in them.

► Anything you don't like about them but accept as part of them.

► What qualities or behaviours you approve of or admire in them.

Now sort this information according to the logical levels (see page **48**). Do you filter according to some levels rather than others? Consider: do you have to admire or approve of someone before you can like them?

▶ Think about the history of your relationship with each person. Did you like them at the very beginning? Or did your liking grow? Can you pinpoint any incident which made you realise you liked them, or which increased your liking?

▶ Look at all the information you have gathered, particularly those factors or incidents which were most important or decisive, or which brought about the change from merely knowing to actually liking the person.

▶ Ask yourself what it is that you really enjoy about this person?

▶ Suppose you were to do exactly the same again – but with you as the subject.

Steps to liking yourself better

Start enjoying yourself. What *do* you enjoy about the way you are? At the end of the day, take a few moments to ask yourself what you most liked about you today. Include everything, however trivial or superficial it seems. Perhaps you thought carefully about the way you chose the colours that you wore; perhaps it was something you did – the way you managed a telephone call, or a colleague. Perhaps it was something you refrained from doing, or something you thought.

EXERCISE

1. Make a list that begins 'I like myself because...'

2. Make another list that begins 'I like...about myself.'

Sort this information according to the logical levels so that you can see where your self-liking – or lack of it – is located. This may also show you some bases you can build on: for example, 'I keep my word' and 'I'm conscientious' both emphasise the connection between your values and your behaviour.

Ask yourself how much the degree of your liking for yourself depends on your behaviour or your capability? If you can identify changes that are needed on these levels, and take steps to make them, how will that affect your self-liking?

Say 'I like myself', and notice how you respond. What is your body telling you about how comfortable you are making this statement?

If you are not comfortable saying it, ask yourself 'What stops me?' and 'What would happen if I did?' to obtain more information.

Finally, think of the people you like most, and the people who like you most. If they like you, dare to trust that you're worth their liking. And dare to like yourself as they do.

How to Manage Your State

▪ *Being in a State*

You have been up half the night with your partner, who has a stomach bug. It's raining and because you are late the only space in the car park is right at the end. You stagger into work the next morning feeling like death. You get soaked. Before you can finish the work you had nearly done when you had to leave early yesterday, your boss rushes in with a project that has to be done urgently. You are surly with her, and snap at your secretary. You forget to phone home to find out how things are going there. You are in a state.

Colloquially, to be in a state is to be having a pretty intense and negative experience. In NLP, though, as we saw on page 77, states can be either negative or positive. So what are we talking about when we talk of 'states'?

A state is a coming together of a number of psychological and physiological events and behaviours, which lasts long enough to be recognisable by observers or the person concerned. A state may involve both particular thoughts and feelings and physiological characteristics such as respiration rate, muscular tension, blood pressure, facial colour and temperature changes.

Some states are pleasant, comfortable and enjoyable. Some are wonderful, even ecstatic. Others are mildly or highly unpleasant. We like some states, and hate or fear others. Good management of our states makes us more effective at home and at work – and greatly enhances our self-esteem.

We tend to develop our own repertoire of familiar states: 'I relax when I'm listening to classical music'; 'My mother always winds me up.' Sometimes we recognise these states at the time, particularly in relation to specific stimuli. Exams and tests are widely seen as triggering anxiety, birthdays are expected to make people feel good. Christmas certainly has its associated state for most people, but what that is varies enormously. Where some people will become excited or euphoric as they look forward to it, and self-indulgent and relaxed on the day, others will experience anxiety, dread and depression as they anticipate and then experience a very different sort of event.

One way to understand how states work is to look at them in families. Often children can be incredibly sensitive barometers of state changes in adults.

Ian remembers working with a couple who were having difficulties with their little boy, Sam. He seemed to have a lot of tantrums, and to become disruptive, attention-seeking or whingey at the slightest frustration. However, the rest of the time, he was fine and fun: lively, affectionate, cooperative. They couldn't understand what was going on.

Ian asked them to really pay attention when Sam seemed to 'flip', and to notice the exact circumstances so they could discuss these when they next met. What emerged was a pattern which the parents just hadn't seen before. Most of the 'flips' took place at times of transition: between one event and another; between one place and another. When he was being collected from nursery, or a friend's house. When it was time for bed. When mother or father were getting Sam ready to go out of the house.

So what was happening, exactly, at these times? A number of things. Together, the parents and Ian made a list of possibilities. There was a change of focus at those times and so the adults' attention shifted from Sam onto the next thing they had to do. They often felt pressured; there was often a greater sense of urgency; musts and oughts and have-tos crept in (you must get your coat on quickly...). It was as if Sam was picking up this tension. Ian explained how they were functioning as a system and building a pattern which NLP calls a calibrated loop. Calibration is a process of fine adjustment: both child and parents were winding each other up because of what they were observing in each other. In this case the loop they had created was a vicious circle.

Knowing about the pattern was one thing; but how could the parents change it? Ian asked them to build a similar profile of what made up the states they really enjoyed together, and to look for the messages that their son might be receiving there. Mostly, these enjoyable occasions were ones where there was little or no time pressure, where activities could be negotiated, where the little boy felt he had a say – and where the parents didn't feel pressured. It seemed likely that Sam was picking up on his parents' more relaxed state, and that he was receiving a very different message from them: that he mattered and had more of a say in what was going on.

So now the parents had some information for away-from changes, and also for some towards moves (see away from/towards in meta programmes, page 56). The couple agreed that when they had to collect Sam from somewhere, they would make the transition as clean and crisp as possible: they would explain to him that they would be leaving in two or three minutes, or when he had finished: they would keep the focus of their attention as much as possible on him throughout. But above all, they agreed to take the pressure off themselves and not try to cram so much in. If they changed their state it seemed highly likely Sam would act differently – and sure enough, he did.

They began to recognise that Sam's 'flipping' was actually a kind of litmus test which told them very accurately that *they* were experiencing disruptive changes of state. Now they knew how to change this.

If we look at Sam and his parents, we can see that a number of interlocking features were crucial to creating the experience:

▶ **Feelings and states** such as irritation, sense of pressure, resentment, anger, and, on the other hand, relaxation, playfulness, absorption.

▶ **Pace,** for example, leisurely or hurried – thoughts such as 'must', 'ought', 'should' (some taking place in internal dialogue, some actually spoken).

▶ **Bodily experience and body language** – for example, tension, speed of movement, tones of voice, anxiety, degree of focus on the moment or becoming distracted, disjointed, busy.

Children are very aware of states. Wendy vividly remembers an occasion when her daughter, aged about two, caught sight of an argument taking place between two adults on a TV soap. She watched the argument, which was entirely verbal, for a couple of minutes, then asked, 'Mummy, why are those two people hurting each other?' Without understanding the adult words, she had been able to read their body language and tones of voice to pick up what was going on.

We could summarise and say:

▶ A state consists of a number of interlocking features.

▶ Each one is important.

▶ A change in any one will inevitably affect the state as a whole.

▶ States, and state changes, involve sequences (action – thought – feeling in many different orders and combinations).

There are many ways in which we can change states that are unpleasant or ineffective, and recreate or enhance ones that are good.

So far, we've mostly been talking about negative or 'bad' states. But of course, there are plenty of 'good' states, too. Our aim is to ensure you have far more good states. The secret of effective state management lies just as much in finding out about your good states, how you create them and how you can have more of them, as it does in avoiding or minimising bad states.

Motivation can be important here. If you are driven more by the wish to avoid unpleasant states, your motivation is an *away-from* meta programme. If you are motivated by the desire to create and maintain pleasant states, you're working on a *towards* meta programme (see page **56**). While the attention of many people is often drawn to unpleasant states and they use an away-from motivation to seek change, as coaches we've found that it really pays to give just as much attention to seeking out and cultivating good states.

The benefits of going to third position

Recognising a state depends on noticing enough detail – but not getting lost in it. Just as those parents became observers of their own behaviour, so state recognition and state management can help us observe and understand our behaviour, rather as anthropologists study unfamiliar societies. When we change our perceptual position (page **68**) and go to third position, we move outside our usual feelings, experiences, beliefs and assumptions and notice what they are. Isn't it fascinating that this person – you – behaves like that? I wonder what that behaviour means to him or her? I notice that he/she always does that every time that x happens: why?

Going to third position does more than give us information. It immediately changes our relationship with the situation. When a state is unpleasant or dysfunctional, taking third position gives us a helpful distance from it. When it's a pleasant state, noticing the detail, strangely enough, doesn't distance us but actually enhances our enjoyment or immersion in the state. It's as though realising exactly what is giving us the pleasure, or working so well, magnifies its effect. We can enjoy it more, or do more of it. It's like really paying attention to every mouthful of a wonderful dish: realising exactly what spices or herbs give it its flavour allows us to appreciate it even more fully.

If people aren't feeling good they often try to distract themselves, but sometimes this can make an unpleasant state get stronger. The parents' arguments with the little boy usually started with something quite small: saying 'It's time to go now', for example. Then he would react, and they would react to his reaction, and he would react to their reaction... and so on. Once they understood about states and had learnt to recognise them, they were often in a position to catch problems even once the escalation had begun. Paying attention allowed them to prevent many of these family arguments developing, but it also allowed them to rescue situations that had initially slipped past them.

▪ *Mapping Your Own States*

It's pretty clear you wouldn't want to spend your life experiencing limiting and unpleasant states, but some people do. How much of your time would you say you spend there? Maybe you'd opt for helpful and pleasant. Fine, how much of your time do you spend there? Sometimes things can be pleasant and yet limiting, especially if you just keep doing the same old thing. This is a good description of someone who rarely leaves their comfort zone. Other times a state which may be unpleasant can be very helpful as when you sense danger. The crucial question is, where are you spending most of your time?

▶ Be really curious about these states, and about exactly what information you are getting from yourself. Gather information. Make notes if you find it helpful.

▶ Check the history of your states. Sometimes it can be really helpful to ask yourself questions such as:
  - Does this state remind me of anything?
  - How old do I feel when I'm in this state? (Sometimes you can feel much younger than your chronological age, and this may tell you when you first experienced this particular state.)
  - What do I **really** want when I'm in this state?

▶ How do others react to these familiar states of yours?

▶ What states do you enjoy or find problematic in the people around you? Is there any pattern to your reactions? If so, does that tell you anything useful about you?

▶ Ask yourself which states you want to have more of, and which you want to change in any way.

▪ *Changing State*

NLP is the art of the how-to, and, more particularly, of the effortless how-to. In modelling people who are excellent at what they do, NLP has always been particularly interested in people who do things easily. More and more these days, in every field, the emphasis is changing from linking achievement with effort to linking it with effortlessness. If there's an easy way to do it, why not use that? More incentive, less effort.

It's the same with state changes. Just because a state is a complex thing, that doesn't mean it has to be hard to alter. In fact, from our experience as NLP coaches, our understanding is that it's the reverse: if you alter any part of a complex entity you will be altering the whole. Just like a recipe: if you add another ingredient, or take one away, the result is different, sometimes subtly, and other times quite dramatically. Major change can be brought about by an apparently small ingredient – try adding garlic!

These are the essential elements in changing state and they can occur in any order. You need to:

1. Recognise the state.

2. Change the state.

3. Ask yourself what you really want.

Recognising the state

Being sufficiently in touch with yourself to recognise that something is going on gives you the opportunity to change it. Gather information about what triggers a state, when it happens, what changes it and how you are with this state – do you like it, fear it, want to get rid of it or fear losing it?

Changing the state

Recognising the state and getting curious about it can actually sometimes be a way to break an existing state. But we may need to do more to break state more rapidly. The free-style skater who falls halfway through their programme will need to break the state of irritation or despair brought about by the fall in an instant if they are to retrieve the rest of their performance, as will the salesperson whose last call bombed.

Here are six ways to change your state.

1. **Change your use of physiology** One element of a state you can change easily is its physicality. If you're sitting, stand up and move. If you're moving, stop, sit down. If you're restless, run and then slow down. If you're tense, stretch. And so on. Simple changes like these can have profound effects. Regular physical exercise has been clinically demonstrated to have a marked beneficial impact on depression, for instance – more so than most medication. Ask yourself what you need to do physically to bring yourself into a more resourceful state. Then do it.

2. **Go to third position** See yourself from another vantage point as a concerned observer. Get that different perspective.

3. **Move through time** If you are experiencing something unpleasant, change your relationship with this point of time. Take yourself out of the here-and-now by rerunning a memory of something enjoyable in the past, rehearsing something good in the future, or reminding yourself that next week, next year, or even in an hour's time, you will not be in the state you are now. You may even have forgotten all about it. The problem will have been solved one way or another – 'This too shall pass'. You will have learnt something from it.

4. Put your state in context See the experience in a larger relevant context. For instance, if you've had a row, remind yourself of all the things that you liked about the other person before the row, and imagine a time in the relatively near future when the old harmony could have been re-established, because those qualities were so important to you. And if you realise their importance was in the past, and the row has shown up that they matter less now, thank yourself for the learning and notice how it changes what you feel right now.

5. Learn to build a resourceful state Sometimes we need to find some inner strength or calm before we can even think about addressing the issue that's come up. So how do you create such a state for yourself? Maybe you just do something different for a little while to give yourself a break; or you encourage yourself by thinking of similar occurrences in the past which you ultimately handled well; or you construct a plan which makes things seem manageable again; or maybe you have particular anchors which make you feel good and strong. None of these necessarily make the issue go away. However, they make you much more resourceful in dealing with it.

6. Use your positive anchors What makes you feel good and strong and ready to deal with the challenges of life? These are your positive anchors. Just seeing a particular person can do it, hearing some particularly stirring music or doing something physical can be just as powerful. Begin collecting these by noticing what makes you feel the way you want. Then you can use them as triggers when you choose.

Ask yourself 'What do I want?'

As ever, asking yourself what you really want is the beginning of shifting yourself from inactivity, passivity, dependence or helplessness towards empowerment. If you are in a state you hate, or one that irritates people you care for, or one that makes you ineffective, knowing what you really want opens the way forward. Once you do, use the well-formedness conditions (see page 63) to check how well-formed your goal is.

What if your goal is to change a state? Is it, for instance, a well-formed outcome to feel fine even though you've just lost your job? At one level, no, because there's proper mourning to feel, perhaps anger, bewilderment, relief and plenty of uncertainty. At another level, yes, because you can both engage with those feelings and you can start to profile your strengths and skills, perhaps with the help of others who know you; you can take decisions about filling your empty time meaningfully and constructively in the short term, do the things you need to do to ensure survival at every level, and begin asking yourself what you really want for your future. All of these will begin to change your state for the better.

The message of NLP is that we can change our states, not that we should try to banish or ignore them, even if that were possible. It's a message of movement rather than stuckness, of choice rather than impotence, of personal ownership and influence over our lives and over ourselves.

Tips for changing your state

1. **Engage with your states** Find out more about them. Get really curious about the details: how do you do this state?

2. **Engage with your body and its experiences** Notice the physical components of your states. Notice how there are patterns to this too. Become curious about recurrent physical symptoms such as tension in neck, shoulder, stomach; headaches, migraines, allergies. Don't stop short when you have identified a physical cause (allergic to wheat, long hours at the computer). Ask yourself about exceptions – when doesn't this happen? – and about links with emotion or with particular situations or people. One client, for instance, always got sick when the boss was away, while another always got migraines at weekends. Look for the information in the experience.

3. **Get curious about other people's states** Observe others, and ask them questions about their states. Model what works. Add to your repertoire of states. Build more options and more choices.

4. **Start asking for more, for better, for longer** From where we stand, if someone gets excited about something, by definition that tells us it's worth getting excited about – for them. Yet some people don't know how to respond to extremes of good feeling any more easily than extremes of bad. If the feeling is their own, they may downplay it (it's not so wonderful, really, anyone could have done that...) or even change state by reminding themselves of something mundane that still needs to be done.

One reason for this may be a kind of self-protection: good things don't last, so better remind myself of that now rather than come back to reality with a bump. So people change the wonderful state before something or someone changes it for them. Sometimes there's a cultural fear of making other people conscious of how much better your state is than theirs – don't let on lest they become envious and try to do you down.

Whatever the reason, it's our experience that taking time to enjoy, relish and learn how to recreate good states enriches our lives and does not in any way have to diminish other people. So find out how to have more. And then have more. The skill of state management allows you to have more of those feelings you enjoy and to modify those you don't. In this way you *can* have your cake and eat it.

How to Discover Your Sense of Purpose

People with self-esteem invariably have a sense of purpose. A sense of purpose connects with our sense of self in the most fundamental way: for some people it relates to their sense of what's beyond their own identity – their spirituality. For some it's the core of who they are. For others it's the essence of what they value and believe. In other words, having a sense of purpose involves the highest logical levels – spirituality, identity, beliefs and values. And, of course, once we discover a sense of purpose it enriches and informs us at these levels too.

Another way to describe a sense of purpose is to say it's a sense of meaningfulness, which informs and directs our actions, however large or small, and which connects them coherently to each other and to the future in a way which is congruent with who we are.

Jeff left university and went into teaching. He liked children, and in his first job in a London borough worked hard to share his love of his subject with his pupils in a way which would catch their imagination and be meaningful for them too. After a few years, though, he found himself becoming disillusioned, not with the children or their parents, or indeed with the community they lived in, but with 'the system', which he saw as disadvantaging and marginalising them. The pressures of the job began to get on top of him, and he realised that he was starting to become irritated with the very pupils he had felt so committed to. In these difficult circumstances, he was beginning to lose the sense of purpose with which he had entered teaching. After a period of ill-health, he decided to leave teaching.

In contrast, a woman who had always supported her husband in his business was suddenly widowed in her early fifties.

> Freda's children had left home and she felt bereft of all that had been dear to her. Though she continued to manage the business quite successfully, she felt that she was just going through the motions. Her sense of purpose had been dependent on her devotion to her husband: in working with him in something he had created, she had taken on his purpose as her own.
>
> In the midst of her turmoil and loss, a friend showed her how to do patchwork, thinking it would help her fill up her spare time and draw upon her sense of design and colour. To everyone's surprise, the patchwork 'took off': Freda loved using her hands, found she had a real flair for putting colours and fabrics together, and became interested in copying traditional quilt designs and making her own variations into tablecloths and cushions. Her daughter took some of her work to show buyers at major London stores; they liked the work; it sold around the world and people began to commission one-off quilts and wall-hangings. In her early eighties some of her quilts were featured in national magazines and in an exhibition at Liberty's. Living alone in the country, her creative side had come out as never before. She had found a new sense of purpose, and it made her life meaningful in a whole new way. She had discovered abilities which she had not been aware of during her husband's lifetime, and which had given her an independent source of identity and self-esteem.

Thomas J. Leonard, the founder of Coach University says, 'A vision is a beacon that is **quite** clear to you once you see it; a goal is what you set when you can't see the vision.' Vision and purpose go hand in hand. The distinction between vision and goals can be explored in a number of useful ways:

► Goals are, at least potentially, attainable: purpose is not finite. It goes out and provides the fuel that gets us to those attainable destinations.

► We can be misled about goals if they are not well-formed; we are rarely misled by a sense of purpose.

▶ Goals can fail to come up to our expectations; a sense of purpose continually rewards us.

▶ We can be in conflict about goals – different parts of us can want different things, or we can want things short-term which get in the way of what we want long-term: purpose unites the different parts of us and informs both short and long-term.

▶ Goals are always in the future: purpose is an expression of self. It grows out of our past and relates present to future.

▪ *Recognising Purpose in Yourself*

There are some useful litmus tests for purpose.

It goes beyond basic needs. In the 1960s the American psychologist Abraham Maslow made a distinction between 'survival needs' and 'self-actualisation needs'. Survival needs include food, shelter, warmth – things without which we would die. Self-actualisation needs are the things which give our lives meaning: love, interest, challenge, creativity, purpose. He pointed out that unless our survival needs are met we can't begin to notice, much less satisfy, the self-actualisation needs. The need for a sense of purpose is one of these – and if you have been struggling at a survival level you will not have had any spare energy to think about things that go beyond it. Survival honours your purpose: that you are reading this book suggests that whatever may have happened in the past, you now seek to focus on self-actualisation.

A sense of purpose goes beyond achieving the basics – or even the goodies – in life. Whereas these are frequently specific and concrete, purpose is usually abstract and more inclusive. A new car is a goal; being able to travel freely and widely may be a means to a purpose. Chunking up a level (see page **31**) allows us to see this more clearly: travelling might mean being able to enlarge your horizons or become more creative.

A sense of purpose is something which feels congruent with you at every level. As we said earlier, a goal may fit with a part of you, but not with another. Goals can provoke conflict between parts of ourselves: purpose doesn't.

Purpose may evolve or change the way it seeks to express itself; but it doesn't run out. The young teacher who became disillusioned eventually retrained as an art therapist and set up a private practice. He also did voluntary work two days a week in a hospice for terminally ill children. He still wanted to share his love of his subject; he still wanted a role which allowed him to teach skills to others. His purpose hadn't changed: he had found a new setting which he felt allowed him to express it more freely.

▪ *Finding A Purpose in Life*

A sense of purpose is usually driven by beliefs and values. Because of this, it's likely to involve some, or many, aspects of someone's identity. And it may go beyond that, even, to incorporate a higher level yet, which Ian sometimes just calls beyond identity. This highest level of all involves a sense of connectedness which may be religious or spiritual, or link our own individual life to a sense of greater meaning in the universe, in nature or in time. A sense of life purpose is often likely to involve this highest level of all.

Some people know when they're young what their life purpose is. Most people discover it as they go along. One way to bring a hidden life purpose to your awareness is to reflect on the patterns of your life so far. What are the issues that you've been concerned with? What are the things that have got you excited? What are the values you have sought to promote, or to defend? What really matters to you? NLP has shown us how patterned our thinking and behaviour can be – however unconscious our life purpose may be, it may have been informing and guiding us all along.

It may be helpful to illustrate from our own experiences here. Earlier in the book we explained how Ian's unhappy time at school, and the contrast when he was encouraged to take charge of his own learning at the polytechnic, helped shape his career as an enabling, encouraging teacher. We'd say that these experiences helped develop in him a passionate concern with the way in which learning happens and how it can affirm people – or not. This in turn led him both to NLP and to formulating his own specific ways of encouraging learning. Initially it was through teaching face-to-face but the same purpose – of giving each person a fuller sense of who they really are and what they're really about – can also be honoured in different ways through other media such as tapes and books, and now the Internet. And so it goes on.

Wendy was fortunate to have a very different kind of experience at school. She went to a progressive school which encouraged pupils to take a great deal of responsibility for their own learning from an early age, and which also involved them in the day-to-day running of the school and in decisions about it. The school valued people as individuals, each with their own nature and their own ways of contributing to its community, rather than emphasising academic achievement first and foremost. Its pupils went on to a range of different professions and into law, teaching, the creative and performing arts, green issues and politics. The experience of being part of a community like this gave Wendy a similar sense of life purpose to Ian's: to share information, to encourage learning, to empower. Both of us have worked as therapists, as trainers, as consultants and as coaches. Each of these roles has allowed us to explore different aspects of that life purpose.

We have been fortunate in discovering our life purpose. We have also been able to use our knowledge of NLP and its tools to translate that sense of purpose into action. But what if you haven't yet found your sense of purpose?

In our experience, people sometimes can't discover their purpose because they have learnt not to value, or to tune into, themselves. Many people have learnt to confuse self-awareness with 'selfishness', and self-consideration with 'self-absorption'. If you are one of them, an important first step to finding your life purpose may be to deal with these beliefs and the personal history that developed them. This doesn't mean writing off your past or dismissing what you learnt from it. One of NLP's major contributions has been to show us that human beings are learning creatures; and that many things which we think of as 'given' are in fact things we learnt in one set of circumstances – and which can be modified or changed in others. We can honour our past in what the NLP pioneer Robert Dilts calls our 'museum of personal history' without being held immobile by it forever after.

If you feel you have been limited in this way, many of the skills we have already explored in this book, and continue to explore as it goes on, will have begun to show you ways to become more in touch with yourself and more congruent internally and externally throughout the logical levels. While life continues to show us new opportunities to explore and exercise our life's purpose, it's our experience that the core of it is usually there once we look. And to that end, you may find it helpful to ask yourself the following questions:

1. What am I passionate about? What really gets me going/turns me on?

2. Just what is it about this that involves me so much?

3. What does it do for me? Take note of the answer, however strange or unexpected it seems. Then ask yourself 'And what does *that* do for me?' and each time you get an answer keep on asking the question, until you reach a point where there seem to be no more answers. In NLP terms, you are chunking up: as you question the purpose behind each answer you get, you are focusing on higher and higher levels of significance. When you reach the stage where no more answers are forthcoming, you will be discovering the purpose behind the passion.

4. What did you really, really like as a kid? Is that still important to you? Using the laddering questions, check out with yourself what purpose was involved. Is that purpose still valid today? How are you furthering it today? Or has it changed? Or have you lost touch with it somehow?

5. Take time to think through your answers with yourself: attentively, sympathetically, encouragingly. Now as your own best coach, consider what you need to do next.

▪ *Creating Self-esteem*

Improving self-esteem is certainly magical in its effects, but the real magic is that it can be created. Every day offers us opportunities to strengthen our sense of self, to like ourselves more, to recognise and manage our states, and to discover and realise our sense of purpose.

We've focused on four particularly important how-tos – how to strengthen your sense of self, how to like yourself more, how to manage your state and how to discover your sense of purpose. These four headings are useful to focus your questions and their answers – but trust your own instincts when you notice things we haven't talked about. Building self-esteem is an ongoing process, not because we never get there but because there are always more opportunities for becoming a more developed, a more rounded, successful and happy human being. Testing and trusting the information that comes from your own senses and experience is one of the best ways to make that journey both rewarding and enjoyable.

Next steps

1. Give yourself five minutes at the beginning of each day to plan how you will use it to affirm your self-esteem. Run through today's events in

your mind. What beliefs, attitudes, physiology, clothes, actions will help you stay congruent with yourself and reinforce your sense of self-worth? Are there any traps you see coming up? How will you manage them so that you emerge with your self-esteem intact? What kinds of internal dialogue will help? Which internal mentors – people you know who affirm you, people you don't know but look up to, people whose skills and behaviour you'd like to emulate – would you like to carry with you in your mind as you go through the day?

2. At the end of every day, ask yourself:
   ▶ What did I like most about me today?
   ▶ How many states was I in today – and which of those were most resourceful and enhancing of my sense of self? How did they come about? What triggers could I use another day to get into those states again?
   ▶ What states were less resourceful for me? What triggered those? How could I not get trapped into them again?

3. Nominate your favourite fault. Looking back over the day or the week, choose a fault or limitation that cropped up and dented your sense of self-esteem. Ask yourself, what might a really good friend think about that fault? Given that our actions always serve some kind of self-purpose, what might this fault have been trying to achieve for you – either nowadays or when you first began to think or behave like that? Even if you want to change your patterns now, applaud this fault for its good intentions. How can you take care of the same intentions in a way that lets you like yourself more?

4. At the end of the day or week, choose your five top self-esteem moments. Replay them again in your mind. How are you going to take them forward into tomorrow – or next week?

CHAPTER 13

Building Good Relationships

RELATIONSHIPS HAVE A huge impact on how we feel about ourselves and our lives. Modelling people whose relationships, whether at home or at work, are successful, and people who find this difficult, shows up what's actually going on. If you follow effective models, you can revolutionise the way you relate to other people: you can build a better team, feel better about yourself, have a more equal and a more satisfying personal relationship, get on better with your kids. And if you model what doesn't work so well for you, you can find where things go wrong, and where adjustments – sometimes surprisingly small ones – will make all the difference.

In this section we are going to explore four main how-tos of good relationships:

1. How to build a 'we' which goes beyond 'me' and 'you' (or 'me' and 'the team').

2. How to see things from different points of view – the skill of taking different perceptual positions.

3. How to invest in the future.

4. How to know when to stop investing and pull out.

We'll use NLP to help clarify what's involved in some common dilemmas and errors, and to provide practical and positive guidelines for making your relationships work well, at home and at work.

Personal and work relationships have many things in common: both involve communicating effectively with others and learning to dovetail your wants and styles with theirs. So much of what NLP shows us about effective relationship building and maintenance applies to both. We vividly remember a teenager we knew shouting angrily at her father one day: *'You wouldn't treat your secretary this way!'*

This raises an interesting issue: why is it we are often more restrained at work than at home? Isn't it strange that people often feel free to say the first thing that comes into their heads, to put aside conventional politeness, to behave with less consideration, when they're with the people they care most about? This is something NLP can help with. In Chapter 16 we will be focusing specifically on work contexts, but in this chapter we're going to explore excellence in relationships, whatever the context. We show how you can create and maintain a win-win relationship, with your partner, your kids, your boss – and your secretary – without giving up anything that's central or important to you.

To start with, we'd like to emphasise two important points:

1. Identity is crucial for relationships.

2. Building good relationships depends on being true to yourself.

▪ *The Crucial Role of Identity*

Only when you are solid enough in your sense of self are you in a position to undertake the sharing, negotiations and compromises that form the ongoing conversations that are integral to friendship, productive work relationships and intimacy. It's like money: if you have enough you can lend or give and still be solvent. If you have enough sense of who you are, and enough respect for that self, warts and all, you can enter into the many kinds of dialogue which make up relationships with others without fearing you might be giving all of yourself away or risking emotional bankruptcy. So the work on self-esteem which we suggested in the previous chapter is invaluable.

It's also true that good relationships rest on this personal viability being mutual. Where others have a pattern of demanding, or being needy, it is difficult to have a healthily satisfying relationship with them. Of course, it's quite possible to have a relationship in which one person leans and the other props; in which the domineering approach of one dovetails neatly with the self-effacing doormat of the other; and such relationships, whether professional or domestic, may seem to work for a while. But in the longer term, they can get very stuck. This has important implications when you are embarking on a new relationship, and when you are wondering whether to pull out of an existing one, which we discuss later in the chapter.

▪ *Being True to Yourself*

> This above all: to thine own self be true,
> And it must follow, as the night the day,
> Thou canst not then be false to any man.

Polonius famously gives this advice to his son Laertes just before a long journey, in *Hamlet*. And it's good advice for life's journey, too. Being true means many things. It means knowing, accepting, respecting and liking yourself in the ways we've explored in Chapter 12. It means knowing what you want, and being prepared to ask for it. It means paying attention to the information you get through your immediate, physical responses as well as through your conscious thoughts and beliefs. It means refining that awareness so that it becomes more subtle and more automatic. It means engaging more and more with what is, and evaluating what others or your own internal dialogue tells you ought, must or should be the case before you act on it. It means being prepared to consider that what is easy, enjoyable, stimulating and fun might actually be better for everyone concerned than what is dutiful, effortful and weighty. It means learning that fun is not the enemy of seriousness, but may actually provide a shortcut to the profound, and be a better touchstone of what really matters.

Our experience as NLP coaches tells us that:

1. **Relationships that work well are built from a secure sense of identity** The more you strengthen your sense of self, the better your basis for relating to others at any level. This doesn't mean becoming more selfish – only more self-aware and self-respecting.

2. **Relationships that work have a clear awareness of boundaries** These are the boundaries between self and other; between roles and responsibilities; between overlap and separateness; between sameness and difference. And all parties show a respect for the boundaries not

just in what they say but in what they do. Being clear about what you want, about what you're prepared to do, about what is your responsibility and what is not, and expressing these things clearly, effectively and directly to others, all help make relationships work better. The American poet Robert Frost expressed it well in the line 'Good fences make good neighbours.'

3. **An important skill in any relationship is the ability to take different perceptual positions** Moving freely and swiftly between them is vital too. We'll explore this more fully later in the chapter.

4. **Many patterns of relationship can work effectively** What's crucial is the process, not the specific content. You can work effectively in a team that has a clear hierarchy of status and management – as long as everyone knows the rules and responsibilities and communications are clear. You can work well in a task-oriented team with little or no hierarchy – as long as the different roles are clear and people respect and communicate clearly with each other. You can have a brilliant partnership where roles and responsibilities are shared – or one where they're divided according to traditional gender roles, or according to personal skills and preferences – as long as both of you are in agreement about it. You can share interests and time, or have divergent interests and spend time independently – as long as you are both satisfied. You can have lots of sex, or no sex, as long as you both want the same.

NLP reminds us that it's what works that matters. So in this chapter we're concerned with the processes that make relationships work, rather than with specific settings. And by modelling people who make their relationships work, NLP provides us with lots of how-tos we can all use to sustain and nurture ours.

5. **The more attentive you become to feedback without regarding it judgementally, the better it guides your responses** This means you can be more effective in dovetailing your outcomes with others and you'll also find it easier to build harmony – or to know when it's best to cut your losses. If your partner, child or colleague didn't get the message you intended, take it as feedback which you can use to improve things. Take the blame out of it: it's not your fault – or theirs. Asking how exactly they understood what they did, and how exactly you could improve that particular piece of communication, is the way forward. A curiosity frame opens up the discovery of new how-tos, whereas a blame-frame blocks the way forward.

6. Assumptions frequently clog up relationships Becoming more explicit about what you want, what you feel, what you think is happening, and avoiding mind reading, projection and untested theorising or fantasising will help make things run more smoothly and harmoniously.

How to Build a 'We'

'We' doesn't just happen, in anything more than a grammatical sense: it has to be built. It's easy to say the word – 'We'd love to come' – but it does not always mean what it seems to. You may have said 'Yes' to an invitation just like this, and you might be right in assuming that your partner would also like to attend. Or not. You might even be right in thinking that your partner would like to attend, but in the event you each spend the evening absorbed with different people. You went to the party, and your partner went: 'we' didn't go at all.

Or perhaps the situation is a work one. Two huge firms are about to merge, and a working party has to be set up to negotiate the processes involved. Each MD says 'We'll be there.' But what kind of 'we' turns up? A businessman we coached described the nominees from his side in merger negotiations: each had been sent for different political reasons by different subdivisions; several had specific 'agendas' to look after; some were effectively nominated to cancel others out. Though the word 'team' was used, there was actually no 'we' about it.

▪ *What is a 'We'?*

A 'we' feels like something which exists in its own right, and which is more than the parts added together. Some definite processes have brought about a chemistry between them, just as baking makes a cake out of the separate ingredients. There is a sense of belonging, of being able to describe, and refer to, this entity of which you are a part.

Organisations recognise this when they arrange 'team-building' days. Being appointed as part of a team doesn't in itself mean that people feel like part of a whole, or behave like part of one. Something else has to happen.

Teams, or marriages, have certain characteristics. We're going to explore what these are, using logical levels (see page **48**). So just what does building a 'we' involve?

Identity

This is the who of the 'we'. The 'we' has a sense of what it means to be itself. Its members can and do talk about it, and about what it is like. It may be a 'troubleshooting team' or a 'conventional marriage' or 'an open partnership'. Have you noticed how some couples are much more a couple than others? The expression 'They're an item' points to this. They're not just two individuals going out together or cohabiting: they are more than this. A good question to ask yourself is: What sort of a 'we' is this or are we? How would I describe it or us? Building and reinforcing we-ness at the level of our identities can be done in many ways: the corporate logo and byline; the company colours; using the word 'we' or 'the company'. And we can take this further by linking the we with its characteristics: 'As far as the team is concerned...' 'You know what our family is like...' 'A pioneering firm like ours...' Every time you refer to the we-ness and to its characteristics, you are reinforcing it. So in your most important personal relationship, you might want to start asking yourselves – what do *we* want?

Beliefs and values

This is the why of the 'we' at the level of beliefs and values. The 'we' stands for something, perhaps explicitly, like 'family values', or implicitly, like loyalty to each other or love. An organisation may stand for customer service, or cutting-edge research. Values get reflected at other levels, such as behaviour and environment. Where there are disagreements or conflicts, there is often a value or belief issue involved. Shared values, on the other hand, help build 'team spirit' and give meaning and a sense of what it is to belong to this particular 'we'. A good question to ask is: what does this 'we' stand for? What would it seek to preserve, or defend under pressure? What kinds of other groupings does it see as very different and why? Asking these questions often helps you bring implicit or even hidden values to the surface.

Capabilities

This is the how – the skill-base of the 'we'. This may mean the kind of traditional role-patterns of making money and homemaking, or it may mean trained and complementary work skills. There may be things this grouping is good at doing, and things that are outside its repertoire. While a work team is likely to know what its skill-base is, families and partners are much less likely to know consciously what their specific capabilities are – or even to think in these terms at all. Yet some families are brilliant at giving confidence to their members, where others undermine it; some partnerships are good at relaxation but poor at achieving in worldly terms; some function well in the short term, others are good at planning, and so on. Few people think of the family, or their partnership, in these terms, yet it's illuminating to ask yourself: what does this 'we' do well? What could it do better?

Behaviour

This is the what of the 'we'. Any visitor from Mars – or anyone taking third position (see page **69**) – would be able to describe the unit's characteristic behaviours if they observed it for a while. Maybe it's a team that's big on meetings and only moves forward on a project when all views have been heard. Or perhaps it's a couple who are all over each other, and the relationship is electric with sexual chemistry. Or a family, on the other hand, that may just be endlessly bickering.

You can easily assume that's just how the company, the couple or the family are. But certain actions and behaviours may be crucial to how well – or how badly – the unit performs. Ian and his wife Paulette, for instance, make a point of always going away for a few days that include their wedding anniversary and they always go somewhere neither of them have ever been before. In this way their behaviour contributes to building the 'we' of their special times together.

Good questions to ask are: how does this 'we' go about things? What does it do? What processes, knowledge and skills are involved? The unit's behaviour is down to internal and external processes: capability is involved. And where it is, it can be learnt, improved, sustained or changed, once you ask 'how' it does what it does.

Environment

This is the where and the when of the 'we'. Families, teams and organisations each have their characteristic environments that tell us something about them. The physical environment we create and the things we have around us can express some important things about the 'personality' of the organisation, team or relationship. Equally important, though, is the when – how often you actually get in contact, whether that frequency is sufficient and whether the timing works for those comprising the 'we'. These wheres and whens can add, or detract, significantly, from 'we-ness'. Wendy remembers once visiting a large school – or trying to, for she couldn't find the way in! Some hospitals can be equally forbidding, with additions, huts, corridors and temporary signs redirecting you hither and yon. So consider, what kind of message do visitors to your office, or your home, get? Are they included or excluded? Are they made part of a 'we' or not, and is that appropriate?

Whatever the setting, good questions to ask are: how is this we demonstrated in its where and when arrangements? And is this what you want?

Offices can give very different impressions not only to outside visitors, but also to their staff. A scientist taking up a new post commented that the lab she had previously worked in gave each person a good 4 feet of desk space, and a personal pinboard. People had room for plants and bric-a-brac. In the new lab she had about 2 feet of desk space, which was not separated in any way from the areas allocated to her colleagues and thus tended to be encroached on. There was no space she could personalise, and nowhere she could pin up charts and working documents, never mind photographs or postcards. Her previous job literally made space for its workers. In the old lab there was also a daily pattern of stopping for a shared tea-break, with cakes being provided by different workers in turn: in the new lab people only met once a week as an entire group for a ritual Friday tea. Whatever the values of the two institutions, their where and when environment arrangements gave very different messages to their employees.

A probation officer who had for a number of years worked near home was offered a promotion in a team some distance away. He had young children, and was very aware that the increase in travelling time involved in the new job would mean that he would see less of them.

He and his wife agreed that since he might often be home late, they would treat breakfast as the important, unhurried family sharing time of the day. They wanted to make sure their family values – loyalty, shared experience, caring about each other – still had time to be expressed and felt, even though this meant getting up a little earlier.

Each of these examples shows a different way in which the logical levels (see page **48**) were significant in detracting from, or building, a sense of we.

The 'we' check

▶ Using the logical levels, describe the kind of 'we' characteristics of your relationship, your family, your team or your organisation.

▶ Are things how you would like them to be? If not, what characteristics need to change?

▶ Of the things that could be changed to increase 'we-ness' which ones are within your control?

▶ Find a change you can easily make, and make it soon. Monitor what happens as a result.

The sense of 'we-ness' can vary, from coherent and strong to flimsy and unreliable. Here are some litmus tests you can use to explore particular relationships you are involved in.

▶ Do you feel 'on the same side'?

▶ Does the whole feel greater than the sum of its parts?

▶ Does the 'we' pull together in adversity, and share in enjoying success?

▶ Do you like the other(s) who are part of your 'we'?

▶ Does belonging to this 'we' add significantly to your sense of self, to your confidence, to your enjoyment, to the skills available to you?

▶ Does belonging to this 'we' limit you significantly in any way?

▶ Do you trust the other(s) involved?

▶ Do you consult before acting?

▶ Do you consider the effect of your actions on the other(s) or on the 'we' before you act?

If you've answered 'Yes' to a number of these items, it's telling you that your relationship works for you in a number of important ways. Look at any you haven't ticked, and ask yourself what would have to happen for you to say yes. In this way you're building a profile of what works, and what could work even better. And by being specific about what would have to happen to change things, you're using the negative feedback to help build recipes for success. Be particularly cautious about any reservations at an identity level: finding limitations here may signal that important work is needed to improve things – or in extreme cases, that you need to think about whether the relationship is really worth continuing with.

▪ *Ways to Build a 'We'*

In our experience as NLP coaches, people who are good at building relationships have a number of key things in common. We've turned these into a list of how-tos.

1. Get clear about your own identity, needs and wishes

You can't build a 'we' without first having a strong first position (see page **68**). This is why teenage relationships usually come to an end: young people are in the process of discovering who they are, and this tends to mean that they either project their hopes onto their partners, later discovering that the partner was not quite what they thought or wanted, or find that the negotiations inevitably involved in building a 'we' are too stressful, undermining or difficult. It takes a strong sense of self to admit you are in the wrong, or don't know; it takes a strong sense of self to stand up for what is important in a way which is assertive rather than aggressive or manipulative – or to ask for what one wants at all.

A strong sense of self can be cultivated. It may have been affected by childhood experiences, but it isn't set in concrete by them. And it can be attended to alongside the second and third positioning that building a relationship also demands. We'll come back to this later in this chapter. A good relationship at home or at work meets the majority of important needs for its members, and also has ways of monitoring and negotiating the way it does this. Building ways of discussing the 'we' that you have with your partner, your children and your colleagues can be one of the most productive investments you can make.

2. Act as if the 'we' already had a separate existence

One of the key ways to do this is to behave as if the 'we' had a separate and valid existence of its own. As with so many other 'as-if' behaviours, this actually helps create the very situation you want. Let's look at some examples.

Julian and Liz were having problems in their marriage. Each complained to friends about the other: *'He never...' 'She always...'* Each was stuck in first position, and blaming the other for doing the same thing! Though they had been together for some time, they tended to behave as though they were free agents in making decisions about hobbies and social engagements: they told each other what they were doing – often after they had arranged to do it. They saw this as part of being 'open' and 'flexible' – but actually it often caused conflict and one or other resented not being consulted.

Julian brought this up with his coach. The strategy they evolved was that every time an invitation was offered to Julian he would ask the 'we' what it wanted before replying. When he told Liz about this she said she'd like to try this out as well. That conversation in itself produced a new sense of collaboration. By the end of it they had gone further still. They agreed that when either of them felt angry, upset or aggrieved, they would present the problem to the 'we' as a problem it had, rather than one they individually had. If Julian was late home and the dinner spoiled, they would remind themselves that it was neither his problem (thoughtless, can't keep to time) or Liz's problem (oversensitive, controlling). The problem – and its solution – belonged to the shared 'we' that was their relationship. They found that treating problems in this way, rather than bickering over who was at fault, helped them sort out the problem faster – and the experience of exploring it and finding solutions together really added to their sense of partnership.

3. Agree on the rules of the 'we'

Building a relationship takes time. We have to learn to think and behave differently from the way we do when we just consider ourselves. People often act as though it's enough to be together, rather than deliberately aiming to dovetail their individual behaviours, wishes and skills. Talking about future goals and about how each partner's roles and responsibilities relate to these can help an intimate relationship just as much as a work team. Being explicit saves you from the pitfalls you can get into through making assumptions. It is amazing how many people get into long-term relationships without considering major issues like children, careers or lifestyle preferences. 'Well, I always knew I wanted children, but now he says he doesn't' is a sad but not infrequent cry.

Of course, this doesn't mean that every last detail has to be gone through at the outset; but being clear about your wants and what you are prepared to negotiate, and asking the same questions of your partner, can save irritation, conflict and even heartbreak.

4. Look for things which satisfy all concerned

Where possible, make being part of the 'we' a pleasant, productive, satisfying thing for all members – everybody wins. This isn't the same as bribing others to do what you want: the manipulativeness in that is rarely missed by the person being bribed! Where you have a choice, go for options that will satisfy your partners and yourself. It's easier to do this if you can put yourself in their shoes and imagine what would work for them. So ultimately, the skill of going to second position (see page **68**) is a vital tool in building a successful 'we'.

5. Give legitimate space to each 'I' involved in the 'we'

Being part of a 'we' doesn't mean that everything has to be done together. It doesn't mean having to share every thought or feeling. The richness of the 'we' is built on a creative dialogue between separateness and sharing, individuality and collectivity. So each 'I' has to have its time and space. Separate activities and interests, recognition of differing skills, time alone – these are all ways to nourish the individual members so that they have more to bring back to the 'we'. This may mean encouraging your partner's independent interests rather than insisting you do everything together. It might mean encouraging a member of your work team to develop an area of responsibility, or a new skill, or a way of doing things, that are special to them rather than insisting that they do things your way, or the way they have always been done.

6. Find ways to allow your differences to enrich the 'we'

We all function differently. Differences can be a source of misunderstandings and conflicts, but they also enrich relationships at home and at work and build a broader resource base for the 'we'. Get into the habit of noticing the differences and then asking yourself how this particular difference could enrich your 'we'. If you tend to favour the grand visions, you may find a colleague who dots every i and crosses every t irritating at times; but organisations, teams and families need both these skills. How could you ensure that the best use is made of both kinds of skill?

7. Identify the things that enhance the 'we' – and do more of them

Get into the habit of noticing what's going on when you feel the 'we-ness' most keenly. Is it when your team is faced with a challenge, or when its members are working calmly to a routine schedule? Is it when you are relaxing together, or when you are working on a project? And just what is it about those situations that helps enhance 'we-ness'?

A young woman went to a coach because she felt stressed and was having regular two-day migraines. She was self-employed and in a long-term relationship. She felt that although her work helped pay the mortgage, it wasn't as satisfying as she wanted – and the same was true of the relationship. In fact, she had thought of splitting from her partner some years before. Her coach asked her when she *didn't* have migraines. She said immediately: 'When we sold our house in London and moved here: we had enough profit to live on for six months while we worked together on the new house. It was very hard physical work, and we both enjoyed it. I only had about one migraine during all that time.' Until the coach asked her, this young woman hadn't realised that her migraines had any pattern to them – and she hadn't realised that she and her partner were at their best together when they were cooperating in a very physical way on a project that meant a lot to both of them.

8. Check your future plans

Get into the habit of checking out future plans to ensure that they express or enhance the 'we'. Begin evaluating ideas or decisions in the here-and-now for their impact on your 'we' in the future. It may be convenient in many ways to have some of your team members working from home – but what impact will that have on the dynamics of the team as a whole? Some people will not see others as often – or at all. Productive updating and casual sharing of ideas that may have happened over coffee or when people bumped into each other in the corridor won't happen because people will have to make a deliberate effort to phone, fax or e-mail each other. This won't be all bad, of course; but if the full implications are thought through then plans can be made to allow for any downside and the team won't have to lose out.

The situation is similar in personal partnerships. Many couples don't anticipate and plan for what will happen when the kids grow up, or when one or both partners retire. Yet both these changes can have major impacts on them as individuals and as a 'we'. Planning to avoid, or manage, the worst scenarios you can think of in terms of the 'we' to which you belong usually means they don't have to happen.

9. Deal with negative feelings

When you are irritated or annoyed, deal with the feelings yourself. Take a breath. Take a moment. Recognise and respect your irritation. What's it about? If the cause is a one-off, and if showing your irritation won't take the 'we' forward, consciously decide whether to raise the matter or to keep silent. Deal with your feelings yourself. If the cause repeats a pattern, look at the pattern. Find an appropriate moment (which may not be now, in the heat of the moment) to bring it to the attention of your partner(s).

10. Deal with genuine irritations

Don't let these fester. If leaving the pattern, or the incident, without comment or correction will be significantly detrimental to you as an individual, or to the 'we', say something as soon as you can. Make it clear what you object to, and why you think the situation is damaging.

11. Recipes for success

Where you are unhappy about something, make sure you also say what you *would* like – give others recipes for success. People can't do much with comments that are generalised or woolly. They need to know exactly what is being objected to, and what they have to do to improve things. If we want people to change, NLP demonstrates that it really helps to frame what we say in a 'towards' way rather than an 'away-from' way. You may not like this or that – but what would you really like them to do instead? Giving others recipes for success is a great tool for building 'we-ness' at home and at work. Being specific also helps you to offer comment at the right logical level, so that it is less likely to be taken at an identity level. It's also helpful for you, as asking what you do want can become a good tool for checking out and developing your first-person strength – and thus offer more to the relationship.

> Marianne, one of our clients, finished a long day's work and rushed home to cook the evening meal for her husband and teenage children. As it happened, they had got home first, and were comfortably watching television. Marianne found herself feeling lonely and upset as she started cooking the meal. But she had learnt through coaching how useful it was to tell others what she really wanted rather than simply criticise them. She realised that she didn't want her family's help in cooking: what she did want was company. So she said: 'I'd really love it if someone came out here with me,' and was able to enjoy talking with her daughter about what had happened that day.

12. Minimise pressure

Conflict or weaknesses in a relationship can be reduced. If you or one of your partners is inclined to be poor at time-keeping, or over-fussy about detail, you could get irritated or even annoyed. You could mention the problem as one that affects the 'we'. And you could also ask yourself if there are ways in which you could minimise the impact of this characteristic on how you feel, and ways round any problems it might cause. Don't cook soufflés which have to be eaten at a specific time – or find another way to ensure that your partner is home and waiting when the soufflé is cooked. What is the point of being 'in the right' if it makes everything go wrong? If a team member at work is slow, careful and detailed, find a way to use these skills to act as a check and a finisher-off of work done by other team-members who are more gung-ho in their approach. Most teams need a range of skills – ensure yours are deployed in the right places.

13. Praise and reward freely and generously

People often notice how quick others are to criticise and how good performance or good behaviour gets taken for granted. Make it one of your goals to praise frequently, immediately and specifically. Reward actually makes all parties feel good, and builds reserves of trust and liking which stand the 'we' in good stead when there are problems or crises.

All of these ways of behaving can help you and your partners to develop a positive cycle in your relationships with each other, building a more secure and resilient sense of 'we-ness' which can be rich in itself at the same time as enriching the separate identities that go together to make the whole.

How to See Things from Different Points of View

'He doesn't understand me!' 'She really knows what I'm going through.' Comments like these tell us how important it is in our personal relationships that the other person has the ability to imagine how it is for us. But the real trick is to be able to do this in real time, while you're actually interacting with the other person, and NLP shows you how to do this.

▪ *The Value of Taking Different Perceptual Positions*

The angle you look at something from can shape your perception. That's at the root of the NLP tool of taking different perceptual positions (see page **68**). When we use this tool we can, in the privacy of our own heads, see a situation from many different angles, get close up, or step into another's shoes or even pull back outside the scene for a moment. It's a brilliant reality check: when we shift position, it's usually easier to figure out how it is for others and to achieve a better way of engaging with them. This is true both personally and professionally.

We could also have called this section 'How to See Things the Way Someone Else Does' or 'Hearing How it Sounds to Them' or 'How to Step into Someone Else's Shoes'. When you want to enhance any relationship it is really useful to be able to see, hear and feel things the way the other party does. People who are good at relationships, whether at home or at work, are usually good at all these things, whether they learnt it unconsciously or deliberately. What NLP shows us is that there's a structure to getting inside someone else's world which can be learnt and refined. There are three key positions you will want to explore.

First position

This is the 'I' position – the place of personal experience. At its best, it's the place of thinking, feeling and bodily experience. It's the here-and-now. Potentially, it's richly sensory. It's where you often feel most alive. This is true whether the experiences are pleasant or unpleasant. At least you are feeling *something*. First position is where you know what you like, know what you want and set out to get it. It's the place of feeling good in your own skin, of taking care of your own needs, of designing your own future, of feeling 'all of a piece with yourself'.

But there's another side to first position. It can be the basis of selfishness rather than self-nurturing, of thoughtlessness rather than thoughtfulness. It's a place where you can get stuck, a place where you go round the same old loop again, where you didn't see it coming, and can't see a way out. It's a place of banging your head against a brick wall. Metaphors like that tell us how immediate and strong the experience can be. It's the place in which you can get cut off from others, and from 'reality'. Of course, you're in your own reality, but if you're stuck in first position you have no means of checking it out. This is where you fantasise, or project your own feelings onto others. This is where you make assumptions and don't know you're making them.

Second position

In this position it's all about imagining how it is for someone else. You can do this in a number of ways:

▶ Assume their physiology and just try it on for size. Think this feels odd? In the martial arts this is a fundamantal technique for students who wish to emulate the master. You'll be surprised how much you learn about what it's like to be someone if you stand and sit, breathe and walk like them, even for just a few moments.

▶ Having assumed their physiology, start speaking as if you were them, starting sentences with 'I'. Again, you'll be surprised at how words will flow and you can construct a version of events from their point of view. Also talk about yourself while still in their shoes. This may give you still more information about what it's like from where they are.

Both of these you can do on your own. As you become more adept you'll be able to do this in your head without anyone being able to see anything from the outside. When you've really mastered this skill you'll be able to do it in real time when you're actually with the person.

You don't have to know someone in order to go to second position with them. If you see someone looking lost and confused in the supermarket, for example, you recognise something of what's going on for them from their behaviour and expression, and draw on your own experiences of feeling like that to imagine how it feels. The more skilled you become at doing this generally the more quickly and easily you'll be able to do this, ultimately even with people you just read about. This can be incredibly useful if you want to model people who are outstanding but whom you're unlikely ever to have direct personal access to.

Being able to go to second position is the basis of empathy and of caring, of tact and kindness, of anticipating and taking care of other's needs, of being able to put yourself in someone else's shoes, of working out when you need to say 'Sorry' for something you did or didn't do to them. But being able to go to second position is also the basis of good team management and sound decision making:

Colin used his ability to go to second position to run a thriving business. He had his own construction company, and maintained a friendly and informal atmosphere around the workplace. Though he had high standards and expected his men to keep to them, he gave them time off if they needed it.

He kept a sharp eye out, and was equally able to tell the difference between people who weren't pulling their weight and those with genuine difficulties. 'I'd like you to come into my office for a chat...' he'd say: the 'chat' might turn out to be a sharp talking-to, an offer of help or a promotion. It seemed like he just had a natural talent for reading people. 'How does he do it?' people sometimes said. In fact, Colin listened, watched and thought about his workforce, but it was the way he did this that made him so effective. 'They make this business,' he used to say. 'If I know what's going on for them, I know what's going on around the business. That's why every so often I put myself in their shoes.'

At its worst, going to second position is where others' needs always seem to come first, so they can take you over, dominate and exhaust you. You lose yourself in empathising with others. Colin, on the other hand, didn't just go to second position with his staff. He had a strong first position, and this, in conjunction with his observational skills and clear sense of purpose, helped him maintain an effective balance between being supportive and being task-focused.

When you want to go to second position with someone, you can use what you have observed of them, calling up your memories of how they behave, what they stand for, how they approach things, what kind of opinions they have. We have coached many clients in how to do this. It's a great tool for managing upwards if you step into your boss's shoes for a moment. But it's just as valuable if you do it stepping into the shoes of someone you love. When you have a moment, try this: walk about as they do for a few minutes, sit in their kind of attitude, move at their kind of pace. This will give you an experience of being in the world which may be very different from your own. If you are a laid-back, reflective sort of person you may find the world very different if you stride rapidly to the bus stop, or rush up the stairs two at a time. What things seem different to you at that speed? Very likely, it will involve more than just the tempo of physical movement. Do you feel pressured – or perhaps energised – by going so much faster than you're used to? Moving around like that, looking out through their eyes, how would that you over there seem from *this* perspective? Does this explain anything about how this other person tends to react to you or others?

One of the core presuppositions of NLP relates specifically to taking second position, and it's an incredibly helpful tool in building good relationships: in a nutshell, the meaning of your communication is the response it elicits. To unpack this, the real meaning of anything you communicate is what the other person, team, even nation, understands by it, not what you thought you meant. What matters is what is actually understood by the receiver, rather than what was intended by the communicator. Going to second position allows you to check out what the other person might understand by something you say or do or perhaps have already done. Imagining yourself in the receiver's position gives you a chance of improving what you say or do in advance. The important thing to remember is that communication is filtered by how it's perceived: if someone gets a different message from the one you intended, that's not their fault. Nor is it yours. Once you know what message they did receive, go to second position and imagine how they will be thinking and feeling now. That's what you need to tailor your next communication to!

Third position

This is the engaged observer position. In this position you are able to view both yourself and the other(s) involved in a situation from outside, pulling back from the intensity of emotion you might be feeling in first position. This is not the same as being dissociated, which is a strongly distanced, self-protective state and a primary spontaneous mechanism the brain uses to get away from trauma or pain.

Going to third position is emotionally different: it is perfectly possible to have an emotional response from third position but it will be very different from the feelings associated with being in first position. You might, for instance, be afraid in first position but feel compassion for yourself or irritated with yourself when looking at things from third position.

At its best, it's a position where you can 'get off the firing line', 'step off the roller-coaster', 'get another perspective' on things. Being able to do this properly is almost always really valuable. It can allow you to get a different bearing on what you are doing, or about to do, or on what's happening to you. It's also a way of monitoring how you're doing.

In third position you can gain access to your own 'wiser self', so it enables you to cultivate a relationship with yourself. As a result you'll be able to encourage or advise that first-position self who may be struggling, hurt or doubtful. As soon as you go into third position, bad things will seem less bad because you will see them differently and find other ways to understand them, and good things can seem even better, because you can see why they are going well. Third position is where things aren't so 'in your face'. It can be a place of self-nurturing and self-support.

EXERCISE

Try this: think of some instance in which you have felt upset.

- ► Now physically stand in one position and feel this upset for just a moment. This is first position.

- ► Next step out of that position. Shake it off, literally – so you don't carry it with you.

- ► Go some distance away – say 2 metres or more – and step into a new physical space where in your mind's eye you can have a look at the you who's upset. This is what we call third position.

- ► Now, in third position, have a look at that you in first position. How do you respond to that you there? What would you say that you need? Notice how you react differently from this position. (If there's no difference you haven't really 'left' first position behind.) Often this is the beginning of being able to do something different in real life too.

Third position can also be a place where you understand 'where others are coming from', and how that relates to where you stand. It can also be a place where you can fit together different views, or different information, to get a fuller understanding of a situation – like putting together the pieces of a jigsaw.

To be successful in relationships, we need to be able to take all three positions: each has a great deal to offer us.

Let's take a look at an example of how the same situation might seem from each of these positions. Imagine you've worked really hard to get something done, either at home or at work, and are feeling pleased with the results of all the effort you've put in. You'd like your partner, or your boss, to notice your achievement and appreciate it. But when he or she arrives, they just start telling you about what they have been doing, what a difficult day it's been for them, and so on.

In first position you're upset, feel neglected and even hurt. Their behaviour is the opposite of what you wanted. You resent their lack of interest.

When you make an effort and go to **second position**, you find that you're beginning to feel rushed and preoccupied too. Your breathing quickens and you start to feel agitated. What a dreadful day. But at least you can begin to unwind by talking about it to a sympathetic listener (that's you, as they see you).

When you start to go to **third position**, you realise that the two parties in the situation are just not communicating. The you over there in first position wants praise, and wants it right now because you've been working so hard. That you is impatient and wants others to be instantly accommodating. Your partner/boss, on the other hand, isn't actively ignoring what that you has done. They're just feeling so pressured that they haven't any attention to spare for other people. From third position, you tell your first position self to be less self-absorbed and more patient: after all, you've had a productive day and your partner/boss usually appreciates you. You can help things along by giving them time to deal with their irritation and frustration. If you pace them in their experience first, they'll be much more able to enter into yours.

▪ *Perceptual Positions and Different Meta Programmes*

Once you've taken the different perceptual positions detailed above, you can start to add in meta programmes (see page **54**). Once you recognise, for example, that your boss tends to approach tasks in a procedural way, whereas you are naturally more inventive and option-orientated, you have some important information. One aspect of the situation is, of course, that your differing approaches can cause friction. So try seeing the world as he does: spend a few minutes directing your attention to the kind of things he notices. How does it feel? While you're being 'creative', it may look to him as if you're cutting corners. What to you is flexibility may seem to him like playing fast and loose with prescribed procedures.

Jack and Rose were moving and needed to clear out their attic, but every time Jack mentioned it, Rose found a way to divert the conversation. Thinking about this, she realised that she felt overwhelmed. The job seemed huge – and one of the things that made it seem huge to her was the way Jack talked about doing it in one hit – 'We need a blitz on it.' So she told Jack how this made her feel, and said that she would really prefer to do a bit at a time. 'I find myself not wanting to do it together, because then I'd have to do it all at once.' Jack thought about this, and realised that he certainly had been talking about it as one huge job – because that was how he saw it. But putting himself in Rose's shoes he realised that it would seem overwhelming. It actually was a big job but this didn't bother him. Given the choice, he would in fact prefer to do it in the same way as she wanted – in smaller bursts. Jack went to second position with Rose and accommodated her different style of chunking (see page **31**). By so doing he was able to find a way of ensuring they could do the task together and build a shared experience. At the same time he also got to clear the attic in a way which made the task easier for them both.

Tips for taking different perceptual positions

To strengthen your first position:

► Ask yourself what *you* want.

► Ask yourself what's really important to you.

► Build a habit of noticing what you feel and think – and remind yourself that your experience is a good place to start from.

► Start the day by asking yourself, 'What shall I do today that will increase my sense of well-being?'

To strengthen second position:

► Get curious about other people. Ask yourself questions like, 'What must it be like to be ...?' 'What would have to be true for me to act as .... does?'

► Step into their shoes: try on their use of physiology and behavioural mannerisms such as rate of speech.

► Imagine being on the receiving end of your words and actions. If you wouldn't like what's coming your way, what needs to change?

To strengthen third position:

▶ Begin to think systemically. See the bigger system of which you are a part, be it your office or your family or your love relationship. To do this effectively it will be very useful to go to second position with any others involved – you're not going to get the bigger picture if all you have is your own first-position perspective.

▶ From this bigger perspective ask yourself:
  – 'What is going on here between these people?
  – 'What is particularly striking about this way of engaging?'
  Begin to build a significant relationship with yourself. Take situations in which you are involved, step into the mindset and physicality that goes with others for a moment. Then step out, shake it off and have a look at yourself from at least 2 metres away. How do you respond to that you there?

▶ In addition, become curious about your own, and others', meta programmes. Think of them as resources for different needs. What approaches would help most in what situations? What limitations might there be – and how could they be offset by using these resources more fully?

▶ And, though it may seem obvious:
  – Find out what works – and do more of it.
  – Find out what doesn't work so well, and do less of it.

How to Invest in the Future

One of the things that distinguishes good relationships is that they are not just vibrant in the present, but also take active steps to nourish their future. This sense of a future may be embodied in organisations' business plans, or in a couple deciding to get married. It's quite possible, in business, or in personal relationships, to drift into the future, but the fact is that what you're doing now shapes the future you can have. Patterns are forming that will persist. So if you want to build successful relationships, it would be a smart move to start investing in their future now. In terms of relationships, what can be limiting is to ignore the information in the present that bodes ill for the future. Other things being equal, time alone will only serve to continue and deepen any patterns that are forming right now.

▪ *Thinking of the Future: In-Time and Through-Time*

One of NLP's great discoveries is that people experience time in different ways. As our discussion of meta programmes on page 54 shows, some people are in-time: they are involved in the richness of the moment and may find it harder to imagine the future or to see how the present and past relate to it. Other people naturally have a through-time perspective: they have an overview of events and their connections, which usually makes them good planners and able to see consequences. But it may also mean that they are not so 'into' what's going on right now and they may envy those who are really engaged in the passion of the moment.

Ideally, what we want is the ability both to live in the moment fully in-time and have a vision of what's needed for a satisfying future through-time. To become more in-time, just swing the past behind you. Have it connected on a line of time behind you that runs up to the present which is located in your body, which then runs on into the future out in front of your body. To become more through-time, place your past over on your left (in front of you), the present just in front of you and the future to your right, again in front of you. (If you are left-handed you may find past on the right and future on the left works better for you.)

If you tend to be more in-time, you can, if you wish, learn to 'take a longer view' by briefly switching your time-line to through-time. Remember, too, that acting in the present on the basis of what feels right for you, or what isn't working, will set new patterns going that can build up over time to the changes you'd like. The important thing is to pay attention to your experience, to ask yourself what you really want, to trust your feelings about it and know that you can make your future *now*.

If you're more of a through-time person, remember that if you want stronger bonds or closer and more intimate relationships, being able to be fully present now, in this moment, with this person is going to be essential. You can start to do this by going in-time. It will probably feel pretty strange at first, though no more than it does for them when they switch to through-time. If you doubt the value of doing this, just take a through-time look at the future that would await you if you were never really fully present in the best moments of your life, or not that close to anyone.

Jean had been married for many years to a man who had – in her eyes – changed dramatically from the day they got married. Previously considerate, he became self-absorbed, withdrawn and dictatorial. She couldn't really believe this, and kept telling herself that he must still really be the man she married. Believing that marriage was for life, she soldiered on, and tried to find comfort in hobbies and keeping up with old friends. After many years, she became friendly with a man who attended the same evening class. Eventually, he asked her to leave her husband, and she knew in her heart of hearts that she wanted to say yes. But she found it really hard to make the break. She couldn't really imagine what her future could be like. She had lived one day at a time, and one day at a time had added up to twenty years, a lifetime which she now felt had been largely wasted. In talking with her coach, she realised that what had been a good survival strategy – 'One day at a time, sweet Jesus' – on a daily basis had also prevented her from taking a longer view and seeking a better life sooner. She needed to discover what she really wanted in her future. Eventually she decided to leave her husband and find a place of her own, so that she could test out the new relationship and give it time to develop. This time she wanted to have a future and a way of realising it.

Many people put up with things at home and at work on a day-to-day basis, unaware of or sometimes deliberately choosing to ignore how this has cumulative negative effects. This can include working in an unsatisfying job just because it pays the mortgage: over months and years this can dull enthusiasm, cause mental and physical stress and erode enjoyment in life.

From this viewpoint, nothing we do is neutral. Everything either contributes to our sense of meaning, purpose and enjoyment in life, or detracts from it. Ian remembers the day when he was standing in a long queue in the Post Office. The person next to him was seething with frustration and said, 'This is such a waste of time', and Ian thought, 'No, this is a waste of my life.' Whenever you're thinking about time, you might experiment like this by substituting the word 'life'. 'This is a waste of my time' would become *'This is a waste of my life.'* 'It took too much time to do that' could become *'It took too much life to do that'*; 'I can't spare the time' would become *'I can't spare the life.'* On the other hand, 'That was time well spent' becomes *'That was life well spent.'* Sometimes just changing one word can enable you to realise what's really involved. Then you can decide if those are the consequences you want.

Taking a longer view also gives us a good tool for evaluating the present. One-night stands may confirm that you are attractive, and provide excitement and pleasure. And indeed that might be what you really want right now. If you imagine this pattern going on into the future, looking back five years from now, say, is it going to give you what you want? Or if you push it all the way – as you can with any significant behaviour that has an effect on your relationships – imagine it running till you die. How would that be for you?

▪ *Investment is Cumulative*

We want to offer you a metaphor for building better relationships. Suppose you were to think of yourself as investing in them. One merit of this metaphor is that it allows you to get clear about what's right for you. It's definitely not romantic, but curiously, relationships – including romantic ones – are often enhanced by thinking of them as investment opportunities and give you interesting insights.

The investment of time, energy and behaviour you make is cumulative over time – whether for good or ill. Recognising this allows you to monitor the present much more closely, once you know what you want: does what you are doing today contribute to what you want, or detract from it? It also allows you to appreciate, probably with a sense of relief, that making the changes you want need not be a major event. In a personal relationship, for example, talking more about your feelings to your partner need not begin with a huge outpouring about deep or intimate feelings. You can start with simple things like: 'I feel rather tired this morning', or 'I was disappointed when John didn't think my plan was that exciting.' Sharing more of your wishes for the future can also start in a low-key way. For example, 'I really hope we'll be able to go abroad this year.'

Building a new habit can be done one day at a time. And the investment – in this case, in a level of openness and intimacy with your partner – can grow gradually. Once you are in the habit of expressing how you feel about small, safe things, it's easier for both of you to talk about larger, more risky issues when they crop up.

What counts as investing in a relationship?

Positive investment in a relationship can mean many things. Though the content will be very different, notice how all of these apply to both personal and professional relationships:

- Spending time together

- Spoken appreciation

- Caring and sharing

- Parity in attending to chores and tasks

- Thinking about the future and enjoying memories of the past

- Support when things are difficult

- Spending money on them (presents, equipment, resource allocation)

- Going to second position in order to build rapport and anticipate needs.

Each of these, of course, can also have its negative counterpart. You can disinvest by not doing them and so make things harder, less pleasant and less rewarding. Check each of the items we've just listed to help you evaluate the current worth of your investments at home and at work.

Stocktake your investments

If you are going to make a financial investment, you want to know you are going to get the value of your investment back, preferably with added value. Looking at personal and work relationships in this way can sometimes raise some very useful questions and give you another take on what you're doing. For instance, the woman who had lived out her twenty-year unhappy marriage day by day had made a huge investment: she just had not noticed how her daily emotional 'premiums' were mounting up. And in her case, the value of her investment had actually fallen.

So the bottom-line question is: is your investment worth it?

Is your investment worth it?

Here are some questions we've found useful. Just ask yourself:

Personal

▶ Is it personally fulfilling?

▶ Is there a sense of shared value now – and the probability of shared value in the future?

▶ Do you share a number of interests?

▶ Do you respect each other?

▶ Do you have a sense of drawing on the past, and being able to build for the future?

▶ Do you find each other interesting? fun? stimulating? supportive? encouraging?

▶ Do you surprise each other?

▶ Do you draw out the best in each other, making each other feel good about being the person you are?

Professional

▶ Is it professionally fulfilling?

▶ Is it personally fulfilling?

▶ Is it stimulating to be there?

▶ Are their values your values?

▶ Are your skills called upon, and valued?

▶ Do you have a sense of a team, and teamwork?

▶ Do you feel valued for who you are as well as for what you can do?

▶ Do you have a sense of a future with these people, this organisation?

Do you have other personal criteria that help you judge whether you're making a good investment? Notice events which you use as litmus tests.

To give you an example, Wendy and her husband have been together for over thirty years. But she remembers, when they were first living together, having to make a decision about whether the relationship was worth investing in. To begin with, they split everything down the middle. The tin-opener that had originally belonged to her husband broke: a new one had to be bought. In deciding to contribute to the cost of a replacement she knew she was making a long-term investment in the relationship itself.

Getting the best value from your investment

▶ **Demand the best future you can** Find out what you really want; reality-test it using the well-formedness conditions (see page 63). Don't blind yourself to any signs that you're not getting what you want. Take them seriously, whether they come to you in terms of observable events or behaviours, gut feelings or powerful dreams. Allow yourself to receive information from your unconscious as well as your conscious, logical mind.

▶ **Imagine the future together** A friend of Wendy's once completely surprised and delighted her by saying: 'I'd really like to know you when you're eighty.' Can you imagine yourself and your friend or partner being old together? What things does this tell you about how you anticipate the relationship developing – or how it really is now? For how long can you imagine staying as part of your present work team or organisation – until you retire? What does your answer tell you?

▶ **Chunk down your long-term goals** so you can start making progress towards achieving them right now. Take a long-term goal you have in your personal or work relationships and ask yourself what you can do today that will contribute towards achieving it. What can you do next week? next month? by the end of this year?

▶ **Use feedback to help guide you** People who invest money generally monitor the progress of their investment on a regular basis. Use feedback from events, thoughts and feelings to help monitor the progress of your relationship investments. If their value seems to be slipping, don't just wait until it slides some more. Ask yourself what steps you need to take to check the fall you've noticed and to help correct it.

▶ **Check out with yourself: would I ever leave?** What would have to happen to make me? This is about finding out your own threshold for withdrawing your investment. Find what constitutes your own bottom line. If your partner hit you?... even just once?... If your boss made you work late yet again?... If you didn't get that rise?... If you only got half the rise you wanted?... If the kids fought over the TV channel yet again...? Some of these things may seem quite trivial, but in fact people often do take major actions on the basis of 'last straw' events, as a recent study on the causes given on divorce petitions showed very clearly. This doesn't mean, of course, that squeezing the toothpaste tube in the middle is the underlying reason for a marital break-up, but rather that small indicators, if unchecked, are taken as typical of something else: in terms of the investment metaphor, as a sign that the investment is not paying off. So if you find your 'last straw' seems trivial even to you, ask yourself what it really stands for, and why it signals a poor return as far as you are concerned.

The underlying meaning of investment as a metaphor for relationships is that an exchange is taking place. It's fair and honest to expect that relationships should be meaningful, and rewarding, to all parties involved. All manner of exchanges are possible and viable – so long as they satisfy both (or all) parties. But if they don't, or if imbalances in the exchange are too great or too prolonged, you ignore them at your peril.

How to Know What to Do When Things Aren't Right

In this section we're going to look at some common dilemmas that occur in relationships, both at home and at work, and show how NLP can help you clarify the issues and choose the right option.

▪ *Staying Yourself*

Here are some things that we've found helped the people we've coached. Some involve specific NLP techniques: some are less specific but built on the NLP principles of curiosity and acceptance.

▶ As always, awareness is the key. Build a good notion of what you are like as a unique individual, using our discussions of meta programmes, representational systems and sub-modalities (pages **54**, **73** and **80**) to help you. Find out how you go about things, as the unique individual you are. Ask yourself the questions we suggested as an outline for modelling to get further information or check details. Practise going to first position by checking out how you feel, what you think and what you want.

▶ Tune in to yourself every day – several times a day. Make a habit of it. Each time you check yourself out, you strengthen your sense of self and make it less likely that you will get swallowed up by anyone or anything. If you are not sure what you think or feel about something, test it out either by picturing it or by saying it – internally or out loud – and notice how your body responds. Do you feel a sense of reservation, holding back, irritation, anxiety? Do you feel energised, positive, enthusiastic? The more often you ask, the quicker you'll get at responding – and the smaller the signal you'll need.

▶ Think of times when you really felt yourself – and of others when you felt unsure or eroded. Jot down all the details you can think of about each, and use contrastive analysis to find out what are the differences that make a difference for you. Jot them down too, as part of a self-monitoring record.

▶ Give yourself some time just for you every day. Perhaps it might be a short period of meditation, a walk around the block, time for your favourite occupation or a relaxing bath. You could use the time deliberately to think about things, or do things for yourself – or you could just enjoy being in your own company.

▶ Write an inventory of yourself. Include things you like and dislike, things you are good at, find difficult, are passionate about, curious about, get compliments on, regret, hope for. Include big items and little ones, things most people would readily understand and private, 'silly', quirks and idiosyncrasies.

▶ Allow yourself to react when someone treads on your individuality. Let them know that this is what's going on, and that it's not acceptable. You don't have to be rude – but making your boundaries clear helps everyone in the long run.

Laurence and Tanya had recently moved to the country, where they bought a comfortable old house with a large garden. Laurence was partly retired, but Tanya worked freelance as a consultant and often travelled away from home. They were hospitable people, and were happy at first to have friends to stay. But as their first summer in the new house progressed, they began to find themselves getting tired, and rather resenting their friends' visits. Tanya also noticed that even old friends often assumed they could just relax and be on holiday when they came. She started to resent this. She and Laurence were having less time together, and sometimes they got irritable with each other about the chores associated with having guests. Talking with a friend who was a coach, Tanya realised that it was time to set some boundaries. She made it clear to the next set of visitors that while they were welcome, they would need to help. She explained that she would be working some of the time, and the rest she would be on holiday with them: either way, she needed them to pull their weight. Much to her surprise, her friends quite understood, and they enjoyed sharing both fun and chores together.

▪ *Balancing Work and Home*

Mike was 26 and ambitious, with a job in a go-getting recruitment company. He enjoyed the work, and was in line for a promotion. He liked working with clients, and was good at forming and cultivating relationships with them. Once he got to work, he tended to become immersed in it. He would even forget to do things for himself, like go to the bank or make essential phone calls that could only be done in the daytime. In particular, he found it difficult to bring the day to a close, and often worked late. His partner Henry, who worked from home, began to get angry, and felt that he was putting work before their relationship. Henry resented the way he felt 'Mike forgets us when he's at work.' Even when Mike promised to get home on time for some specific event, such as meeting up with friends, he would often just 'forget'. The relationship was in danger of breaking.

When Mike's coach asked him what he really wanted, he replied that he really wanted to succeed at work – *and* he really wanted the relationship with Henry. He just couldn't seem to keep both in mind at the same time. His coach explained people who are really effective in 'balancing' their lives have developed ways of relating home and work as they go along. Some people use their diaries to ensure that 'home-tasks' get done during the working week; others make a point of phoning their partners during the course of the day. Mike was actually not particularly good at planning even at work, so he thought that better diary management would help him in both areas of his life. He didn't like the idea of having to remember to phone Henry, but was quite happy for Henry to phone him every day to ensure that he remembered to leave on time – or to let him know that he needn't. He also decided that he would ask his manager if he could go on a time-management course. Balance wasn't a question of allotting equal shares of attention to home and work, but rather of getting better at juggling the two in relation to a shared understanding of values and goals.

For us it was interesting to hear what happened next. Because Mike had started to address the issue, the relationship improved as Henry felt taken seriously. After a few months, they decided to sell their flat and move closer to Mike's place of work, since this would cut his travelling time and, quite literally, help him work 'closer to home'.

Balancing home and work can involve a number of things on each of the logical levels (see page **48**). It may be about the identity issues involved, as it partly was for Mike. It may be about values, as it was for Henry. It may be about capability – effective juggling is a skill that can be learnt, as Mike began to discover. It almost certainly involves behaviour, and the way this expresses, and is felt to express, priorities and values as far as both sides are concerned. So if this is an issue for you, think about the logical level(s) at which it is an issue, as this will start to indicate where you might intervene to effect change.

Sometimes Nature lends a helping hand, too. One executive we knew worked long hours, sometimes coming in at weekends. He found this hard, as he commuted and hardly saw his young child. His boss was very unsympathetic – until he too became a father, when all of a sudden his time-keeping became more elastic and it became permissible to be late because of disturbed nights and doctor's appointments! As is often the case, a change in the boss's own circumstances had helped him go to second position with his staff.

▪ *Finding the Right Time to Raise an Issue*

When you wonder what the right time to raise an issue is, ask yourself – the right time for whom, and the right time to achieve what? Two key NLP guidelines can help answer these questions. The way your message is received depends not only on the way you present it, but also on what your receiver understands by it. So first consider: are you clear about what you want to say? And can you say it in a way the other will be able to hear? Then ask yourself: what state do you need to be in to say what you need to say? But it's equally important to consider what state they need to be in to hear what you have to say. If you raise an important issue about work allocation with your boss just as he is rushing off to make a presentation, he may not hear you, and he will almost certainly be irritated by your interruption of his train of thought.

Sometimes people put off raising an issue because it never seems to be quite the right time. In such situations, it's vital to ask yourself what you really want. It may never be the perfect time to raise the issue, but if it is the right time in your life to achieve what you want then it *is* the right time to raise it. Stop prevaricating and just do it!

▪ *Is It Really an Irreconcilable Difference?*

Irreconcilable differences almost always centre on cherished beliefs and values, or our sense of identity. That's why resolving them can be so difficult. People can get very stuck and entrenched when they feel any violation of these core elements has occurred. Sometimes it even seems they're committed to keeping the difference irreconcilable. Usually, though, that's to do with asserting and trying to preserve the importance of the values or their identity.

A more useful approach we've found is to regard an irreconcilable difference as one where you haven't found a means of resolution – *yet*. Adding this one word changes the time-frame so that impossibility becomes possible: it's a one-word reframe (see page **72**) of the situation.

In coaching we've found it useful to get really clear about a number of specific questions:

▶ Do our clients with irreconcilable differences want to achieve a reconciliation? If the answer is yes, we want to know why, because this makes it very clear to all concerned what is involved and worth working to preserve. If no, we still want to know why because the value statements that come out will guide future decisions and behaviours as they set up a direction they want to head in.

▶ What specifically is it that is irreconcilable? Frequently, the descriptions we hear at first are riddled with holes: there's a lot of deletion. When you start filling these in you sometimes find that the more complete description changes how the person is thinking about the issue anyway. This of course becomes true a hundredfold when all parties start really clarifying what it's about. Often there will be distortion and generalisation happening too. To get the specifics, use meta model questions (see page 51).

▶ If they have the will, do they have the means to move towards reconciling their differences? This is more a capability issue. Sometimes people need to learn new communication skills and new ways of interacting. Sometimes it isn't the difference that's irreconcilable but the means of expression.

One couple Wendy worked with 'couldn't reconcile their differences at all'. Using these three questions really helped take things forward. Their answers to these questions showed that what they actually wanted was fairly similar. But they went about achieving what they wanted in very different ways – their meta programmes were in strong contrast. This meant that they didn't *do* things in the same way, and they didn't have a way of *communicating* what they wanted successfully either. They recognised that their aims were actually not all that dissimilar: both wanted to build a successful business and have a good home. They learnt how their meta programmes differed: the wife was very in-time and enjoyed life in the moment, finding it very difficult to plan ahead, while her partner, who took a more through-time perspective, couldn't understand why she often spent money on impulse instead of saving it, and got distracted from other things she'd agreed to do to help their plans forward. Learning to respect each other's approach as valid was the beginning of being able to discuss and achieve what they wanted together. It meant considerable adjustment for each partner, but knowing that they were committed to each other and to values and goals they shared helped them work at understanding and managing these important differences.

In dealing with irreconcilable differences, one NLP approach is to chunk up (see page **31**) from details to the larger, or more significant, issues involved, finding out what the issue means to each partner, and what that achieves for them. Sooner or later, a value or goal will emerge that they can both agree on. They may go about realising it in quite different ways – and that may be the problem – but the value is a shared value. For example, when a couple divorces, there may be an argument about whether the wife keeps the family home or whether it should be sold so that both partners can afford to buy accommodation. The mother may argue fiercely that the kids will be better in the home they know; the father may argue that if he gets somewhere bigger than a bedsit he can have them more often and give them a better time. Both appear to be rating the children's experience very highly, and wanting the best for them. Recognising that you have some important value in common usually makes it easier to negotiate on lower logical level issues.

Sometimes, however, the expressed disagreement about home and kids may also be a way of fighting out other issues. You may never have established a true 'we-ness': even though you have managed to share house and home it may have been as two individuals living alongside one another. For such a relationship, the advent of children, which brings competition for time and resources to the surface, can be the test which shows up an inherent weakness. In fighting for the needs of the kids you are also fighting for your needs as individuals. Any resolution here will need to take account of this; and it's unlikely that you can become reconciled unless you truly want to rebuild your relationship on a different footing.

▪ *Do You Stay or Do You Go?*

Let's look at two examples, one involving a personal relationship and one from a work setting, following each problem through to its resolution.

> Ross and Catherine had got together as students on a work-camp. They enjoyed being together, had a fling and then were dismayed to find that Catherine was pregnant. Ross had a coach already, and decided to talk it through with her. At this point he really wanted out of the relationship, but he felt sorry for Catherine and responsible for their child. Neither wanted an abortion. Should he stay, or should he go? Ross

decided to offer to buy a flat in the same block as his girlfriend, so that he could share in childcare and be an active part of their child's life without actually living together. He could afford the money, and the time commitment; but he could not afford to live in an intimate relationship with someone he did not care deeply for.

Desmond had seven years left till retirement. As a long-serving police officer he could look forward to a good pension if he stayed. But he had become really disillusioned with the worsening social problems in the town he worked in, and felt that his seniors were making things worse by taking a hardline approach with youngsters on the estates where he had worked for twenty years. He wanted out – but he had a lot to lose. Desmond decided that he could afford to take early retirement, as he was a widower and had always been frugal. He started looking for part-time work, and offered to help out a friend who owned a taxi by driving the cab for him at nights: he was used to shifts and didn't find night-work a problem, and because of his police experience he knew the area well. He also decided to become a volunteer at the local community centre. He couldn't afford to abandon the community where he had served, and built up good relationships, over so many years.

People often say that they 'can't afford to leave'. And by 'afford' they often mean that much more than money is involved. Ross couldn't afford to feel badly about himself for leaving his former girlfriend and their baby. Desmond was worried whether he could afford to take the risks of leaving a secure job and looking for work at his age. But even with finances sorted, he couldn't afford to feel he had let down the estate kids by withdrawing from the networks he had been part of for so long.

One way to look at the issue of leaving is to find out what kind of costs it involves for you. The NLP questions *What stops you?* and *What would happen if you did?* are two good ways to find out what exactly is involved. Finding out the exact dimensions of your dilemma puts you in a position where you can begin to explore a range of possible solutions.

Tips for deciding about a relationship

▶ **Ask yourself what you really want** This is essential information – you can't decide until you know. Leaving a job, an organisation or a relationship is a big step, and you deserve your own best attention. So do the other parties involved.

▶ **Pay attention to your gut feelings** When we make big decisions, we need every part of ourselves contributing. Logic, training and conscious thought give us substantial help; but they need the counterbalance provided by gut feelings, which sometimes show us the limitations of rules, assumptions and logic itself. As we've noted elsewhere, we are made up of many interacting systems – and we need them all when we are about to leave known territory and launch out into the future.

▶ **Don't put up with second best** Many people are afraid to make demands, or feel they aren't worthy, or believe that only exceptional or very lucky people get what they want. It's our experience as coaches that most people can get a lot of what they want if they allow themselves to know what it is, check how far their goals are viable and well-formed, and act as if they deserved to achieve them.

▶ **Create compelling futures and use them for extra information** Use the information on representational systems and sub-modalities on pages 73 and 80 to help you create an imaginary future that's as powerful and attractive as possible. Check it out by creating a number of different versions. NLP calls these 'compelling futures' because the power of your imagination can make them so realistic, and fascinating, that they're compelling. When you have created more than one version of the future, and each is equally compelling, you can test them against each other in a way that's really helpful. One of our colleagues called this 'branching roads' because it helped his clients to branch out in new and different directions, and 'try them on for size'.

If, like many people, you create negative compelling futures – for example, anticipated disasters that frighten you in the here-and-now, make you reluctant to take risks, or leave you avoiding things that haven't happened yet and may never happen – you can use the same skills and strategies in reverse to defuse, de-intensify, dissolve and dismiss them. Involve your most powerful representational systems and their most influential sub-modalities to restructure those disaster movies, to change the outcome of the arguments and to add encouragement to your internal dialogue. You'll find you can transform old habits, frame by frame, word by word!

We knew one middle-aged learner driver who ran disaster movies: she was going to run into thick traffic; she was going to look stupid because she wasn't in the right gear and the car would stall at a junction; she wasn't going to be able to stop in time if a pedestrian stepped out between parked cars; she was going to crash. She constantly ran critical internal dialogue, even though her instructor was encouraging and told her she was making steady progress. She failed several attempts at her driving test, and eventually asked an NLP coach for help. He realised that whenever the scenario got scary, his client stopped in a panic. She never gave herself the opportunity of transforming it. The coach helped her use her powerful imagination to continue these interrupted visions and to rescue each situation she was afraid of. She learnt to steer herself out of trouble; to practise smooth gear changes in her head; to rehearse different possible responses to emergencies and to drive through her imagined disasters to a situation of competence and safety. This also helped her build a vision of what she did want that was equally clear and powerful, and as she found she could take control of these powerful internal experiences she began to drive with much more confidence and skill.

▶ **Ask 'Why not?'** This question is really a reframe: it shifts the emphasis from the away-from position (Shall I leave? Why should I? Would it be justifiable? What would happen?) to a towards stance. Why not lead a better life? grab a chance of happiness? end the dissatisfaction of how things are currently? It's a loaded question, just as the question 'Why?' is. But it's a question loaded in favour of the future, not the past; of new discoveries rather than old miseries; of possibilities rather than dreary certainties.

Sometimes there really is a 'Why not?' that you hadn't thought about – and this question shows that up too. Either way, your choice will be more informed.

▶ **Dare to dream** Over the years this has become an increasingly important theme in some of the major training sessions Ian runs because it is so easy, yet so rarely done. Dreaming goes beyond what we know. It gives life to fantasy and hope. It creates possibilities, and finds solutions that go beyond your current ways of thinking. Dreaming comes in many forms: creating hopeful visions, daydreaming, night-dreaming – and just plain old imagining what it would be like if...

▪ *Next Steps*

Good relationships are central to our humanity, and one of the fundamentals that make life worth living. They enrich us in so many ways. So take a moment now and ask yourself:

▶ Given everything we've covered in this chapter, what is the most important piece for you?

▶ How might you take it forward?

▶ What will be your next step?

▶ When will you begin so that you can enjoy even better relationships?

CHAPTER 14

Maximising Your Brain Power

KEEPING OUR BRAINS in good working order is obviously pretty vital for success in just about anything we take on. And in this chapter we'll be showing you how to.

Earlier in this book we described how, in NLP terms, people literally construct the 'reality' of their experience through internal processing. In fact, this offers people such a wealth of practical information that NLP has sometimes been called the 'Brain-User's Guide'. And knowing how to use your brain more fully and effectively is one way in which you can maximise your brain power. But you can also grow your own brain power – quite literally: while the number of brain *cells* we have actually declines from our mid-twenties on, research has demonstrated that the number of *connections* between brain cells can continue to grow – provided the brain is exercised and given new material to deal with. The power of your brain, in other words, doesn't just relate to the number of brain cells you have: it relates to the use you make of them, and the way this stimulates the brain to grow new connections between cells.

When NLP models people who use their brains effectively, it shows that new challenges, new learning, and new connections are what keep the brain in good trim. It's been demonstrated relatively recently, for example, that people who keep mentally active into old age are less likely to develop diseases such as Alzheimer's. Activity doesn't have to involve academic learning, though it might: doing puzzles, reading books and papers, listening to radio, learning or practising new skills are all ways in which you can continue to stimulate your brain and encourage the formation of new neural connections. All the outstanding people who were modelled in the early days of NLP, such as Milton Erickson, went on working at an outstanding level into old age. And one important reason was just that: they went on working into old age. The problems and challenges they faced in their ongoing professional work actually helped their brains stay in good working order, just as regular exercise helps the body stay healthy and mobile.

In this chapter we've chosen to highlight four ways in which you can boost your brain power.

1. **Making the most of what you've got** The brain works in a number of different ways and at different levels of awareness. This section draws on NLP to show you how to work at these different levels, and ensure the fullest range of mental functioning.

2. **Being more creative** People sometimes think that creativity means inventing something totally new. We've found it more useful to think of it as the process of making new connections. This isn't reserved for the artistic or the inventive: everyone can do it. Creativity involves giving ourselves permission to be playful and inquisitive, versatile and flexible. It involves looking for multiple solutions rather than settling for just one. You don't have to be a special kind of person to be creative: NLP shows it isn't a 'given' like the colour of your eyes. It's something you *do*.

3. **Accelerating your learning** By modelling people who are good learners, NLP has identified what it is they do that makes their learning both rapid and effective. Using the strategies developed from observing them can help you become faster and more effective in your learning too.

4. **Improving your memory** Again, the ability to remember isn't something fixed. We want to explore the connection between two key processes involved: storage and retrieval. Often these are confused. You may find you can improve your memory dramatically by learning how to encode accurately in the first place and how to easily access what you have stored.

How to Make the Most of What You've Got

Too often people talk as if they were born with a certain 'amount' of brain power. Believing this is a very effective way of limiting what you can achieve. We've found it's both more useful and more realistic to begin by assuming we don't actually know in any fixed sense what we or anyone else is capable of. We've also found it extremely useful to flush out any limiting beliefs our clients may have about their ability to learn. So that's where we'd like to start.

▪ *Self-limiting Beliefs*

Take a moment to check out any self-limiting beliefs you may have about learning. Here are some common examples:

- I'm not academic.

- I was no good at school.

- I'm too old to learn.

- I can't do maths.

- I'm not creative.

- I've got a poor memory.

Some of these are limiting because they assume that mental ability is fixed and can't be changed, and some because they assume that personal history, or age, limit achievement. NLP doesn't claim that everyone can become an Einstein or a Michelangelo – only that everyone could learn something from them and as a result expand their own abilities. This is important because when you believe something which is limiting, you will indeed be limited by it.

So a good place to start, if you're seeking to make the most of your brain power, is by becoming really curious about how you currently operate, and what else you'd like to learn.

▪ *Extending Your Current Range*

Back in Chapter 3 we outlined some important NLP discoveries about the way people process experience. If you've already begun to build a profile of how you use representational systems, identifying which sub-modalities are most influential for you, and what your natural meta programme preferences are, this would be a good moment to revisit it, or to jot down some notes. Remember, every strength potentially has its limitations.

So: how are you using your brain, and what makes you special in the way you process information, create an internal world and behave in the external world? Everyone receives information through their senses, and NLP shows us how we use those same senses to process it internally. Yet although each of us has access, at least potentially, to information from all of our senses, we tend to favour a couple only. And that's a limitation, because we could make use of all five. So we want to show you some ways to use more of what you've got. We're going to come at this in eight different ways. You choose which ones will give you maximum leverage.

1. Build your mental versatility

One of the most common complaints we hear as coaches is people saying they're not very imaginative or not very visual. Suppose you think you're 'not very visual' because you don't seem to make pictures easily, and you feel limited by comparison with people who have 'vivid imaginations'. We often find that these self-styled 'unimaginative people' are strongly kinesthetic. If you are one of them, your ability to attend to, replay or create physical and emotional experience internally is actually just as subtle and rich in a different way as the brilliant images of someone who visualises easily. Furthermore, you can develop your ability to process visually if you choose, really quite easily. We'll show you how in a moment.

Everyone dreams – whether they are naturally visual or not in waking life – usually five or six times a night. Dreams are the ultimate whole-brain experience. Elements from every sense may be present in your dreams: bodily sensations, strong emotions, moving pictures, even smells and tastes can all figure, however little of the detail you remember in the morning. People who say they're not very visual generally have no difficulty remembering a nightmare that was so vivid it woke them up. That's pretty impressive for someone who isn't very visual! Your dreams make it clear that you already have all it takes to lead a rich and powerful internal life in any of your senses.

So there's no need for you to think yourself limited in the waking world.

Here are some simple exercises to help you build your mental versatility.

EXERCISE: Mental Workout 1

Spend a few moments imagining some activity or event you enjoy. Notice what you're most aware of first. If what you notice are the kinesthetics, pay attention to how you feel. As you do so, start to look around in your mind's eye and see what goes with this experience visually. Next pay attention to the sounds that are part of this experience. (Sometimes this may include the sound of silence.)

If, on the other hand, you began by focusing on the visual dimension, now you need to add a soundtrack. So what are the sounds you'd be hearing? Run the movie again, adding in those sounds. And what would you be feeling in your body?

Run your movie again, adding these in too. If your lead system was auditory, let the sound lead you to the pictures and the kinesthetic sensations.

What you're doing here is overlapping from a sense which is familiar to ones which are less so. As you do so, you're helping yourself to build your skill in using your representational systems more fully, fluently and automatically.

EXERCISE: Mental Workout 2

You can help yourself engage different representational systems more quickly and effectively by deliberately using the eye-accessing patterns which are associated with each (see page **43**). Notice which direction you naturally tend to look in as you see pictures, hear sounds and feel feelings, in order to check whether your accessing corresponds to the pattern. Many people share the pattern discussed in the section on eye-accessing patterns, though some people reverse it and others may have their own variations. Change it if necessary to reflect your patterns – but remember the original when you're observing others. Knowing your own patterns is necessary if you want to access them deliberately.

Think of another pleasant scenario, and decide on which of your less favoured representational systems you'd like to engage. As you begin to run through your scenario, look in the direction that accesses that system. For example, if you're picturing a walk along a beach and want to access what you could hear, look horizontally left. Again, practice will help you.

EXERCISE: Mental Workout 3

When you read about sub-modalities, which did you find were the most influential for you? If your lead system is auditory, are you most influenced by tone? or pitch? or volume? What happens if you make the sounds in your favourite scenario more mellow? or crisper? or higher? or more distant? Play with these variables until you get the sound quality just how you want it.

Then take one of your less familiar representational systems. Let's suppose it's visual. What kind of picture quality have you been getting, as you added visual information to your pleasant scenario? Use the analogy of the visual controls you have on your television to help you improve your picture: brightness, contrast, colour balance. You can also add definition and distance. You can go black-and-white. You can freeze-frame. Altering these variables will have an effect: find out which are most influential for you. See page **80** for a fuller list of sub-modalities.

EXERCISE: Mental Workout 4

Take one of your meta programme sorting preferences. Let's suppose you're someone who likes the 'big picture' – in other words, you prefer your information in large chunks. Take an issue, or an event, that's familiar to you or that occurred recently. Think about it just as it comes to you naturally – but notice what that involves. Suppose it was a business context and you thought: 'The way forward for our company is through developing initiatives at a departmental level.' Perhaps you had an idea about where you expected things to be in a year's time. Now chunk down. Think of what might be involved for one department to become more involved in developing initiatives. How might they do that? What sorts of events, discussions, processes might be involved? Now chunk down again. Take a single individual in that department. What would he or she have to have in mind, and do, in order to contribute to developing those initiatives? What would help them keep this need in mind on a daily basis as they got up in the morning, went to work and did their daily tasks? The specific content is not what's important: what builds your mental muscle is training yourself to move more freely towards the extreme on the meta programme that's less familiar to you. As you succeed in becoming more flexible, you build your brain power – and you also get more understanding of how different people function, which helps you interact with them more easily and effectively.

2. Give yourself even richer experiences

One way to do this is to remind yourself from time to time to pay attention to all the sensory information that's coming in. If you're enjoying a good meal, it's likely you'll be paying attention to taste and smell. Spend a moment ot two paying close attention to colours, and to textures. Notice contrasts – between smooth and crunchy, between contrasting or complementary flavours. What words would really describe your experience, or those textures?

So many of the arts enrich by stimulating our senses. Bringing different senses together can do this too. Walt Disney's film *Fantasia* visually expresses various pieces of music. You can do this too. Creating new experiences like this is a way of enhancing your sensory experience and making yourself more versatile and flexible at the same time.

3. Cultivate your dreaming

Pay attention to your dreaming and your daydreaming. Dreams are important to us in many ways, by:

▶ Actively processing information and feelings.

▶ Always involving many senses, so the experience is very rich and 'textured'.

▶ Giving us valuable information about what is going on in our lives, either directly, or more often in a disguised or symbolic form.

▶ Being strongly sequenced, though often in a way which is emotionally rather than logically organised.

▶ Drawing upon a rich range of unconscious, associative, creative links between many kinds of information.

Some people remember their dreams; others tend to forget all but the most dramatic as soon as they wake. When you do have one of these, take time to run over the story in your mind before the events of the day over-lay it. Relive the story of that dream. Remind yourself of the events, pictures, sensations and other sensory information it involved. This was the product of *your* mind. Marvel at your own creativity!

If you get into the habit of asking yourself, when you wake, 'What did I dream?' you may at first only remember a few particularly strong feelings or vivid images: jot them down anyway. Some people keep dream diaries. Don't rush to interpret them, and don't assume that there is necessarily a single clear meaning which can be interpreted according to psychological theories or books on dream significance. We have found that the most useful assumption to make about dreams is that they have significance for you, the dreamer: they come from your internal storehouse of feelings, experiences and images, and are an active and useful way of processing that is quite different from – and just as useful as – the processing that belongs to the logical and conscious part of your mind.

Often, a strong feeling will be your first clue to the meaning a dream has for you: note it, and wonder about it, but don't rush to tie it down by conscious analysis. The real work of the dream is often done simply in the dreaming of it: the conscious mind doesn't always have to understand, and when it tries to translate dreams into its own terms it may be limiting it, just as poetry translated from another language usually loses something of its more subtle reach of meanings.

The value of dreams

Dreams demonstrate a different level of mental functioning from con-scious, disciplined thought. When you pay attention to them, and even cultivate them, you are learning to become familiar with, to trust and to draw upon a fuller range of your own mental resources: in other words, you are using more of what you've got.

The mind works both consciously and unconsciously. Conscious thought is formally taught in our educational system. Its strength is its systematic and disciplined way of handling information. Its limitation is that it tends to be rule-bound and too narrow in its problem-solving approach.

The brain also processes information at an unconscious level: mostly, this is associative and depends on links, similarities and feeling. This processing produces dreams, as well as much of our other 'creative' or 'expressive' experience. That's why we are often surprised by the spontaneous connections we make or insights we have, and by our imaginative inspiration: it isn't what we'd have come up with consciously at all, yet it seems somehow completely 'right'. This way of thinking works 'laterally' – it expands, goes sideways, finds multiple avenues rather than just one.

We need both kinds of functioning if we are to make the most of our brain power. Logic and intuition, discipline and divergence, are all vital tools that enrich and enable us. But whereas we're used to working with the conscious mind, in part because we are aware of it and can monitor it as it works, many people are less at ease in trusting and using unconscious processes. Paying attention to your dreams, and deliberately cultivating daydreaming, are both ways of stretching yourself into this area.

So let's look at the value of deliberate daydreaming. Where dreams come unbidden, you may find it useful to deliberately evoke the conditions for daydreaming, if, like many people, you have not really valued the activity.

How is it valuable? Daydreaming brings us escape and relaxation; visions of the future that inspire and help us bring about what we have dreamed of; solutions to apparently insoluble problems; inventions and creative possibilities. Daydream states allow the unconscious, associative parts of the mind to work in their own playful and imaginative ways, bringing not only pleasure but results that deliberate, attentive, rational thought doesn't. We need space in our lives for both ways of processing if we are to realise ourselves as fully as possible.

The key to daydreaming is to be in the right state (see page 77). There is a kind of automatic abstractedness that goes along with daydreaming. Mostly it just seems to happen – but when you know about creating and changing states, you can choose to make it happen.

Here are some ways you can cultivate and work with your daydreams.

► Notice when you have been daydreaming. Is there any pattern of circumstances that helps bring about your particular daydreaming state? Some people find that repetitive, relatively automatic, activities such as jogging, ironing or walking create the right state. Perhaps it's a warm bath, swimming a few lengths, or sitting in the garden. Or it may be swaying to the movement of a train, staring into space, looking out of the window of a bus on the way to work, or going on a long drive. Once you find what helps you daydream, use it and make space for it in your life on a regular basis. Let daydreaming come to you, and notice what kinds of windows it opens from your ordinary world onto what other kinds of possibilities. Some of your best ideas and inspirations may come at these times.

► Next time you have a decision to make, or a problem to solve, set up the circumstances so that you can trigger your daydreaming state – and allow yourself to explore your problem or decision in this way. When you've done so, make brief notes of what you experienced and discovered. Add that to your conscious thinking on the subject: you now have much more information, and the advantage of having engaged more of your mental resources.

4. Play to your strengths

Some people have a strong belief in endeavour, and in trying to take on and improve personal weaknesses. At its extreme, this approach can mean that you spend time and effort bashing away at your limitations, often feeling miserable and worthless, rather than recognising and enjoying your strengths. While it's enriching to add to your repertoire, there really is no obligation to keep on doing what you're bad at, or find difficult – unless you really want to. Success and achievement do a great deal more for you than repeated failure.

We're not saying that you shouldn't try to improve at something that really matters to you, whether it's becoming a better parent, manager or hang-glider. And becoming really good at something means engaging actively with your limitations. But one of the best ways to do this is to know what your strengths are and play to them: NLP shows clearly that that though effort is often involved in developing excellence, misery and lack of self-esteem aren't.

Tessa was a bank teller. She liked customers, and they liked her. She was also efficient at her work, and her manager thought she could be a real help to new staff learning the job. But when he asked her to make a presentation to the new recruits, Tessa was terrified. She was quite happy working with individuals, but she hated speaking in front of a group. It reminded her of being asked to read aloud at school. Her mouth would go dry and the words simply wouldn't come out. She tried to convince her manager that someone else would do the task better; but her manager asked her to think it over.

Tessa thought about it, and talked with a friend, Sara, who had been on an NLP training course with Ian. Sara asked her what she thought she was really good at, and Tessa said without a moment's hesitation 'dealing with people'. What she meant was dealing with them one at a time. But as they talked she began to see these new recruits as individuals too. She decided she would plan a little talk and write down simple headings with real-life examples, and that she would pretend she was talking in turn to individual people in the group rather than the group as a whole, and make eye-contact with them as she had seen confident presenters do. She played to her strength, managed her first presentation much better than she had expected and told her manager she'd like to do it again with the next group of new recruits.

5. Feed your mind

Since body and brain are so interconnected, it makes sense to remind ourselves that making the most of what we have includes taking care of ourselves at every level. 'I feed my body,' said one of our clients. 'What do I need to do to feed my mind?'

NLP emphasises that mind and body are interrelated systems. It's not possible to feel something without that feeling being expressed, or encoded, in the body's physiology, as we can see if someone goes suddenly white with fear or red with anger, stiffens with apprehension or relaxes when reassured. Changes like these can take place in seconds, and are easy to spot, but people are often also aware of changes that can't be seen: 'My stomach just knotted up when I heard that,' or 'I felt really warm inside when she smiled.'

So how can you 'feed your mind'? Remembering how mind and body connect, you can nourish your mind physically, emotionally and intellectually. Think of feeding it on each of these levels on a regular basis in order to help it function and grow. We have some questions to help you.

Food for Thought

Physical

▶ What do you do to take care of your body? Did you take any exercise yesterday? Is exercise a daily part of your life? Both of us know from our own experience that regular daily exercise not only makes us feel fitter but keeps our minds more alert and active. If you don't have a regular fitness training programme, start by walking more. You don't have to join a gym or invest in expensive equipment to begin to get into shape. And as your body gets fitter, your mind will feel more alive and become more responsive too.

▶ Did you get enough sleep last night? Do you normally? Sleep is when you do most of the maintenance work on your body. So you want to restore yourself and be in the best shape possible.

▶ Remember, you are as good as your last meal – that's the fuel your brain is currently running on. If it was junk food, you're making it harder for yourself. If it was wholesome and well-balanced, your brain will be getting better sustenance for what you're asking it to do.

Emotional

▶ How rich is your imaginative and emotional life? You might be very active physically, but never look at a novel, or see a play or movie. You might work hard at a job that involves your mind, but forget to have fun and play. Use the balance wheel (see page **132**) to help you find out what areas of your life you may be neglecting, and then begin to re-balance yourself.

▶ What relationship would nourish you emotionally? Give it a high priority.

▶ Spend time with children. They are usually more open to their experience and their feelings than adults, and more direct in showing them. They are also fabulously creative and playful.

Intellectual

▶ What else can you do to feed your mind? Keep asking questions. Remember how young children ask them all the time – and they are great learners. Asking questions and wondering about answers will stretch your mind.

▶ Choose to watch a programme or read an article about something unfamiliar to you. You don't have to become an expert – but just dipping into a different world is a good mind-stretching exercise.

▶ Ask other people questions about their lives and work, and really pay attention to the answers. Imagining how it might be to live their lives is good food for the imagination, and develops your ability to take second position as well.

► Learn to meditate – over thirty years of research on TM (Transcendental Meditation) make it clear that this particular form of meditation certainly improves overall intellectual performance and mind-body functioning.

6. Make the most of your time here

Paying attention to the full range of your sensory experience enriches your mental and physical functioning, and enables you to realise your potential more fully. It also helps you transform how you relate to the process of time itself: in accessing internally stored information, you can learn from the past, enjoy its riches more fully and correct the effects of limiting decisions and past traumas. You can gain more information from what's happening in the present, and learn how to achieve the outcomes you want in the future. By becoming more attentive to here-and-now sensory information, you can enjoy things much more, and cut the time it takes to adjust to experiences which seem likely to be difficult or negative. And by developing the ability to imagine and create your own compelling futures, you can lead yourself easily and effectively towards achieving your goals.

Making your life more varied, and making the most of each moment rather than drifting passively along, can help preserve and enhance your sense of autonomy into an alert old age. As one of our coachees said, 'I remind myself that life isn't a rehearsal. This is it. So I'm not going to waste any of it.'

NLP modelling of people who stay mentally alert into old age reveals that in addition to keeping their minds questioning and engaged, they tend to have a personal quest or passion. One elderly friend of ours still manages her home and tends a substantial vegetable garden even though she is badly affected by arthritis. All her life she has had a passionate interest in politics. As she talks, her mental alertness and her questioning attitude remind us of someone in their youth.

Passion is about energy and involvement. What's vital is to have a passion – the focus is less important. If you don't have a current passion, think back to what really excited you as a child. Or what you have secretly been promising yourself to do if you won the lottery or had a legacy. What could you do today to make that dormant passion live, so that it could help you make the most of your time here?

7. Be in charge of your habits

We're all creatures of habit, programmed to store and repeat what we have learnt. In many ways, this is a very useful attribute. It means that many skills, once learnt, are thereafter available for use without further thought or need for amendment, unless something changes. The skills of speech, walking and reading, are potentially available to you for the rest of your life. But having a built-in tendency to repeat patterns also means that you may equally easily go on repeating ones that don't work so well or that limit you in some important ways. Smoking and nail biting are good examples of patterns that once had a purpose, but which have often become outmoded by the time you want to change. But the very effectiveness of the habit makes you think change will be difficult. Dependency, lack of assertiveness, and being forthright and tactless can also become habitual. We even talk of people as being 'set in their ways', as though something which was once fluid has become rigid.

NLP has demonstrated beyond question that people can change, if they want to and they know the way. Sometimes it takes help. But no one has to be the victim of their habits if they don't want to be. And taking charge of your unwanted habits is one way you can maximise your brain power. It's a bit like reviewing your computer files to see which you need to keep and which need to be consigned to the recycle bin. Why waste unnecessary space in your head – and your life – with old programmes?

Any habit develops through repetition, and as it gets repeated we become less and less aware at a conscious level of how we do it. The toddler learning to walk won't remember the first steps he took unaided. This is also true of changing a habit: once it's been accomplished, and a new pattern begun, repetition helps install it ever more securely. If you want to become more assertive in your relationships, the first time you say 'No' and really mean it may feel like a major step. But day by day it will become easier for you to know what you want and ask for it, until it's as much a habit as being a doormat once was.

8. Remember, it's never too late

It's never too late to learn a new way of thinking, feeling or behaving. We have both worked with people in their seventies, eighties and nineties who really wanted to learn new things, and who succeeded. Wendy vividly remembers a meeting of the European Veterans' Athletics

Championships in the early 1980s, which her husband helped organise. There were high-jumpers in their seventies, and steeplechasers in their eighties. These people were still stretching themselves. There are almost always runners in their sixties, seventies and eighties competing in the London Marathon. And the Open University has many elderly graduates. Age isn't a barrier; attitude is.

Some years ago there was a TV series about people having new experiences: a miner who had spent a lifetime down the pit retired and took up painting at an evening class. After a few years, his paintings were being regularly exhibited in one-man shows. Two elderly ladies walked every summer in the Himalayas. They had always wanted to go, went once and then made it an annual trip. Even increasing infirmity didn't stop one of them: she just arranged to be carried. An elderly man we knew was going gradually blind. Playing the piano had always been important to him, and so he set himself the task of memorising all his favourite pieces while he could still see and learn the music. That way, he would still be able to play for himself.

We knew a businessman who ran a major national company for many years and yet learnt seven languages in the half-hours he spent every day commuting to work on the train. 'I can learn anything I want to in that half an hour a day,' he said.

So you can go in new directions, or continue to develop your existing skills, throughout your life. And if you care enough, and learn the skills you need, you can change interpersonal habits too. We have coached people in their seventies who wanted to use NLP to improve their long-term relationships. And while you may feel you need expert help for some changes you want to make, the NLP approaches and tools in this book will take you a long way in themselves. You might begin by looking at the well-formedness conditions for outcomes on page 63. What do you really want? If you really want something, it need never be too late.

How to Be More Creative

▪ *What is Creativity?*

People often confuse creativity with originality – and then feel despondent because it seems so difficult, even impossible, to be truly original. But we can all be creative, because, as we've said, creativity is about making new connections – and that's literally true neurologically. Creativity is the mind's growing edge. It may involve risk: it always involves discovery. By creating new connections you build your brain power and develop your mental and interpersonal flexibility. Every time you link two things together, you create a third entity. And that new connection can itself connect with other ideas, other possibilities. Imagine the impact this could have throughout a system like the brain!

The results can be astonishing. Neil Armstrong took his famous first step on the Moon in 1965. And that event changed our relationship to the Universe. It confirmed the potential of human inventiveness and skill: it told us, if we want it enough and can find out ways, we can solve problems that were impossible before.

We suspect that this event gave many people a very powerful – and liberating – belief about human capability. And now there are long-term plans to visit Mars.

Being creative on an individual level has the same potential: when you connect things together, you go beyond both of them; and you have the possibility of forming new beliefs about yourself and your potential. We remember talking to a teenager who loved learning. She found it so exciting. She said: 'Sometimes I feel that my brain's literally stretching.'

Children are naturally creative, and each one of us has been a child. So we have all been creative, even if we don't consciously now understand what that involved. Children show their creativity in the way they discover their environment and make their own meanings out of it. As a toddler Wendy's daughter, Charlotte, used to love playing with all the plastic bowls and boxes that were kept in a cupboard under the sink. All Wendy needed to do was to open the cupboard doors and Charlotte would keep herself busy and happy for hours. Many children have imaginary friends, and create worlds with their toys. They don't need elaborate props or equipment: the meaning comes out of themselves.

Creativity is about making links and connections: to be creative, you need to give yourself permission, and time, to make new connections. It's about process rather than product. You can be creative at work or at home, when problem-solving, gardening or resolving arguments. You can be creative with words, materials, ideas and food. You can be creative with your surroundings or with your thoughts.

Another important aspect of creativity is that it results in something new even if every ingredient is already known and familiar. An insight is creative, because it's a new conclusion from information you already had. It's the new perspective that makes the difference.

Above all, being creative returns us to a state not so different from that of Wendy's daughter in front of that open cupboard. It's about being absorbed. Enjoying what you're doing. Paying a lot of attention to detail. Having a grand vision. Being excited. Playful. Wondering what would happen if...

▪ *Barriers to Creativity*

These are the most common barriers to creativity. See which – if any – apply to you:

▸ **Lack of time** Actually, this is not as important as it sounds: the linking process we're talking about only takes seconds. It can happen any time, anywhere – provided you are in the right state and pay attention to your own experience. So creativity is more about the quality of the time you have, and the freedom in your mind to be receptive to yourself.

▸ **Fear of being judged** This is the kiss of death for any brainstorming session. Creativity results in unusual ideas and perhaps even being different in some way. Differences can be thought of as strange, odd, challenging by some people. Fear of being considered weird, stupid or even just different will kill creativity.

▸ **Lack of self-esteem** If you do something creative, you are going beyond the bounds of what is familiar, to yourself and perhaps to other people. Sometimes when this happens, people fear that because their idea, or action, or invention is different they must be somehow strange and wrong. When you're not sure about yourself, being different in any way – even in your thoughts – can feel very risky. The danger is that you give up your new insight just so you can blend in.

► **Fear of failure** This can be a powerful inhibitory mechanism. But by definition, if you're making a new connection there can be no inherent 'right' or 'wrong' about it. So failure can only have two meanings:
  – It didn't work in the way you wanted or hoped for.
  – Someone else didn't like it. But so what. Over the years Ian has had people comment on how he generates so many successful projects, and ask him how he does it. He usually points out that these projects constitute about 10 per cent of what he's actually imagined. The other 90 per cent either didn't work or never got off the drawing board.

Creativity is not the preserve of the genius. Einstein was brilliant but he may not be the best model of creativity for most of us. You don't even need specialist expertise to be creative. And the fruits of your creativity may manifest in very everyday ways. The international knitwear designer Kaffe Fassett is a really good example. At twenty-eight, having never knitted before, he became intoxicated with the textures and colours of wool. Having bought about twenty colours, his first thought was to find an experienced knitter who could make up the patterns he had in mind. 'Gradually it dawned on me that I must learn to knit, and design as I went along... Over the next few years I ignored many of the rules that seem to paralyse most knitters into sticking to monochrome garments. Merrily, I combined colours and textured yarns, made knots in the middle of rows, and used up to twenty colours in a single row in some of my more ambitious efforts' (*Glorious Knitting*, Century Publishing, 1985). And he revolutionised knitting. He used the most simple of stitches (he wasn't an 'expert'), allowing colour, texture and pattern to 'paint' the designs he had in mind. He gave lectures and ran workshops, one of his main aims being to convince people 'that they can make something really beautiful and life-enhancing'. People often assumed that because he had started out as a painter he had some essential expertise that they were lacking. 'I want to try to convey to you that a sense of colour is not something you automatically know about; you discover and rediscover its secrets by playing with it and, above all, by constantly *looking*.'

If at any time you doubt your ability to be creative, remind yourself that five or six times every night, you create an entirely new dream, which you script, direct, act in and watch, which can involve all your senses, change times and places and have an impact that lasts long after it is over. This creation is so effortless most people don't even recognise it as such!

▪ *How to Be More Creative*

▶ **Find the right frame of mind** Explore the state you associate with being creative. Find out what triggers and maintains it. What's your best time of day? the best setting? Do you need to be alone – or perhaps on your own in the midst of a crowd? Do you need silence? or background music? Build a profile of your creativity state. Don't rely on its occurring by accident. Make space and time for it on a regular basis.

▶ **Cultivate dreaming and day-dreaming** Pay attention to your existing creativity rather than dismissing its fruits as 'just a dream' or 'just woolgathering'. Don't waste what you may already be discovering by ignoring it.

▶ **Ask yourself 'What if?' and 'What else?' and 'How else?'** Don't stop with the first idea or answer you thought of. Always go beyond, find more and different ideas.

▶ **When you hit a problem, pretend your usual solution isn't available** This can work at all kinds of levels. If your computer crashes, how else might you do the work you were planning for today? Could you use a tape-recorder? make mind-maps? use the phone? If you normally argue face to face, what would happen if you wrote your feelings down instead? Some solutions may be no better than the ones you're used to: others may offer you brilliant new opportunities. There's an NLP saying: if you always do what you've always done, you'll always get what you've always gotten. Creativity is doing something different.

▶ **See how many different results you can get with the same ingredients** There's a cookbook called *Recipes 1-2-3*, by Rozanne Gold (Grub St, 1997) in which every recipe is made out of only three ingredients. Some recipes use the same three ingredients but different processes or quantities to come up with different results. Ian's used the same principle in creativity workshops: take some everyday office object (paperclips, Post-its, rubber bands and so on), and figure how many different ways you could use them in combination. Combining is the key.

▶ **Know the rules – and bend them** In many different fields, variations on existing themes or rules are the basis of success, whether it's in jazz improvisation or the raised bed with desk- and storage-space underneath.

▶ **Think of different ways to do the familiar** Change the order in which you do familiar things. Change the usual implement for something less expected. Use your less favoured hand. As soon as we break routine, we move from a state where we are on automatic pilot to one where we are alive and alert. If you play with using your non-dominant hand, you'll exercise unfamiliar brain connections and help build new links. Try using the 'wrong' hand to clean your teeth, or brush your hair. Feels strange, doesn't it? Build ambidexterity, because you'll be building new connections in your brain.

▶ **Look out for the difference that makes the difference** When you come across something that strikes you as different, original or new, ask yourself where the key difference actually lies. In the case of Kaffe Fassett's knitwear, the difference is often in the use of an unexpected colour: a line of turquoise in a predominantly pink and purple pattern, for example, which 'hots up' the other colours and makes them more vibrant. Part of his creativity lay in being able to look at whole balls of wool in colours like these, which don't naturally seem to go with each other, and realising that just a touch of the unexpected would in fact make all the difference.

▪ *The Disney Creativity Strategy*

In Chapter 3 we encountered the work of Robert Dilts. Dilts, one of NLP's earliest pioneers, has written extensively on the strategies of genius and has modelled a number of outstanding people, among them Walt Disney. The Disney creativity strategy (see page 39) which Dilts developed gets people to separate out three essential roles that contribute to the process of generating creativity – the dreamer, the realist and the critic. Too often these roles get confused, or one will dictate to the others. For many people the critic is the dictator, but it's important to remember that the word 'critic' means someone who evaluates, not just points out what is wrong.

When Ian uses the Disney creativity strategy in organisations, he sometimes locates each role in a different room, so that people know that when they go into, say, the Dreamer Room they dream, or into the Critic Room they are critics only. NLP often makes use of physical space in this way: specifying what goes on where helps us get into the right state and know what is expected, and physically moving is a good way to change your state. The three roles of dreamer, realist and critic can also be separated in time. You can allow yourself dreaming time, and record your dreams in notebooks to come back to later when you're ready to think about how they could be put into practice (realist) and what criteria or problems that might entail (critic). However you separate the roles, the important thing is to know which one you're in at any particular time, and to give each enough room to do its job.

Creativity is a natural activity in human beings. Cherishing, encouraging and making use of your creativity is a major way to maximise your brain power, whether it's in finding new solutions to old problems or in finding new directions in life, whether it gives you more fun in your leisure time or more skill and ease at work. So what would you like to apply your creativity to? It's your choice.

How to Accelerate Your Learning

Everyone has been a good learner. By the time you read this book, you will have acquired a multitude of complex physical, mental and interpersonal skills, as well as an immense body of information about all kinds of things. Most of this you may well now take for granted. You will also have learnt a number of skills or beliefs which limit you or make things difficult for you in one way or another – perhaps including some doubts about your ability to learn, or to learn fast enough. And as most of us are holding down jobs and/or raising kids, and generally leading busy, if not frenetic, lives, learning things faster would be a very welcome skill to acquire.

In our experience as coaches, one of the most important ways to accelerate learning is to clear some negative learnings and assumptions out of the way. Every seed is programmed to become a complete example of its species – given the right conditions. As many of us know from experience with plants in our offices, houses or gardens, even plants that aren't doing well have an astonishing ability to recover and grow healthily once the right conditions are restored.

If you want to know how to accelerate your learning, it will be useful to engage in a little self-modelling. When you were a child you learnt a phenomenal amount in a very short time, not just information but also social skills, body-mind co-ordination and much, much more. So how did you do this?

We'll be showing you here. NLP can help you identify the right conditions for your learning, and what is currently blocking it, so that you can once more be free to learn as effectively as you did when you were a small child.

So how *did* you manage it all those years ago? The first five years of life represent the most amazing accelerated learning programme ever developed. Not all of this learning is necessarily 'good', of course, in terms of its usefulness in later life – you can learn to be intimidated or overly anxious – but certainly small children learn thoroughly and with every part of themselves. They learn without labelling what they are doing as learning. They begin to map out their world through the fullest use of all their senses every waking moment. This is truly total immersion learning. Virtually everyone, then, starts out as a fast learner.

▪ *What Fast Learning Involves*

Learning is perceived as relevant by the learner

When we're little, the world is fascinating because it's utterly new to us. We don't yet have sorting mechanisms that tell us some things are 'more important' or 'more worthwhile' than others. Everything is new, everything gives us more. Learning is highly meaningful for a number of reasons: because it's interesting, because it relates to some immediate goal, because it is rewarded, because it helps us to model someone who is important to us, because it will give us more autonomy, power or means of self-expression – and because we're curious and just want to know.

All these reasons give us important incentives to learn fast and learn well. In NLP terms, these are toward motivations. The process of learning is something the learner actively wants to do.

> **TIP** Make sure you are motivated – have a good reason for anything you want to learn, and know what it is.

The learner is very focused in the here-and-now

Very small children pay a lot of attention to what is going on around them and what they're doing. They're not thinking about how today compares with yesterday. Those concepts – and the concerns they can bring with them – come later. They're not running multiple scenarios – and thus they're not distracting themselves. They can, and do, get distracted, but then they're totally immersed in the distraction! Attention is 100 per cent.

> **TIP** Catch wandering thoughts. It may help to write down things that require action later, so that you don't have to carry them alongside what you're currently doing. Having done so, bring yourself back to the here-and-now.

The learner is totally immersed in their experience

At this stage, learning is done in a highly associated state which produces high neurological and physiological engagement and enables the learner to make huge strides very rapidly.

> **TIP** Choose your timing, and your setting, and your state to give yourself the best chance of becoming immersed. Cultivate the art of being fully associated in your experience. Start learning by doing. (See page **26** for more on association.)

All the learner's senses are involved in their learning

Children don't think about how they learn, or should learn. All their senses are on-line to pick up and process information. This means that what they are learning can be encoded in multiple ways, making it more rapidly and effectively part of them.

> **TIP** Engage more of your senses in the act of consciously learning. Always consider how you can render even formal learning visual, auditory and kinesthetic. For instance, you could make notes, construct models and literally walk things through (kinesthetic), create mind-maps and use coloured pens (visual), or play music by Baroque composers such as Bach or Vivaldi, which has been shown to enhance concentration and learning (auditory).

The learner's efforts are frequently praised or rewarded

Very little children usually get plenty of praise for trying to do things, as well as for actually achieving them. Even if there comes a time when the grown-ups start to take their skills for granted, there has usually been a good grounding of positive encouragement for first efforts at sitting, crawling, standing, talking, and walking. With luck, a foundation has been laid, which can become the basis of self-encouragement in their willingness to take on the risk of trying new things.

> **TIP** Find ways to praise and reward yourself. Use encouraging internal dialogue. Break your goal down into stages and give yourself treats for accomplishing each stage.

Thinking in terms of success and failure

The learner hasn't yet learnt to think in terms of 'success' and 'failure' – so they aren't easily daunted when something doesn't work out. In fact, being frustrated is more likely to make them want to try again.

Very small children mostly don't get labelled as failures when they try something that doesn't work. Children's first words, or first steps, are too exciting and too major for most adults to discount them as not good enough. A new walker who falls is likely to be encouraged to try again.

> **TIP** Be kind about your mistakes and limitations. People who endlessly criticise themselves tend to become disheartened. Those who forgive errors and lapses make better progress.

The learner paces himself or herself

When they lose interest, or get tired, they simply switch to something else or fall asleep. They haven't yet learnt to override their instinctive awareness of their own states, to pressure themselves unduly or to make unreasonable demands of themselves.

> **TIP** Pace yourself – don't drive yourself too hard. Even when you're doing well – perhaps especially when you're doing well – have a break. And don't move the goalposts because you achieved something sooner or more easily than you expected.

Processing what's been learned

The learner sleeps long and deep, which gives the unconscious mind time to process what's been learnt, and the body time to recover from exertion and build its strength.

Sleep is a major ingredient in successful learning. It allows the body to rest and repair itself after exertion. Mental exertion requires energy and stamina, so any kind of learning is potentially tiring. Learning is processed and stored unconsciously – which is why we relatively soon forget the actual processes that are involved in even complex skills like walking, talking or reading. And sleep is a time when the unconscious part of the mind is very active in processing new material and making connections.

> **TIP** Respect your body's need for rest. Give yourself enough sleep time to process what you've learnt.

So now we've seen the criteria for fast learning. But as we continue our exploration of it, it's crucial to understand that it's not just about learning new, very clever techniques. Becoming a good learner again is often primarily about clearing away the patterns you have learnt to be limited by, and putting the original incentives and conditions back in place. Instead of jamming your foot on the accelerator, try taking your foot off the brake first.

▪ *Factors that Inhibit Learning*

In our experience as coaches, there are some things which commonly inhibit effective learning. We've listed some of them, but see if there are others you think are particularly relevant for you. Having identified which apply most, you'll be ready to start turning things around.

- Loss of full attention

- Lack of rewards

- Lack of incentives

- Experiences of failure

- Adverse judgements by others or by self

- Diminished self-confidence

- Fear – for instance of making mistakes or being wrong

- Self-limiting decisions

- Critical internal dialogue

- Perfectionism.

▪ *Turning Things Around*

Now that you've started to identify which factors have inhibited your learning, see if you remember any specific events which seem particularly significant. NLP has shown how powerful such 'one-trial learning' can be, and it also offers a number of great ways to change what was learnt in this rapid way. Many of these advanced techniques are best done with the help of an experienced NLP coach or practitioner, but there are also many effective NLP ways of helping yourself:

▸ Reframe any negative experience as learning – and ask yourself what is the positive learning gain you could get from it.

▸ Become aware of what's going on in your internal dialogue – and make it less critical or more encouraging.

▸ Separate what you do from who you are – so that you don't confuse behaviour or capability issues with your identity.

▸ Recall childhood learning problems with this in mind – so you can update and 'edit' any inappropriate voice-overs you may have recorded.

▸ Give yourself permission to make mistakes – and then ask yourself what you have learnt through making them. Break down learning goals into smaller, manageable, achievable chunks – and then focus your attention on one chunk at a time.

▶ Take the pressure off – give yourself enough time to learn. Alternatively, give yourself such a short time-frame that you can't do it in the usual way. You can improve your reading speed, for example, by deliberately scanning the written page too fast to get the sense. Do this for a minute or two and you'll find, when you go back to reading for meaning again, that you're reading faster. You've adjusted your basic and familiar speed.

▶ Keep some of your learning targets secret from others – so that nothing rests on how much progress you are making.

▶ Engage as many of your senses as possible when you are learning – so you encode your learning vibrantly. Can you see it, say it, do it? Be really inventive.

▶ Teach someone else what you have learnt – then you'll know how much you've really understood it.

▶ Imagine situations in which this learning will serve you in the future – so you're already prepared to activate this new potential.

▶ Finally, ask yourself what will be good enough, rather than perfect, when you are learning something, and make learning fun.

The better you are at learning, the more choices you have about what you can learn and how you can learn it. As a young journalist, the writer Arthur Ransome was sent to Russia by his newspaper to report on the Russian Revolution. He needed to learn how to speak Russian so that he could gather information from the people actually involved in events, so he went and bought as many children's books in the language as he could. He knew that the vocabulary would be relatively restricted, and the grammar clear. An interest in the stories would also make him want to read on and find out what happened next. He found this process so successful that he not only became a fluent Russian speaker – and married Lenin's secretary – but used the same method later to help him learn other languages.

Being an effective learner is vital if you want to be an effective leader. The better you are at learning the better you'll be able to teach and empower others, whatever their age. We know a great leader who happens to be a pre-school teacher. She's often involved in helping the children with tasks like putting on their jumpers or tying their shoelaces. She found that they learnt best if she chunked the process down for them: so to start with, she would put their arms into the jumper and pull it over their head. All they had to do was pull it down and straighten it. When they could do that easily, she taught them to put their arms into the jumper and their head through the neck-hole while she held the jumper for them. Finally, they learnt to get the jumper gathered up and ready themselves. When doing shoelaces, they progressed from learning the final tying of the two loops, to making the loops, to crossing the laces and pulling one through the other. By reversing the stages in each of these processes she'd chunked the learning so the children could concentrate on one thing at a time. This way they naturally mastered the skill and made it their own.

▪ *Learning and States*

Because of the complex interaction between body and mind, many processes may be involved in learning. If we learn something, what we store in memory will involve not just the 'content' but also our state when we learnt it (see page **77**). Learning, in other words, is state-dependent – helped or hindered by the state we are in when we're learning.

How does this work? Your experiences at school, for instance, could colour how you feel when you are in a formal learning situation as an adult. If you felt anxious about mathematics, you may well find that the thought of learning mathematics even as an adult brings up similar feelings.

NLP gives us the means of becoming aware of our states, and of changing them where they are limiting or unhelpful. It shows us that effective learning is about having an effective relationship between three things:

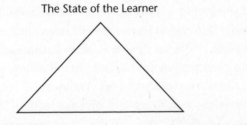

The State of the Learner

The Content Learnt   Strategies for Learning

Of these, the content is in a way the least important element! If you're not in the right state, it becomes harder to use even the best strategies. If you are in the right state – as you were in the earliest years of your life, where your attention was engaged, you were not worried about success or failure, and where you were prepared to be curious and try things out – and if you know or are shown the most effective strategies for this particular kind of learning, then you will learn easily.

▶ To accelerate your learning, think of three times when you learnt something easily. Describe your state in each as fully as you can. (Include mental experiences and thoughts, physiology and physical setting, feelings and emotions.) What do all these have in common?

▶ Think of a time when you had difficulties learning something. Describe that state.

▶ Use contrastive analysis (see page 35) to find the differences between the times it was easy and the times it was hard. Find the differences that make all the difference. In this way, you are pinpointing the key to learning easily and rapidly for you.

▶ Make sure you create these conditions the next time you want to learn something.

▪ *What If...*

Here are three 'What if' scenarios we've encountered, each of which will give you another take on accelerating your learning.

1. But what if I'm a slow learner?

A colleague of ours coached a policeman, Dave, who wanted help in learning the wording of laws and legal cautions he needed to know to pass his exams. He had to learn the exact words, not just remember the general gist. He had a lot of this kind of information to learn, but he was finding it almost impossible and described himself as a 'poor learner'. But he did have a really important motivation: learning the words was part of being a policeman – and he really did want to be one. Fortunately, Dave's NLP coach helped him find out just how he had come to think of himself as such a poor learner at school. In the process Dave remembered how easily and comprehensively he had learnt the entire history of his favourite football team at much the same age outside of school. He'd had all the facts and figures at his fingertips, and, more importantly, he knew all the rules. For Dave, it was a revelation to realise that he knew how to learn this kind of information. 'Maybe I wasn't so stupid after all,' was his comment. Reconnecting with that younger self, who had been a truly excellent learner of exactly the kind of detailed, procedural information that he needed to learn now, was an important step in restoring his confidence and allowing him to learn what he needed for his job.

2. 'What if I have to learn something, and I don't want to?'

It's always worth respecting difficulties you have and asking yourself if you really want to do this learning, or if you just think you should, or if someone else thinks you should. In our experience, people do best what is meaningful for them. Sometimes asking 'Do I really want to do this?' will bring you a clear 'No'. Ask yourself, then, what says you have to. If you find a reason that's valid in terms of some other goal or value you have, that will help to restore a sense of ownership and purpose. But if there doesn't seem to be a reason that has meaning to you at a core level, try giving yourself permission to opt out. If you find this difficult, pay particular attention to the feelings, or the reasons, that come up. They will give you good information, and help you become clear about what the difficulties really are: 'I have to do it: it's part of my job.' So do you *have* to do this job? Is this the only place that will ever employ you? Or are you willing to do this unwelcome task because of the other aspects of this job? You choose.

3. What if it's still hard?

A very successful businessman we know took up running to keep fit. He enjoyed this, but it didn't seem enough. He had always liked cycling, and was a fair swimmer. He decided he'd try training for the triathlon. He found it really difficult physically, and it was hard to drag himself away from work or his family to put in the training. Yet he went on doing it. When a friend asked him why on earth he bothered – wouldn't just jogging be enough? – he replied: 'I do it because it's the only thing in my life I find really challenging.'

How to Improve Your Memory

- 'I don't have a good memory.'

- 'That's too much for me to remember.'

- 'I'm afraid my memory is failing now that I'm getting older.'

These are beliefs but too often people say them as if they were facts. There are some very common misconceptions about memory: that it's an ability that can't be changed; that you only have a certain amount; that it relates to age, and declines as we get older.

Memory isn't about volume and it isn't about content, it's about processes. It's about something we *do*, not something we *have*: it's about remembering.

Remembering is dependent on the connections we make between things. Imagine you're constructing an index. If you have referred to a book, or a person, by only one attribute, you'll have only one data point, and hence only one way of accessing that information. If you have used a number of different data points, each capturing a different aspect, you'll have more ways to access this information.

As coaches, we've found that you can achieve enormous improvements by focusing on two particular aspects of memory: encoding and storage on the one hand and recall on the other.

▪ *Encoding and Storage*

If you want to improve your ability to encode accurately and store information, you'll need to check out:

- Your attitudes, beliefs and feelings.

- How much attention you pay to the information you want to store.

- How your senses are involved in processing the information.

Attitudes, beliefs and feelings

John was an in-house business trainer who used to be good at remembering names. Over the past couple of years he'd come to resent an increasing workload and an ever-growing number of delegates. One day he was heard to say to a colleague: 'There's no way I'm going to be able to remember the names of all these delegates.' John's feelings of disappointment and resentment were affecting his beliefs about how much he could remember – yet within his area of expertise he was quite capable of remembering vast bodies of information and new research. He didn't actually want to remember the names of all the delegates, because in his view there were too many of them. Not surprisingly, he did find it difficult, though many years ago he had made it a matter of pride to learn all their names. But he had felt differently then.

> **TIP** Consider how you think and feel about what it is you want to remember.

Feelings can affect encoding and storage in other ways, too. Do you remember your first day at school? Many people do, often in considerable detail. But what about the second day? Probably not. The reason for this is that day one at school is a special day: you may have looked forward to it, or dreaded it; you may have had a wonderful – or an awful – time. The teacher may have been really kind – or expected you to be able to do things you hadn't yet learnt. The playground may have been a great place to run around in – or a terrifying space where giants a whole year older than you rushed past you and around you, yelling loudly and playing boisterously. There may have been a lot of feeling – and strong feelings can make for vivid encoding.

> **TIP** Engage your feelings to make what you want to remember vivid.

Some feelings are best forgotten, though, and your brain can do this too. If someone has a car accident or other major trauma, they may well edit the memory of it or even have amnesia. Sometimes phobias that started with a traumatic event in childhood get buried in the same way: a person may be left with a terror of certain situations without even knowing why. The brain has stored the information, but in a secret rather than an open file. NLP has ways of working with these secret files but it's wise to get expert help. However, where you sense that ordinary forgetting relates to milder feelings, there are some good NLP ways you can retrieve that information.

Routes to lost information

1. One good way to recover information is to recall the circumstances in which you first gained it. Maybe it was the name of someone at a party? or something you heard on the radio? Remind yourself of as many details as you can of that party, involving information from all sensory systems. Who did you talk to? Where were you sitting, or standing? What music was playing? and so on. As you fill in the context, you may find the detail you want pops up – or that search processes are triggered so that it pops up later.

2. Are you forgetting because you felt uncomfortable, uneasy or unhappy about something? If you need or wish to recover the information, pay attention to your feelings in the here-and-now and imagine they are like beads on a string. Very similar to the other times you've felt the same, feeling like this now is linked to all the other times and because the mind stores like things together, your attentiveness to these feelings now can lead you back along the string to the time and circumstances you forgot.

Paying attention

How much attention do you pay to the information you want to store? One of the most striking things about people who claim their memory is not very good is how good they are at remembering poorly! Suppose you're introduced to someone but as you're told their name you're preoccupied. When later you try to remember their name all you can recall is what was bothering you then and what they looked like. In such circumstances there's nothing wrong with your memory. Your way of remembering – the process of encoding that you employed – has faithfully encoded exactly what was going on. You were preoccupied and this meant you had your own internal dialogue running. So any additional auditory input – like the person's name – would be competing with your internally generated auditory signal. What they looked like is more memorable partly because visual data is generally easier to recall – it's more vivid – but also because that element was less cluttered with internal signals at that moment.

What you attend to will affect what you actually commit to memory. So often, poor encoding is confused with poor memory.

Harry was often in trouble with his wife Susan because he didn't seem to remember things she had told him, or things she had asked him to do. He would forget to buy the odd bits of shopping on the way home from work; he would forget the arrangements for the weekend she had carefully explained to him. She got cross with him, and he got angry and defensive. They both began to wonder what was going on. Sometimes Susan felt he forgot because he wasn't as interested in her, or their life at home, as he was in his work: he really enjoyed his job as an engineer and always seemed to remember things about colleagues and projects, however trivial. One day it all blew up and Susan accused him of not caring enough. After their anger was spent, Harry admitted that he was upset too: he said he was worried about what was happening to his mind. Susan pointed out that it couldn't be his mind, because he did remember some things well: it must be something about how he was doing, or not doing, the remembering. Thinking about this, Harry pointed out that she usually told him things when they were involved in doing something together, such as washing up, or when the television advertisements were on. She told him things when they occurred to her – but it hadn't occurred to her to check whether Harry was really fully attentive. They realised that he didn't actually forget the information, because it had never been encoded properly in the first place. After this, Susan made sure that she had his full attention when she told him something she wanted him to remember: sometimes they laughed and made quite a joke about it. And he stopped 'forgetting'.

Internal processing

Encoding information means processing it internally; and internal processing involves your representational systems or senses. A number of things emerge from this:

1. We tend to find it easier to remember using certain preferred representational systems. So if you are strongly visual, make sure when you are being introduced to someone new that you take a mental picture of their face – and perhaps see their name on their forehead, or like a

badge or necklace close to their face. If you know you find it easy to remember sounds, hear the sound of them saying their name and make sure you record it internally alongside their image, so that when you next see them the visual image calls up the sound of the name. Looking in the appropriate direction to access the representational system you want to store the information in will help ensure you store the information in the most appropriate way (see the description of eye-accessing cues, page **43**).

2. The more representational systems are involved, the richer your internal representation and the storage will be. You can do this deliberately to help with encoding. Involve as many of your senses as possible, in order to make a memory really rich and retrievable by multiple routes. (Anything memorable about the temperature, moisture and pressure of their handshake, for instance?)

3. Some things are best encoded using particular representational systems, which means attending in that system before attempting to encode anything. Consistently good spelling in English, for example, depends on visual processing. NLP investigated what good spellers did, and found that they all take and store mental 'pictures' of how words look. When they need to spell the word, they refer to that internal picture to get the right spelling. The NLP spelling strategy is based on this, and is used successfully to teach people who wish to improve their spelling. Like many of the tools we've alluded to, you could learn this on an NLP practitioner training course (see NLP Training Courses, page **353**).

People who are good at physical skills will tend to store information about them kinesthetically, and they may not be able to explain what they do in words. We know someone who is good at carpentry. When asked by his friend to explain how to use a lathe, he found that he was quite unable to explain – or even to remember how he did it. He had to sit down at the machine and actually work with it himself: his hands knew what to do.

You can develop a facility with any representational system if you practise. This can seem remarkable to others who have not bothered to do so. And this is true of entire cultures as well. Any culture reliant on oral transmission, for instance, will have highly developed auditory memory strategies such as rhythm, rhyme and mnemonics. So while it seems amazing to us, it was perfectly natural in ancient Greece for epic poems – thousands of lines long – to be committed to memory and accurately recited. Such skills still exist in parts of Africa where literacy and computer ownership are low, and also in India.

Conversely, imagine how strange it would be trying to learn a dance by reading a book about it, or learning to sing by looking at pictures of people singing. You need the right tool for the job. So check if you have the right representational system alerted for what you want to learn.

Exploring your memory

► Get really curious about your memory. What do you find easy to remember? What do you tend to forget? Do your own patterns tell you anything about what's important to you and what is less so? or what kinds of representation come most naturally and you store most easily? or where your self-limiting beliefs are?

► Find out how you go about remembering. Do you: make pictures of the information? tell yourself stories? hear someone telling you? try it on and experience? like to get your hands dirty?

► What has to happen for you to forget something? Does your mind 'just go blank'? Do you steer away from something and find yourself thinking of something else? Do you say to yourself, 'I mustn't forget this' – in which case your wording itself is directing your attention to forgetting rather than remembering!

► How do your remembering and forgetting relate to your interest in the information and your feelings about it?

► What kinds of things do you have a 'poor memory' for, and why?

► Do you have a good memory for things you'd rather not? We knew someone who easily remembered everything that went wrong, and every time he was slighted by others. If you do, how are you encoding these experiences? Are you replaying a video? listening to a tape? feeling the feelings? Use the information on sub-modalities on page **80** to pinpoint how you're doing this. You can then recode the experiences using different sub-modalities that make them less powerful. But you will also now know which sub-modalities have worked so effectively to ensure you remembered what you didn't want to. Just start using these to remember what's worth remembering from now on.

▪ *Retrieval*

There are numerous books on improving your memory, which give you standard tips. Rather than regurgitate all of these, we want to flag up how some of these devices actually work so that you can construct your own.

Encoding and retrieval are closely linked. Bruce Chatwin recounts a really good example of how the two processes interact in his book *The Songlines*. Visiting Australia, Chatwin learnt how the Aboriginal culture and history was encoded and passed on through songs that related to invisible paths winding across the land – the Songlines. So the land itself and all its natural features, every hump and hillock, encoded the stories of the ancient Dreamtime from generation to generation.

The Aborigines sing their Songlines as a series of couplets that match the length of time it takes to walk a particular stretch of land. So the land and song are one. In fact, according to Chatwin, they believe that they are singing the land into existence as they walk over it, in a wondrous mixture of geography and mythology. Each tribe has its own territory and Songline, and each knows about the history of its neighbour because of the way their Songlines interlink.

While travelling in the back country, Chatwin gave a lift to a man called Limpy, who wanted to visit a place he had never been to, which was of immense importance on his Songline. After seven hours' driving, and about ten miles away from the valley, Limpy began muttering and gesticulating rapidly as he stared out of the window. He had begun to recognise places he had only previously heard about, and he was singing the Songline to himself. But he was forced to do this in great haste because of the speed of the car: the Songline he knew went at walking speed.

The Songline had been encoded through singing and walking through a landscape with close attention to detail, and in a linear sequence. Every note of the melody was linked to a feature of the landscape, and this made remembering the Songline – and passing it to all tribe members and down the generations – much easier.

When the car journey intersected with the Songline, Limpy's memory of the whole Songline was triggered, but where the man-made road deviated from the Songline Limpy 'switched off' and only resumed the experience when the road met the line again.

A somewhat similar process was used by Roman orators when they memorised complex speeches. They would mentally link each heading of their speech in its correct sequence with the features of another sequence they already knew well – such as the 'landmarks' of a particular building or route. By linking the sequencing of the newly created speech to a sequence they already knew, they 'highjacked' an existing memory to help them remember the new speech.

If you want to use this pattern to help you remember a story, or a presentation, think of a route you know really well. Take yourself along it in your mind, stopping at each major landmark and finding ways to link the sequence of the headings in your story or presentation with the sequence of landmarks. Inventing links will help you create the links you need, and the more ridiculous or vivid the links the easier you'll find them to remember.

The importance of sequence

Sequencing and other forms of categorisation are important features of good memory, because they act as ways of linking and ordering information; and both storage and retrieval depend upon the brain's ability to categorise efficiently. It's easier to store information if it has an appropriate place to go to, and easier to find it if you know where you put it.

We have more than one system we can use: the conscious mind makes use of rational and logical categories, while the associative part of the mind makes use of similarities and links of other kinds. This is how mnemonics work. *Shall Mother Have Egg Omelette*, for instance, is one way of remembering the order of North America's Great Lakes (Superior, Michigan, Huron, Erie, Ontario). Another mnemonic, *Richard of York Gave Battle in Vain*, gives you the sequence of colours in the rainbow. Would it be useful to invent a mnemonic for a sequence you want to remember?

Linking, of one sense with another, of one idea with another, of the known with the unknown or the imagined, is the stuff of memory. When we want to remember something, links are the key to filing it; and when we want to find the memory again, they are the key to retrieval. Telling ourselves a story is one way of encoding substantial amounts of information.

Choosing the triggers

Finally, we need triggers that will help us reawaken the meaning when we need it. Icons on the computer, thought-maps and colour-coding, words or names that stand for whole stories, are all ways to do this. If we say the name 'Cinderella' it brings a story, a set of ideas, feelings and events to mind. We can have triggers in any of our senses. Red, amber and green are triggers on the road. Black and yellow – as used to denote something being radioactive – are common triggers for an awareness of danger. The oscillation between a high and a low tone on a siren tells us one of the emergency services is close by. NLP calls this process of linking a particular stimulus with a set of information and feelings 'anchoring' (see page 24). If we want to be able to access information, or a particular state, using an anchor is an elegant and effective way. For Limpy and his fellow tribesmen, every feature of the landscape was an anchor for their history and their identity.

► Think of some anchors you have for particular memories or states. Songs, smells, colours and places can all act as anchors.

► Think of something you remember easily. What are the anchors you use?

► So how can you apply this skill you already have to what you want to remember?

Improving your memory actually consists of two processes: finding effective ways to encode the information you want, and effective ways to retrieve it. NLP offers us many different ways to make both more effective, and many ways in which each one of us can ensure that our memory is tailor-made for our needs.

However, you do need to get out there and work at it. Improving your memory is just like building a muscle. You have to consistently engage in the activity. If you do, you can dramatically improve your memory and old age will have little or no effect. If you don't, well, memory is a prime example of what you don't use, you lose.

So here are a few suggestions to help you build your sensory acuity and so encode effectively. In all three cases you will be concentrating on a particular way of processing and recalling experience. To become equally adept in all three systems – V, A and K – you will need to practise.

EXERCISE

To improve your visual memory:

▶ Look at a group of objects, say on a mantelpiece, take a mental snapshot of them, then close your eyes and see what you recall in your mind's eye. Open your eyes, look again, close your eyes and see again in your mind's eye – only in more detail. Using the visual sub-modalities (see page 80), notice which ones you got and which you need to begin paying more attention to.

To improve your auditory memory:

▶ Listen to a song you like and hear it in your head. Notice what you remember. Then listen again and hear more. Hear it in your head then hum it out loud. Repeat often. Use the sub-modalities checklist to help you distinguish which auditory elements you need to attend to in particular.

To improve your kinesthetic memory:

▶ Think of a physical activity you'd like to learn. Suppose it was a particular dance step. Find a teacher and imitate them. Learn the steps in manageable chunks and keep repeating till you have this learning 'in the muscle'. Now do this again with another physical activity. If you keep expanding your repertoire, you'll find you won't just get good at remembering a particular step, you'll become much more proficient at remembering whole routines.

Creativity, learning, memory: you've now seen that boosting brain power is really child's play! Building a better brain is, however, one of the best steps you can take on the road to success, as it lies at the root of pretty much everything we cover in this book.

CHAPTER 15

Health, Wealth and Happiness

FOR MOST PEOPLE, health, wealth and happiness are synonymous with the good life. They may sometimes arrive unbidden, but they can also be created, conserved or lost because of the way you think and what you do. NLP gives us ways to find out how people who are healthy, wealthy and happy actively create and manage their 'good fortune'. It has identified a number of key behaviours and attitudes, which we're going to explore in this chapter. Putting these into practice in your life is something you can learn.

The Value of Conserving

Each of these three magical ingredients involves a fundamental human skill – the skill of conserving. We particularly like the definition of conserving to be found in an old 1956 edition of *Webster's New Collegiate Dictionary*. To conserve is 'to keep in a safe or sound state'.

Conserving something is not the same as preserving it. There are some important differences.

Preserving	Conserving
maintains the status quo	encourages and promotes growth
limits new input	allows new input
holds things at a single point in time	is an ongoing process

Conserving is an active process, in which we attend to what we value. It's not about mindlessly holding on and hoarding. In terms of health, it involves nurturing of all kinds – but it doesn't mean you have to live cocooned in cotton-wool. In terms of money, it means regular saving and the management of resources, but it doesn't mean you have to be mean or deny yourself. In terms of happiness, it means noticing small things, taking pleasure in them, revisiting them and cherishing them. Happy people don't fool themselves and pretend that everything is rosy: they just make sure they don't miss anything which can be enjoyed or which will enrich them in some way.

Conserving involves choice – the choice to engage in actively promoting things you value. It starts from who you are (your identity) and what's important to you (your beliefs and values). Conserving draws on your knowledge and skills (your capabilities), and it involves your choosing to do certain things and not others (your behaviour, extending into your environment). Since it involves so many levels of your existence, conserving is one of the key ways in which you can connect your experience into a meaningful whole.

We want to look at how two very different people approached health, wealth and happiness in their lives. By examining the two, we can tease out some of the important differences between a conserving approach and a preserving one.

Brian was the eldest son of an old country family. Once upon a time the family had been quite wealthy. Now they were struggling to maintain an estate. He was brought up to value hard work, and to help on his father's land. Most of the family money was tied up in the estate. They were asset-rich and cash-poor. Brian went to university and did a degree in estate management. He wanted to learn the skills he would need when it was his turn to take on the management of the farm.

When he was in his mid-twenties, his father died suddenly and Brian had to take over much earlier than he had expected. Rather to his surprise, he found he had learnt as many of the skills he needed through his childhood experience as he had through college. He knew about enjoying everyday life in the countryside. He could fix and mend. He could sow and reap and plough if he needed to. When he inspected the estate equipment, he found that though much of it was old, it had been taken care of and was still in good working order. Though Brian had enjoyed being a student, and had expected to work for other landowners for some years to learn the job, he felt confident that with the support of his workers and his family he would be able to manage well. Brian had learnt the secrets of conserving without even realising it. He was healthy, and his choice to take a physically active role on his estate meant that he would go on being so; he was wealthy, not in ready cash but in owning land which he intended to nurture and hand on to his children and his children's children; and he was happy in a lifestyle he enjoyed, in the teamwork of his estate workers and in the support of his family. In one sense, Brian might seem to have 'had it made'. But he also inherited things that were much more valuable: beliefs, values, skills and behaviours which, unthinkingly absorbed during his childhood, gave him what was needed to conserve and to enjoy his inheritance.

Monica was an ambitious and successful businesswoman. She had worked her way up from sales girl to manager to boss, starting her own company when she was only twenty-five. The company flourished. Monica did not enjoy running it all that much, though she was good at it; but she made a lot of money fast, sold out and invested wisely. (She was far more wealthy than Brian.) She knew she would never need to work again. Her investments succeeded in turn; but somehow Monica never felt confident that she had enough security, so she only spent what she needed to have a comfortable house and reliable car. She did not take much time off or have exotic foreign holidays, and she kept herself to herself because she just didn't know if people liked her or her money. She didn't know what she really wanted out of life. Monica found her success hollow, because she only knew how to preserve what she had. She hoarded it and was afraid to use it. But she was trapped because she dared not take risks or try anything new. She worked long hours, first of all in the business and later in keeping track of and managing her investments, and she took little exercise. In preserving her fortune, she was in danger of eroding her health. In a nutshell, she didn't know how to be happy.

It could be said that Brian had an advantage because he had inherited his position; but in our view this is to miss the point. People with inherited wealth can hoard it as Monica did, just as people who make wealth can conserve it like Brian. Where Brian may indeed have been 'lucky' was not in the inheritance itself, but in the attitudes and ways of managing which he learnt from his family as he grew up.

We have found as coaches that being healthy, wealthy and happy is about managing your life in the present so that it is enjoyable now and at the same time helps relate to the future you want. This means taking good care of you and your assets now and for your future. Your assets are not just financial – your health and your state of mind are far more important: ask anyone who's chronically ill or suicidal. It means using these assets – but not using them up. It means nurturing them so that they grow but not putting off life for some supposedly better future. It means knowing what you've got, and keeping track of how you're doing – and then just getting on with your life. It means asking yourself questions like 'What do I really want?'

In the four sections that follow, we're going to look more closely at what's involved in being healthy, wealthy and happy, and how NLP can help. You might find it helpful to take stock at this point, and ask yourself what exactly these things mean as far as you are concerned.

▪ *How You See Health, Wealth and Happiness*

We find it really useful to get clear with a client what it means to be healthy, wealthy and happy as far as they are concerned, because people have very different takes on this and we want to establish a baseline that fits. So take a moment to consider the questions that follow.

What do you think of as health?

▸ Does it just mean you are rarely ill?

▸ Does it mean you can run for a taxi without puffing?

▸ Does it mean you work out at the gym three times a week?

▸ Does it mean you never get a cold? Or that, if you do, it only lasts you a couple of days instead of a week?

▸ How do you know when you are healthy? What do behaviour or feelings tell you? Does your skin look clear and fresh? Is your tongue pink instead of furred and white? Is your digestion regular and trouble-free? Do you feel lively and active? What is your evidence procedure?

▸ What tells you when you are *not*? Do you feel sluggish, or depressed? Do you find even small tasks an effort? Is this the second – or third – time you've had a recurrence of flu this winter? Are your joints stiff? Do you forget even the simplest thing? What is your evidence procedure?

▶ Do you know if your current behaviour is making you healthy?

What do you think of as wealth?

▶ Does it mean you have thousands invested?

▶ Does it mean you have a hundred or two spare at the end of the month?

▶ Does it mean you can easily afford a holiday when you want one?

▶ Does it mean you never have to wait weeks or months before you can afford to buy something?

▶ Would you say you are wealthy? If yes, how do you know you are wealthy? Did you make it, inherit it, save it, or invest wisely?

▶ If not, how would you know if you were wealthy? How attainable does it feel?

▶ Do you believe that you'll always have to scrimp and save? Are you just waiting to win the lottery?

▶ Do you know if your current behaviour is building your wealth?

Do you think of yourself as a happy person?

▶ What does it mean to you to be happy? Is it feeling good when you wake up in the morning? Is it remembering specific events, or people, or having something to look forward to? Can you feel happy if you are alone?

▶ Does it mean having a clear sense of how the present relates to your future hopes and intentions? When you sit down at the end of today, will you be able to identify anything you've done that has made your dreams and goals a little closer? Or will they just seem as unattainable as ever?

▶ Do you feel happy most of the time? some of the time? rarely? hardly ever?

▶ What lets you know you are happy – or indeed unhappy?

▶ Do you know if your current behaviour is making you happy?

Jot your answers down, so that you have a benchmark to refer back to later.

Being healthy, wealthy and happy takes skill – and skill is something you can always learn, once you know what's involved.

▪ *Stocktake of Your Meta Programmes*

At this point it can also be very helpful to remind yourself of your own meta programme preferences. If you wrote these down, look at the personal profile you built before. If not, you could refer to page **54** in Chapter 3 and build your profile now. Knowing your own meta programme profile will help you conserve your health, wealth and happiness, and avoid the pitfalls inherent in some of your habitual ways of going about things.

Each type of meta programme has its strengths and weaknesses. The trick of managing them is, first, to become aware of how you tend to operate, and then to monitor what's happening to make the most of what your style achieves for you while limiting the extent of its liabilities. Once you know what your meta programme preferences are, you can do a number of things that will help you cover the gaps.

Some meta programmes are particularly relevant to conserving. Let's look at the implications they have.

Away-from and towards

If you want to achieve something – in this case, conserving health, wealth and happiness – it's really important to know what kinds of things motivate you. You may, like Monica, have an away-from motivation: you may be very aware of what you don't want. You know that you don't want to be poor, or ill, or miserable. There are quite a lot of useful things you can achieve by this away-from motivation, and the stronger the internal representations of what you don't want, the more powerful such a motivation can be. Monica knew she didn't want to be poor in her old age; she could clearly imagine what that might be like; and this was what motivated her to save, to take out insurance policies and to make sensible investments. Another away-from response would be to use a powerful sense of what it could be like to be weak, infirm or progressively disabled in old age to ensure that you eat sensibly and take regular exercise now.

One obvious limitation of an away-from motivation such as this is that it keeps you focused on what you don't want – fearful or unpleasant experiences. Its other major limitation is that you don't necessarily know what you *do* want, so you can't easily aim for it. Monica was so insistent on gaining and saving that she curtailed her enjoyment of the present, and didn't ask herself what she was saving *for*. So she never knew how much money, or what kind of pension plans, would be enough. She couldn't rest – and she couldn't enjoy the present.

Brian, on the other hand, had more of a towards motivation: he knew what he wanted, both in the present and for the future. He had been brought up to think long-term about the family estate, but he had also learnt to enjoy things in the present. But it wasn't all towards: he had learnt to take care of buildings and machines before they broke down because he knew running things into the ground would be much more expensive, and that's something he didn't want. Likewise, he took care of his workforce partly because he didn't want them to become unhappy and leave him for easier work and better pay. Brian's actions were grounded on the strengths of both towards and away-from meta programmes.

> **TIP** Think how this meta programme applies to something you want to conserve in the area of health, wealth and happiness. In this particular instance, is your natural motivation away-from or towards? Now think how the opposite motivation might help you. Identifying the strengths in both approaches not only gives you more ideas, but also helps you build your flexibility and versatility.

Necessity and possibility motivation

People motivated primarily by necessity will tend to have a strong sense of what they 'ought' to do. They may keep up-to-date with the latest information about what is 'good for them' in terms of exercise and diet; they may be regular and prudent savers. Their form of happiness could derive in part from knowing that they have done 'what needs to be done'.

People motivated by possibility may have a more exciting time, in that they can be good at impromptu fun, seeing options and seizing opportunities; but they may find it harder to remember and carry out the small, regular tasks which conserve. They may get distracted and drift off course.

In different ways, both Brian and Monica were driven to an extent by necessity. However, Brian found it easier to respond to immediate possibilities because of his towards orientation. He was looking out for opportunities that enhanced his enjoyment of the present while also contributing to his long-term goals.

TIP Identify as many necessities and possibilities relating to your health, wealth and happiness as you can. Start a list, and add extra items as they occur to you over the next few days and weeks. What do you *have to* do? What *might* you do? Your aim is to enhance your current approach and to generate multiple approaches and solutions. Brainstorm them before evaluating them.

Small chunk and large chunk

If you're someone who tends to focus on detail – in NLP terms, you sort for small chunks of information – you run the risk of not seeing the wood for the trees because you may forget to check how these relate to your larger goals and longer time-frames. On the other hand, if you tend to go for the big picture and sort for large chunks of information, you can have the most wonderful goals around health, wealth and happiness but you may be less likely to do the little things which cumulatively will produce what you want. The trick is to be very clear how the small chunks relate to the big picture and your overall goals.

TIP If you start with the big picture – for example, 'I want to stay healthy' – ask yourself what specifically you can do today that will help you move in this direction. You could always have a glass of water handy on your desk, and sip it regularly. Do this throughout the day, every day, and you will be putting a health habit in place. Aim to drink at least two litres of water a day. If, on the other hand, you're a 'small chunk' person, and just feel good resting with your family at the end of the day, be sure to remind yourself that this here-and-now, everyday, undramatic time is the stuff of which happiness is made.

Start reinforcing the connection between your specific actions and your overall goals. For example, if you tend to chunk large, ask yourself what you can do today which will make a positive contribution to, say, your wealth. Pick an easily doable action. Do it, and remind yourself that as the title of Brooke M. Stephens' book says, *Wealth Happens One Day at a Time* (Harper Business, 1999). This small thing can be part of the larger achievement you are after. If you tend to chunk small, remind yourself that each monthly mortgage payment you make is helping you to make your home your own. You might want to find out just how much of it you now do 'own' and when the rest will really be yours. One client of Ian's who did this was astonished to find that if he increased his monthly payments slightly he could halve the time it would take.

In-time and through-time

Someone who is naturally in-time will find that the present is literally in the foreground of how they see things, and may block out the images they could have of the future. If they are strongly kinesthetic, as can be the case with in-time people, they may not be able to 'take a longer view' easily, or at all. So whatever grabs their attention here-and-now, whether it is good or bad, will tend to absorb them. In its more extreme form, impulse buying and having fun may consume money or time which could otherwise be used to create and conserve health, wealth and long-term happiness. Equally, they may find miseries, disappointments and failures overwhelming because they find it difficult or impossible to believe that 'this too will pass'. This makes for a real emotional roller-coaster. The art of being in-time is to enjoy the present, recognise and relish the richness it brings you, while developing your through-time skills to ensure you can plan the future and make it happen.

> Judith was very in-time. Her marriage was stormy and unsatisfactory. There were major rows, and often she felt put down, angry or frustrated. But after such a row, things tended to subside. When things went well again, Judith tended to forget how distressed she had been days, or even hours, before. So the determination she had felt so strongly while the row was going on, to change what was going on in her marriage, never got acted on. And so the years passed. Nothing changed, and nothing was learnt. But one day Judith decided enough was enough. That's when she got a coach.
>
> Charles, on the other hand, was a good planner. He ran his own successful business, and had no trouble taking a through-time overview of

how events in the past, present and future related to each other. He was quite successful, but he sought help from a coach because his girlfriend thought him at times 'sort of distant', and because he always felt slightly removed from things. He tended to spend so much time thinking that he felt he missed out on enjoying life.

Judith and Charles were both limited by their meta programmes, as their coaches helped them recognise. Judith learnt to ask herself some important questions which helped her assess the day's events from a more through-time perspective:

- How would I feel if this happened again tomorrow?

- What results would stack up over time if this went on happening?

- Is that what I want in my future?

- How could I respond differently the next time this occurs?

- How would that difference begin to stack up towards a different future?

- If I want something different, what do I need to do now?

Charles' NLP coach taught him how to pay more attention to what he was experiencing and feeling in the present, and to become aware of when he stepped out of what was going on. This had some interesting consequences, one of which was that he began to enjoy sex in a quite different way. Because he was more in his experience he felt much more present: 'Now I know what they mean when people talk about making love. It's better than sex.'

In business coaching we've sometimes been involved in working with teams to get the right meta programme balance so working relationships really work. Anthea and Paul's business was a particularly striking example of how getting the mix right can make the whole enterprise take off.

Anthea was a great planner. She had found an ideal job working for Paul, who was an inventor. He had patented a product and just received his first major order. In the pub one evening he realised that up to now he had been used to working alone on small orders: now, he would have to produce orders in a short time-frame. But he couldn't afford to neglect other projects he was beginning to develop, because he needed to build a rolling roster of work at different stages in order to keep orders and income flowing. Anthea offered to help him manage. She found it easy to take an overview of the different things that needed doing, and thought she would enjoy keeping Paul on track. And indeed theirs proved an ideal combination. Periodically they sat down together to plan goals and consider how Paul's work, and that of their newly appointed part-time staff, related to them. Anthea then took over daily review and management, and kept everyone to their schedule. She made sure Paul attended to current and future customers when necessary, and stopped him from becoming so immersed in his hands-on work that he neglected future developments. The business succeeded beyond their wildest dreams.

TIP Learn to organise your time-line both ways.

NLP discovered that people tend to experience time in a very spatial way, and this can help you find out where you are placed on this particular meta programme. The patterns we're describing are the most common versions, though there are many individual variations. As we discussed in Chapter 3, most in-time people tend to think of time as a line running from behind them (past) with their body in the present and the time line running out in front of them into the future. Most through-time people tend to experience time as a line in front of them running from left (past) to right (future). They can easily see it all, but they are a little removed from it. Once you are aware of how you naturally experience time, experiment with reorienting your natural time-line until it fits the other template. It may feel strange at first, and perhaps even a little uncomfortable. Spend a few moments or minutes discovering how different it is to have this orientation – and what it opens up for you. You don't have to leave it like that; but most people find it very valuable to turn their line around from time to time to assess a situation or experience things differently.

Other useful things you can do:

▶ You can begin to build in times to consider how your current situation relates to your goals, bearing in mind how your current meta programme preferences will be helpful or limit you. At first it will feel strange to operate in a way which may be unfamiliar; but as with all exercises, every time you do so you will be building your strength and enhancing your versatility.

▶ You can model people with different meta programmes and find out how they do it. This will be a good way of gaining operational detail to extend your own skills.

▶ Make a habit of asking yourself at regular intervals how what you are doing, thinking or feeling now relates to what you will be doing, thinking or feeling in the future.

▶ Identify some behaviours that will help you conserve your health, wealth and happiness. How can you make these habitual?

How to Take Care of Yourself

What makes you feel cared for? Most people, when they are asked this question, come up with an answer that involves someone else. One person said that it meant having someone cook for her. Another said it was having a massage. Someone else said it was having tea brought in bed. Perhaps these related to early memories: being fed, cuddled or wrapped in a warm towel after a bath.

Feeling cared for usually involves actions which let you know that you matter. Invariably, we assume that this means we're cared for by another, that we're special in their eyes. However, a question we often ask as coaches is: 'Do you feel cared for by yourself?' It's striking how often the answer is 'No'. Too often people are trying to get from others what they're not giving to themselves. When you start caring for yourself, though, it has a remarkable knock-on effect: others begin to follow your example and care for you too. It's as if you've just become credible: now you're willing to care for yourself, you're someone worth caring for. Truly, 'to them that hath shall be given and from them that hath not shall be taken away' (Matthew 25: 29).

So let's be clear that one of your most crucial caregivers needs to be yourself. Who else knows you so well, spends so much time with you – and also stands to benefit so much?

Some people find it hard to allow themselves to become a priority. But in our experience, if you don't take care of yourself you will eventually deplete the very resources you need to take care of anyone else. So even in terms of other people's needs, it doesn't make sense to put yourself last.

Giving yourself at least an equal amount of care often requires adjusting your beliefs and priorities. It may even impinge on your sense of who you are – your identity. If you think of yourself as a carer, whether professional or not, you may find it difficult to allow your own needs to come into the picture sufficiently.

Make a list of things that make you feel cared for. Now make a list of things you'd do if you were really caring for yourself. It's great having someone else care for you – but it's not enough. So when will you begin?

Taking care of yourself in a regular way that relates directly to your own feelings is much better value than taking care of yourself indirectly. In fact, if you can't, don't or won't do it directly you'll almost certainly find ways of doing it indirectly. This can snowball into results you'd never deliberately choose. Many 'unwanted' behaviours like smoking or overeating can easily become habits because they're quick-fix attempts to give yourself something. Ian was working with a woman who wanted to give up smoking so he asked her why she hadn't. She paused and then said: 'It's the one thing I do for me.'

Taking care of yourself is also an important anti-burnout measure. Otherwise caring for others can be a high-risk occupation. Many nurses and care-workers, for example, become overweight and unfit because they snatch edible treats in odd moments on long shifts and either find it difficult to plan in exercise or just feel too tired. Many doctors drink too much, or become so stressed that they break down or commit suicide. Watch the mothers waiting outside a primary school: how many look exhausted, dishevelled, weighed down? Look at the business people on the train or tube. How many look rested, cheerful, energetic?

But enough! There are simple, regular, easy ways to take care of yourself – provided that you make yourself a priority and take time to find out exactly what things will make you feel cared for.

EXERCISE: Self-care Profile

Look again at your wheel of life (see page **132**). What would need to change here for you to be happy with what it shows you about your care of self? So what are the next steps?

We'd like to give you another approach also. Taking care can happen at many levels: physical, spiritual, mental, emotional. It can include basic necessities and extra treats. It's more meaningful, and helps you conserve better, if it happens regularly – preferably every day.

Give yourself an honest self-care rating out of 10 for each of the following:

- Physical well-being

- Emotional well-being

- Mental well-being

- Spiritual well-being.

Look at your scores again: could they be more balanced across these areas? What could you do in the immediate future to raise your lowest scores? Are you satisfied? Should you be?

Now make a list of what you actually do to take care of yourself under each of those headings. Do you know how to take care of yourself in all four areas? If not, who could be a model for you?

Did you find any serious blind spots? Often, it's only when you take stock like this – or when you hear someone else talking about what they do and realise you have never even thought of that – that you realise what you're failing to honour in your everyday life. How many successful business executives have taught themselves to ignore exhaustion, disorientation, mental and physical burnout, loneliness and jet-lag as they rush around the world? How many mothers of young children have taught themselves to blank out a need for intellectual stimulus because 'there isn't time' and 'I'm just too tired.' Redressing such imbalances doesn't mean that you have to add self-care as yet another chore to your list of 'to-dos', making you feel even more overwhelmed. It means that you need to make active, considered choices about what your priorities are, and good self-care has to be among them.

Rather than just admonishing yourself for failing to take good enough care of yourself, why not give yourself some really good reasons for making it a priority?

▶ Start by taking one of the areas in which you feel your self-care is minimal or lacking, and find out what you are currently prioritising instead. What beliefs and values are involved in your current behaviour? Many people find contradictions here: for example, they may believe in taking time to relax, but somehow just as they sit down they think of something else that needs doing first. Does relaxation ever come first?

► In what ways could you continue to honour these beliefs by actually freeing up time and attention to care for yourself more? Without self-care most other things you do will suffer in the end. Self-maintenance is actually the foundation that provides the energy and well-being you need to take care of the things that are important to you.

It's our experience as coaches that once you find the beliefs and values that underpin your current behaviour it's considerably easier to move from worthy intent to action that delivers.

Tips for taking care of yourself

► Find a variety of ways in which you can take care of yourself. Make sure that you include immediate, simple, cost-free ones that may seem trivial. For example, you could give yourself a few minutes to look at a magazine, or phone a friend or walk in the park.

► Build self-care into a habit. Tack some self-care patterns onto other habits you already have – like cleaning your teeth or taking the dog for a walk – by fitting them in just before or just after your established habit. Making use of sequencing in this way will help your new patterns get established.

► Become curious about the ways other people take care of themselves, and model them. Ask two friends what they do. Would that work for you?

► Experiment. Try something new today, or tomorrow. Can you find one day this month when you could have a whole morning, or a whole evening, or even a whole day to yourself? What will you do with it?

► Take care of yourself every day in at least two different ways. Try two other ways tomorrow.

► Keep a record of the treats you give yourself for a week or two – and then look over it to see how often you really did do things for yourself, and which worked best. Do this periodically.

Dismantling stress

So far, we've been talking about what needs to happen to enhance your caring for yourself. The other side of the coin is to investigate what stresses you. People who are good at taking care of themselves recognise when they are stressed because they pay attention to the feedback their body is giving them. NLP shows us that our experience affects us systemically. Because the different physical systems of your body are interconnected with each other and with your brain, what happens in one part or one area has knock-on effects throughout the system. The beauty of knowing this is that, once you have learnt to monitor what you are experiencing, you can use any changes as potential feedback. If tension in your neck becomes worse, if you suddenly find yourself relaxing in the shoulders, or taking a deep breath, or letting breath out in a sigh, you have feedback about how what is happening is affecting you. Where you have feedback, you can feed it forward into changes which make your life better.

In our experience, habitual responses to stress or stress symptoms are extremely valuable, and shouldn't be ignored. Let's look at an example.

Tony had what he called a 'delicate stomach'. When he was at school, he would sometimes feel sick, or actually be sick, before tests or important football matches. Because of this, he lost half a stone during his university finals. When he started work in an advertising agency he loved designing layouts and dreaming up slogans, but was so nervous about speaking in public that he dreaded presenting his ideas even to small team meetings. Meeting with clients, he hyperventilated, felt faint and just about managed to speak coherently. He went to see the doctor, asking for tranquillisers. The doctor gave him something for immediate relief but went on to say: 'You need to manage the stress, not suppress it,' and gave him the name of a coach who had had a lot of success with stress management.

Tony had got used to his stress symptom. He even began talking about his stomach as though it had a life of its own. 'My stomach's bad today,' he'd say. Or 'My stomach can't handle meetings very well.' Talking like this about a symptom, or an area of the body in a way that makes it seem an independent thing, helps compound the problem. Thinking of this 'thing' as somehow separate, as many people with long-lasting symptoms do, makes you feel even more helpless and out of control.

Once Tony's coach taught him to accept that his stomach was a part of him that acted as his stress-barometer, Tony was able to use its reactions as feedback. In fact, he found it very valuable, and learnt to differentiate between the kinds and intensities of reactions he got in his stomach. It was as if his stomach became his teacher. And there were some things – like speaking in public – it made very clear he needed to sort out. His coach helped him explore the various situations and triggers he associated with stomach pains, and find ways to manage or even avoid the stress. Things started to improve quite quickly, and Tony felt a new self-assurance – and was able to say he was back in charge again.

Tips on dismantling stress

These were the tips that Tony learnt from his coach:

► Respect your symptoms and stress responses.

► Ask yourself what they are telling you (use them as feedback). Try saying 'My symptom is telling me that...'

► Reclaim your symptoms as part of you. Rather than saying 'My stomach/head feels...', say 'I feel...in my stomach, etc.'. Your symptom is your barometer of what is going on for you. Long-term symptoms are likely to give you information about what was happening way-back-when; in the present, they are often triggered by something that was a feature of the original situation which is occurring again in the present. In examining your symptom and the feedback it's giving you, you are likely to gain information about both the past and the present.

► Become aware of the variations in your stress symptom(s) and of their degrees of intensity.

► Remember, learning from your symptoms and learning how to manage what triggers them usually means that their severity and frequency will both diminish. It's really worth attending and investigating!

► Symptoms often tell us about buried feelings and wants. Don't ignore them any longer. Once you have the information about what causes your symptoms, take responsibility for yourself and tell others what you want.

You can begin to build your stress profile by completing the following sentences:

► I find it stressful when... (the train is late, I have to give a performance).

► I am stressed by people who... (are confrontational, ineffectual etc.).

► The part of my body that is most sensitive to stress is... (my skin, my stomach, my head etc.).

► It may be telling me that... (I feel worried, or under pressure, or resentful etc.).

► When I'm stressed it would help me to... (take a deep breath, talk things over with a friend).

How to Be More Healthy

We've looked at health in some detail so far. Now let's see how we can improve it. The first step in conserving your health is to know what it is you are conserving. When you think of health, does it relate to fitness? What tells you that you have it, or don't have it?

Are you wanting to reclaim your eighteen-year-old fitness and energy, or to achieve reasonable fitness for a seventy-year-old? You'll find it really useful to ask yourself three things:

- What is my norm of health?

- What is the norm for my age, gender and body type?

- Does the norm satisfy me or do I want to be even healthier, even fitter?

▪ *What Is Your Norm of Health?*

You probably remember times when you have woken in the morning feeling a little 'off-colour'. You may have wondered whether what you're feeling is tiredness, stress or the onset of a cold or flu. But you knew in the very first seconds of waking that something had changed. How did you do that? One of the basics of human programming seems to be a predisposition to notice change – and that means, of course, to have stored some notion of a baseline against which to compare. (The meta programme similarity–difference describes our individual sorting preferences along this common axis. See page 57 for more information on this.) The better you get at noticing differences, the faster you'll be at spotting signs that your health is not quite at its peak. But equally, developing your acuity in this way will also allow you to notice what improves your health. What about those days when you've felt outstanding? To notice is to give yourself the opportunity to consider why anything you're doing – or not doing – points to how you could enjoy even better health more of the time.

Symptoms as information

The golden rule here is: pay attention to your symptoms. Find out what it means to you before you try to intervene. Whether it is a headache or a bubbling feeling of well-being, pay attention and start becoming curious. People often go to doctors, therapists and coaches to ask for help in 'getting rid of' their unwanted symptoms. In our experience the principal value of a health symptom – be it welcome or unwelcome – is as information.

- What makes it better?

- What makes it worse?

- When does it occur (days/months/seasons and in what circumstances)?

- With whom does it occur?

Build up a health profile of yourself. You may find it helpful to complete the following sentences:

- I am at my most healthy when...

- The time in my life when I felt at my best was...

- I have not felt the same since...

- I usually feel well when...

- I can expect to feel off-colour when...

- I know when I am at my most healthy because I feel...

- I know when I am at my most healthy because I can...

- I know I am at my most healthy because I think...

You may well have been surprised by how much information came to you when you filled in these blanks. These answers will probably have already told you about things you could do, or stop doing, or need to modify, in order to conserve your health more effectively. In our experience as NLP coaches, most people have all the information they need about themselves and their lives – provided they take the time to ask themselves and to listen to the answers.

What is the norm for your age, gender and body type?

Becoming familiar with general norms like these can give you useful information about what you are working with. But it can also be double-edged, if you allow the norm to set your limits. By modelling excellence, NLP shows us that much more is involved in health and fitness, as in every other aspect of life, than mere averages.

Remember that the norm is an average. That gives you a lot of scope! There are plenty of men and women in their seventies, eighties and nineties who are active and independent, thinking productively and being creative in various aspects of their lives, just as, increasingly, there are teenagers who are overweight and unfit.

So the key question here is 'What do you want?' Knowing the norms – both your own personal ones and those of your age, gender and body type – is just a way of factoring in some information you will need to take into account in planning to achieve the kind of health and fitness you want. For example, do you want to be mobile and active in your old age? What do you need to do now to ensure your current physical fitness continues – or to begin to build it before it becomes harder to do so? What do you need to do to conserve, or enhance, your mental fitness?

Will the norm be enough to satisfy you?

NLP tells us a lot about how people achieve – and also about what is involved in non-achievement. Self-limiting happens in the mind; and one of the main ways people do it is by making assumptions about what *isn't* possible. For example, many people assume that getting older means becoming less active, less alert. This assumption can then mean that they adjust their behaviour to their expectation – and by so doing confirm their assumption: truly a self-fulfilling prophecy.

The four-minute mile is a really good example of how self-limiting can work. For many years people had believed that it simply wasn't possible for a human being to run the mile in under four minutes. And no one did, so that proved it... Or did it? Perhaps all it proved was that if you believe firmly enough that something isn't possible you will be limiting yourself very effectively so that there truly is no possibility – for you. Apparently Roger Bannister asked himself some interesting questions. Did he know the difference between running a distance in a particular time and running the same distance in one-hundredth of a second shorter time? No, he didn't. So if he knew he could run the mile in just over four minutes, would he know if he was running it one-hundredth of a second faster? No, he wouldn't. And if he could run it in four minutes, would he know the difference when he ran it in one-hundredth of a second under four minutes? Again the answer was no. Once he had deconstructed the assumption that had limited him – and everyone else – for so long, he became the first to break the four-minute record for the mile.

Another example is that of the New Zealand middle-distance runner John Walker. By the 1980s he had run over forty under-four-minute-miles, and was still running them in his late thirties. What had once been impossible had become almost routine for Walker. He had proved that 'sub-fours' could become a norm, not a rarity, and he was still achieving the same high standards at an age which most people, including athletes, would have previously considered 'too old'. NLP has shown that if you ask yourself 'Why not?' instead of assuming that you can't, or that something is impossible, you open up possibilities, invite new discoveries and push your boundaries further than you've previously thought possible.

Stocktake of health needs

We invite you to consider a health goal of yours. It may be just to get well or be well more often. Or it might be to get fit in some way. You choose. We've used getting fitter as an illustration but you may want to substitute something else.

► What do you believe is possible for you to achieve in terms of your health and fitness? (Could you walk a long-distance path? Could you learn a new physical activity? Could you take up yoga?)

► What would you like to achieve that seems at the moment to be beyond what you think is possible? Try taking a current goal and expanding it just a bit further. (Could you jog, or walk, for half an hour every day?)

► How do you know it is not possible? What evidence, and what beliefs, are involved? (Maybe you're thinking: 'I'm too old', 'I'm too fat', 'I haven't got the time', 'I'd look stupid at my age.')

► What might be the first step you could take towards achieving this goal? What would tell you that you were progressing? (You might need to remind yourself that age itself doesn't stop you.)

► What would be the next step? (Find some comfortable trainers, and some loose shorts or trousers. Walk round the block today, and again tomorrow. Jog a few steps when no one is around – and then when they are.)

► What would be a realistic time-frame to explore just how far you could go towards achieving this goal? (For this week, it might be enough to walk around the block every other day. And perhaps for next week too. Let your own sense of increasing comfort and ease tell you when you can do a bit more.)

► What help and support would you need? (Do you want others to know, and to encourage you? If so, how might they do that?)

▪ *Nurturing Your Immune System*

By this point if you've been doing the exercises you could:

► Have a good sense of what health means to you.

► Know when you are experiencing it.

► Be building patterns of behaviour and self-care that will help you achieve and maintain your optimum health and fitness.

Even so, you will experience fatigue, infection and emotional strain at times. One of the most important components of your health is your resilience. Your immune system is crucial here. *Anything* you can do to enhance its functioning will yield disproportionate benefits. How you live every day can make a huge difference here.

Respecting your body's natural rhythms is one way you can help conserve the efficient functioning of your immune system. Good food, exercise and sleep are others. Ensuring that your diet gives you a complement of the vitamins and minerals you need is another. It's not rocket science, but these things can give your system a huge boost, so let's see what you could do.

Rest

Our bodies are programmed to cycle through regular alternations of rest and activity. We all recognise the daily, 24-hour cycle, but many people notice another major variation as some kind of 'dip' after lunch. Studies of doziness and loss of attention in air traffic controllers in the 1970s identified a smaller, less marked cycle which occurs every $1^1/_2$ hours and which is called the 'ultradian' rhythm. In fact, our patterns at home and work do often reflect this in the spacing of tea-, coffee- and lunch-breaks. It may be at these times that we find ourselves staring out of the window, glazing over, or yawning and stretching.

Power-napping is one way in which some office workers have learnt to respect and make the most of ultradian dips. Churchill napped every day – and then worked on like a powerhouse. Our domestic pets, and small children, all do it instinctively. So you might want to ask yourself how you could build in ways of respecting these ultradian dips in your life. Start noticing when your attention wanders for a moment, when your eyes glaze over or you stare off into space. Perhaps you could take this opportunity to do something that involves movement: stretching; walking to another part of the office for some chore that can be done any time; getting a glass of water. If you really have to stay at your desk, wriggle your shoulders, sit more upright, take some slow, deep breaths. Be inventive about what you can do. If you're at home, you may be able to respect the natural dip by taking five or ten minutes out. If you're studying, take a brief break and you'll work on refreshed. You can also become aware of the signals other people give you that they are experiencing such a dip in their rhythm.

Food and drink

There was a Victorian refrain which went: 'Whatever Miss T eats, turns into Miss T.' Food affects us – and we can learn to notice how. Food allergies, of course, are gross feedback. But we can learn to notice smaller, subtler signs of how foodstuffs affect us. Headaches, joint stiffness, feelings of energy or lethargy may all be telling you how what you're eating or drinking are affecting you. Ian knows, for instance, that if he eats too many sandwiches his scalp starts to feel unpleasantly dry and tight. As soon as he balances up by having a big leafy salad that feeling goes and he feels easier, more relaxed and alert. These personal signals tell Ian what's needed. He's come to this understanding by paying attention to the feelings in his body and through some trial and error learning. Find out more about your own by paying attention and experimenting.

Bear in mind that your symptoms may also be telling you what's missing. To take the most obvious, thirst. Thirst is not telling you it's time to have a drink. Thirst is actually delayed feedback and is telling you you are already dehydrated. If you start to pay attention to yourself you'll be able to pick up the signs earlier and so may not ever get to the point where you have to be dehydrated to actually think about taking liquid! You can refine your awareness even further. If you feel thirsty, take a moment before automatically reaching for another cup of tea or coffee to ask your body what kind of drink it actually wants or needs. You may be surprised at how often you actually want something else – water, soup or a fruit drink, for example – and that you know the answer.

Exercise

So often when people think about exercise they imagine going to a gym or some heavy-duty workout routine. However, as always we suggest that you make doing the right thing easy and enjoyable, because we want you to get a real change. This applies particularly to exercise. Suppose you were to work out intensively with a trainer four times a week, 52 weeks of every year. That would be pretty amazing, wouldn't it? But actually your exercise would only be four hours a week and there are 168 hours in every week. What you do with the other 164 hours is what will really count. Imagine what kind of everyday activities you could do in 164 hours that would enable you to almost effortlessly increase your total amount of exercise. As for weight reduction, you'd be lucky to burn 400 calories in a one-hour workout. So that's a maximum of 1600 calories after your four weekly workouts.

As coaches we find it's how you live as a whole that makes the difference. So don't assume that you have to go the gym to really exercise, or, even worse, that going to the gym takes care of exercise. (Ian's personal trainer has far too many stories of people working out who then have several pints at the bar before going for a nice, juicy pizza!) It's what you do the rest of the time that really counts. And that means you have a whole lot more choice right now.

Ask yourself what small changes you could make immediately that would involve you in using your body more. Could you:

- Walk to work, or walk part-way, instead of driving door-to-door?

- Get off public transport one stop earlier and walk?

- Walk up and down stairs instead of using a lift?

- Go to a colleague's room or desk instead of using the phone or e-mailing them?

- Take a walk at lunch time?

- Walk the dog more often?

- Get a dog?

- Offer to walk someone else's dog?

All these examples have involved walking, because it's the easiest thing to do more of – and the easiest to underestimate. The same is true for climbing stairs. One businessman we know changed his place of work, and immediately started to put on weight. He was completely mystified as he hadn't changed his diet or done anything different. Then it dawned on him that in his previous office his department had been split between the first and second floors and he had climbed the stairs many times every day. He simply hadn't realised how much exercise his old job had involved. Once he did, he decided to get off the Tube two stations earlier not so much for the walk but because that station had lots of stairs. His weight soon dropped back to its previous level, and he noticed that he was feeling much brighter and more alert.

Ideally, you'll do two quite different kinds of exercise. One will be cardiovascular, which gets your heart rate up, builds endurance and burns off fat. The other will be resistance training, which triggers increased production of bone material in your body. This makes your bones stronger while simultaneously building muscle to protect them and giving you better definition. But of course there are many ways to exercise.

The important thing is to be realistic about what you can do – and to make it a pleasure to do it. As coaches, we tend to recommend setting a target that is slightly below your ideal. Better to stick to a plan of exercising three days a week then to 'fail' to meet a target of seven – because the feeling of failure is very likely to make you feel inadequate and may put you off altogether. Plans that are inflexible have a way of not working out. And the principle of little and often that is the essence of conservation goes with them.

Sleep

When we're children, sleep is something that usually just happens: we haven't yet learnt to override our body's signals with thoughts of what we ought to accomplish, feelings of responsibility or social demands. In the West there is currently an epidemic of sleep deprivation among adults. If you want some idea of the consequences, these are magnified in the behaviour of adolescents, who are almost universally sleep-deprived. Most adults need at least eight hours of sleep a night, but many are only achieving six hours or so, creating a *cumulative* sleep deficit. Adolescents, however, actually need more sleep because of all the physiological and psychological changes they are handling. It is currently thought that about ten hours a night would be ideal for them. Given that many teenagers, like their parents, are often only getting around six hours, their sleep deficit can shoot up to four hours a night.

Sleep deprivation is known to create mood swings, impair quick reaction times, produce loss of alertness and impair critical and creative thinking, memory and concentration. As if that wasn't enough, your body's killer immune cells function less and less the more sleep-deprived you are. The risk of your becoming ill because more susceptible thus increases substantially.

Being sleep-deprived can have some interesting side effects. Some people of course just feel lethargic and stagger through the day. Others, though, disguise their sleep deprivation by seeking stimulation as it enlivens them. Put these people in a warm room or a boring meeting and they rapidly fall sleep, a sure sign that the body needs rest. The same applies if they fell asleep watching TV – but they often don't realise because they blame the stimulus rather than own their own response.

The other major consequence of sleep deprivation is that you never really experience feeling ALIVE! So for all these reasons we suggest you take a moment to consider:

- How much sleep makes you feel truly refreshed?
- How often do you get that amount?
- What stops you getting as much sleep as you need?
- Do you get the quality of sleep you need?

Knowing how much sleep you really need is a good start. Having a sense of what your personal margin is, is another. For example, you might feel really rested after eight hours' sleep but know that you can manage pretty well on seven for several days in a row before you have to 'catch up' again. Pay attention to how fresh you feel when you wake in the morning. This is usually a good clue to your sleep status. Use it as feedback to influence what you will do at the end of this day. If you don't feel right when you wake up, you need to commit to handling this by what you will do to make tonight different. Then you'll be getting back in control. If you wake up feeling great, consider what it is you're doing that's proving so successful.

What helps you to go to sleep? Research indicates that we sleep best if we have spent some time in winding down before we go to bed. People who go to sleep easily invariably have a routine. The routine itself varies enormously from one person to another. Whereas one may have a hot bath before retiring, another knows this could make them feel overheated and restless. So what is the best routine for you? Why not deliberately design one just for you? Give yourself the last hour of the day to wind down in this way.

Because human beings are creatures of habit, if you build habits of preparation for sleep you will also build the expectation that you are going to go to sleep. In effect, you are creating a series of anchors (see page **24**) to prepare you for sleeping.

Monitoring what energises you and what depletes you

Researchers in psycho-neuro-immunology, or PNI – which focuses on the relationship between mind and body – have found that you can strengthen your resilience and your immune system in ways that go beyond the physical, and yet give decidedly physical benefits. Remember the old saying, 'Laughter is the best medicine'? And somewhere we know that taking lots of vitamin pills if we do nothing to change a feeling of misery is not going to do it. One of our colleagues asks her coachees to list all the things in their lives which take energy from them, and then make another list of the things which put energy back. Items have ranged from the energy-depleting 'responsible job' to 'mother-in-law' to 'not enough time' to 'worry a lot', contrasting with the energy-boosting 'meditation', 'the seaside', 'working out', 'friends' and 'my cat'.

▶ Make a list of your energy-depleting and energy-boosting items. Some depleting examples might be: housework, writing thank-you letters, filling in forms, having to be polite. Some energising examples might be: phoning a good friend, having a cuddle, dancing.

▶ Consider each of the depleting items. Do you have to have it in your life? Is there any way in which you can reduce its effects? What is the first thing you can do to stop this erosion of your life-energy?

▶ Consider the energising items. Are there enough of them? Do you allow enough time for them? enjoy them for long enough? What is the first thing you can do to enrich or improve the support you receive from these things or things like them?

▪ A Systemic Audit

You can use the logical levels (see page **48**) to help you check your health 'income and expenditure' in more detail.

▶ What nurtures you at a **spiritual** and an **identity** level? And what erodes you?

▶ What in your life is consistent with your deepest **beliefs and values?** What undermines them or conflicts with them? What do you need to do to have more of the former and less of the latter? Find ways to become less engaged with those conflicting activities, people or environments.

▶ How much does your life currently allow you to use your **capabilities?** Do you have enough space to stretch and develop them? Do you have enough stimulus and input to give you opportunities for learning, growth, engagement and excitement?

▶ Do your activities and **behaviours** sufficiently reflect who you are, what you believe and what you are capable of? If not, what can you do, both short- and long-term, to make your daily life more congruent with who you are?

▶ Is your **environment** at home and at work one which supports, or detracts from, what is important to you at all the other levels? If not, what do you need to do to change and improve it?

These are big questions; but NLP shows us that the implications of even quite small items, and small changes, at a systemic level can be major. Be as unwilling to work in an emotionally toxic environment as you would in a physically toxic one. Both will have damaging effects on your health. Don't put up with toxic relationships: seek to change them – or get out of them. Your health may be at stake.

Think about the people in your life: family, friends, colleagues. How nurturing are they? And what kinds of nurturing do they offer you? Practical support? love and affection? laughs? Spend time with those who enrich your life, not those who bring conflict into it, or who drain you without giving in return. Nurturing good friends is not only rewarding in itself, it nurtures your well-being too.

Bear in mind that other people can't be expected to read your mind. The emphasis in coaching is on two things: awareness and responsibility. Become more aware of how situations and people affect you; start telling people how you feel more often; ask for what you want – and encourage them to do the same. NLP emphasises the importance of feedback, both internally from one system to another, from unconscious awareness to conscious perception, and from one person to another. Feedback has an important part to play in conserving our health.

The overall message NLP has for us in relation to our health is: respect your experience and attend to your own needs. It's the same message that coaching has. The information you need is there, provided you pay attention to it.

Useful ways to conserve your health

▶ Think systemically.

▶ Respect, and don't override, your body.

▶ Get good advice, and then take it.

▶ Establish patterns that work for you and that conserve your health and well-being at every level.

▶ Build in rewards, pleasure and fun.

▶ Take action about what erodes or interferes with your health and well-being.

▶ Remember, actions compound, and health-promoting actions compound into health. It's never too late to begin to make these changes.

How to Build Wealth

Building wealth is a pretty simple matter. Yes, really! In a nutshell:

1. You will need to *save consistently* over time.

2. You will need to *invest consistently* what you save consistently over time.

3. You will need to do both *over time*. Only then will you be able to enjoy the magic of what Einstein called the eighth wonder of the world, namely, compound interest.

Yet, evidently, many people don't find it that simple. In this section we're going to look at what wealth can mean for different people, and how NLP can help you create, conserve and manage it. We're also going to explore some of the common ways people stop themselves doing these things, and show you how you can draw on NLP to help change the patterns of thought, feeling and behaviour that may be getting in your way.

A very high percentage of people don't seem to really engage with their finances: they give their power away to banks or other arbiters of their financial worth. Often little changes in attitude can have a big impact on this learned helplessness. Ian has found it makes a difference when he points out to clients that their bank statement is not objective information from an impartial authority, but an invoice from a business seeking to charge you the most it can for its services, and that that business frequently makes mistakes on its invoices – invariably in its favour! However, it's no good blaming the banks. Wealth, like authority, begins at home, as we shall see.

Caroline and Linda worked in the same office and had become friends. It was their first job after university, and after a while they decided it made more sense to share a flat together than to rent separately. As they became used to living together, they began to realise how different they were. While they were both outgoing, Linda was careful with her money while Caroline spent it freely. Linda budgeted her salary, sought out bargains and always seemed to have enough left over if she wanted any special or expensive item. Caroline could somehow never pinpoint where her money went – it dribbled away and she seemed to have nothing to show for it. If she ever wanted something special, she had to go without or to borrow. Her credit card was always up to its limit, while Linda had plenty left on hers. Linda always had her share of the rent and household services, while Caroline sometimes had to rob Peter to pay Paul for hers. What was Linda's secret?

Linda had realised that the secret of wealth – even the limited wealth she had as a new wage-earner – was saving. She never spent up to the full amount of her income. She budgeted for her regular outgoings, and put a percentage of her salary away every month as soon as she got it. So she was always in a position of choice. While Caroline thought this a very dull and stuffy way to behave – she sometimes teased Linda by saying she was middle-aged – she actually envied what it brought. She saw how Linda didn't get stressed out about money. When she felt the pinch she even wondered if Linda wasn't actually having more fun than her. But somehow, when it came to it, she could never resist just one more pair of shoes.

You could say Linda wanted security and choice, and realised it was in her power to have both but that this meant some restraint, while Caroline wanted the excitement and pleasure of instant buying and instant experiences. But that's too simple, because if you had asked her, Caroline would have said that she too wanted security and choice, and she certainly disliked feeling hard-up and not being able to have things she really wanted. One of her difficulties was that the specific things she wanted here and now in the present all seemed so much more attractive than the – for her – rather abstract idea of having some accumulated spending power for the future.

So while we can answer the question 'How can I build wealth?' relatively simply – save and invest consistently over time – we may, like Caroline, need help in adjusting how we construct our way of experiencing things to enable that to happen. And that's where NLP can help.

We're going to look at a number of important questions you need to answer if you want to build wealth. Then we'll focus on some NLP ways of finding and using the answers to help you achieve what you want. So take a moment to consider:

1. What does wealth mean to you?

2. What do you want it for?

3. What stops you from achieving wealth?

4. What do you expect to happen if you accumulate wealth?

To move forward, you will need to take stock of your current situation.

► Do you know what your income is? Exactly? Approximately? Not at all?

► Do you know what your outgoings are? Household and services? Food and clothing? Transport? Insurance? Entertainment? Hobbies? Do you know precisely, or approximately, or are you often surprised by letters from the bank, rejections by the hole in the wall, etc.?

► Do you save? regularly? occasionally? hardly at all?

► Do you have a pension you regularly contribute to?

Many people don't even ask themselves these questions – often because they are frightened of the answers. The answers will change over time, all the more so if you are in the midst of a major life-change, like getting married, becoming a parent or retiring.

NLP and coaching both emphasise the crucial importance of awareness as a first step. If you know how things are now, and you know what you want, you are in a position to make plans and take action that will progressively move you in the direction you want. So even if it's a painful experience, determining your current financial position is the basis of establishing your power and autonomy in relation to money. And as we've already shown in this section, conserving is a principle that underlies healthy living in a much wider sense. The other essential things you need to know are: what constitutes wealth, as far as you are concerned, and what's currently stopping you from achieving it.

▪ *What Does Wealth Mean to You?*

It's important that you know what *you* mean by wealth, so that you have a measure of what you want to achieve. First of all, this means quantifying it. Satisfaction depends on having a clear goal. You can always choose to redefine your goal.

For some people, quantifying it will be enough of an answer: so much annual income, so much invested, so much liquid assets, will tell them all they need to know. For most people, though, wealth may be less to do with amounts and more with the feelings having wealth gives them: security, a sense of ease, freedom to choose. And it's clear that feeling secure, or having a sense of ease or choice, is relative – not absolute. If you've just got a permanent job after years of unemployment or intermittent work, and if that job carries a pension, you may well feel more secure even if your salary isn't huge. When the kids get jobs and leave home, the income that only just stretched for your family's needs is likely to seem more substantial all of a sudden. The meaning of wealth varies not only between individuals but between different times and changing circumstances in any one individual's life.

One way of looking at this is to consider what you have and want in relation to your needs. The American psychologist Abraham Maslow, writing in the 1960s, argued that people's needs range in a hierarchy from the most basic, such as food and shelter, to the most abstract – the need to realise one's full potential. In NLP terms, he was talking about environmental and behavioural needs at one extreme of the logical levels and identity and spiritual needs at the other. In thinking about how wealthy you want to be, consider how your definition of wealth relates to these different levels of need. So often, fantasies about wealth are really dreams about a way of living. So what is this way of living you believe only wealth can deliver? Very frequently, we find we are able to coach clients to start having some of the dream right now. That's because much of it is really about a way of living which stems from a change in attitude, not bank balance.

Often people are operating in the present on the basis of old needs, old patterns, old beliefs. Sometimes they're operating on the basis of needs, patterns and beliefs that aren't even their own. There's a whole generation whose attitudes around money were powerfully formed by parents who as young people went through the Depression and then the Second World War. Some of their children will be operating now on the basis of the thrift that they learnt from those parents. They may feel guilty spending. Others will have rebelled against their parents' cautiousness: live for now, enjoy what's become available, follow the banks' encouragement to borrow. So what are your beliefs and habits around wealth? Are any of these in need of updating?

▪ *What Do You Want Wealth For?*

As we said at the beginning of this chapter, there is a significant difference between conserving and just hoarding. Conserving makes you rich in experience and opportunities, while hoarding gives you monetary wealth without significantly improving the quality of your life.

In modelling people who were really outstanding, NLP found that one thing they had in common was the skill of being specific rather than vague or generalised. Try saying these two phrases to yourself:

- I'd like to be wealthy

- I'd like my net worth to be £

(insert an amount that seems really large to you).

How did you feel as you heard yourself say each of them?

You may have had other feelings, too, and we'll look at these in a moment.

One way to help yourself become specific about what you want is to quantify it. Your stocktake will have given you some benchmarks you can build in.

Let's take a look at the various expenses.

	£
Living expenses	_____
Holidays and travel	_____
Entertainment	_____
Savings	_____
Pensions	_____
Improvements in your everyday lifestyle	_____
New lifestyle items – larger house/car, new equipment	_____
Would you like to retire early? How much would you need to set aside to make this possible?	_____

Once you have quantified all this and added it up, how much surplus would you like? What would you like it for? Here are some possibilities – tick those which apply to you and add any others. Remember to add a percentage for inflation.

	£
To give me security in my old age	_____
To improve my lifestyle now	_____
To leave to my children	_____
To help others	_____
Pensions	_____
To allow me to do… (specific projects)	_____

Looking at the totals may make you feel it's quite impossible. But remember: 'Wealth happens one day at a time.' Building wealth is about day-by-day activities, not huge changes or stop-go alternations between spending and miserliness. Conserving is about building habits.

▪ The Magic of Compounding

The end of the twentieth century was the time when people finally started wising up to the fact that you could establish substantial wealth through consistent, long-term saving and investing. A whole slew of books starting with *The Millionaire Next Door* (Thomas J. Stanley, Ph.D., and William D. Danko, Ph.D., 1996) made clear that the majority of people becoming millionaires were not to be found in the City or on Wall Street and did not lead extravagant lifestyles. Most were content to live modestly and quietly.

What they were doing had no glamour to it and did not attract attention. With their gradually accumulating savings they were investing. (Leaving savings in a bank account would mean they'd never become millionaires.) Investing in companies meant their savings had a chance of growing substantially. Doing this consistently over decades with due diligence and expert advice resulted in an explosion in the number of millionaires in the US and, to a lesser extent, in other Western countries.

Keeping their money invested resulted in returns that compounded over the years. A very high percentage of these investments were purchased for well under £1,000. To give you some idea of what can happen, if we assume a conservative growth rate of 8 per cent, that £1,000 will be worth £2,159 in 10 years' time, and £13,765 in 45 years' time. If you imagine what's sometimes called aggressive, that is higher risk, investing and a growth rate of 21 per cent, after 10 years your £1,000 will be worth £6,727. But after 45 years it will have compounded to £5,313,023!

Of course, the market ride can be a bumpy one, but again time is crucial. Too often people try to time the market, or buy when stocks are at their cheapest in order to sell when they will be at their highest. No one can time the market. It's time not timing that really counts. Often people will invest in a fund and as soon as it doesn't do as well as they expect they sell. Then they miss out on the next upturn.

Imagine a fund that produced 20 per cent compound growth over two decades. Wouldn't that be nice? But suppose for three or four years it has 30 or 40 per cent growth per year, and then for the next four years only does low figure growth. Suppose this pattern is repeated. There are such funds. Sometimes people investing in them make only 2 or 3 per cent. Because many people invest in funds when they are doing phenomenally well and then leave as soon as there's a downturn. Warren Buffet said you shouldn't think of owning a share for ten minutes if you're not willing to own it for ten years.

The truth is that there are many investment strategies for building wealth. Buffet's is just one. They do involve risk, but that risk can be tailored to the individual's comfort level. However, there is a much greater financial risk in not being in the game at all. People often don't realise just how risky it is leaving your money in a bank account while inflation eats away at it, the cost of living rises, house prices go through the roof, and the market *over time* vastly outperforms it.

If you have ever been in debt you will know from the other side how the principle of compounding operates. You borrow; the borrowing attracts interest; the amount borrowed plus the interest then becomes liable for interest; the amount owing increases. Fortunately, the reverse is also true. Any amount you save and invest also attracts interest; your capital is increased by the amount of the interest; your total saving is now larger; the interest is larger. And so on.

But there's another dimension to compounding, too: anxiety that goes along with inadequate financial management also increases over time and as the amounts involved go up. And however confident you feel at twenty that fifty is a long way away, when fifty comes it seems only a very short while to sixty. However apprehensive you may be, now is a really good time to do your sums, work out what you want and begin conserving.

But first you need to know what will motivate you to do it. Remind yourself of your predominant meta programmes. If away-from, what's going to happen if you don't start saving and investing? If towards, what opportunities will greater wealth enable you to enjoy, achieve or discover? Are you referenced more by self or by other? Whose needs will motivate you most? Knowing how you naturally operate allows you to work within that familiar framework, or to deliberately stretch yourself by doing something different.

You may have consciously agreed with all we have been saying so far, and yet have a sense of reluctance or resistance to doing what's necessary to become more wealthy. This is the place to find what information you can get from two very enabling NLP questions, both based on a respect for the information value of your 'resistance'.

▪ *What Stops You From Achieving Wealth?*

It's our experience that when people are clear that they want something, but somehow just can't get around to achieving it, there is a good reason. At some level, a positive purpose is being served. So long as you go on arguing with yourself, or berating yourself for not doing something, you block this important information. The NLP question 'What stops you?' is one way of breaking out of the circle of argument and self-blame and becoming curious instead.

We've already mentioned one thing that stops many people saving in order to create wealth. Caroline in our case study knew she needed to limit her spending – but somehow she always needed to make just one more purchase first. She'd begin saving tomorrow. She was influenced by what she felt and wanted today, which was very immediate and attractive to her, more than by some dim and remote idea of having money in the bank in the future. Caroline was strongly in-time, and in-time people often find it difficult to hold back from something that's attractive here and now in order to serve a purpose that they see as further away. The future literally isn't as clear or as real to them.

In Caroline's case, two things proved very helpful. One was that a colleague who had done NLP training showed her how to turn her time-line around so that she could get a through-time perspective on it. Caroline started to use this new skill to help her plan her activities, and her budget, each month. She also began to tap into this as a strategy for checking whether something she wanted here and now would still feel like a good idea at a later date. When she saw something she liked in the shops she would stop for a moment and imagine times in the weeks and months ahead when she might be wearing it or using it. If it wasn't clear to her that it would continue to be a useful asset, she'd turn her back on it.

The other way Caroline made use of her own meta programmes was to build a link with saving. She decided that every time she resisted a purchase she would take that money out of her account and put it in a savings account. But she didn't just want to rely on non-spending as a form of saving, so she worked out, with Lisa's help, an amount of money she thought she could actively save each week, and made a ritual of taking that money out in cash on a Saturday and putting that in her new savings account. She respected her in-time immediacy and harnessed it to help build her wealth. Later she started doing this on a monthly basis. But at the same time she was also building her skill in using a through-time orientation for longer-term planning and for evaluating the consequences of her actions. She also practised imagining how things would look, feel and sound to her in the future after months and years of this new behaviour around spending and saving.

In Caroline's case what had stopped her was how she habitually constructed her experience of time. What stops you may also often be something to do with past learning, or with your beliefs. When faced with our question 'What stops you from achieving wealth?', one person's answer was: 'It's immoral to have lots of money when people are starving all over the world.' Another we've heard was: 'My parents were working folk, and proud of it.' Whatever your answer, you need to respect it, because it has arisen out of things which have importance and value for you. Once you know how influential these are in preventing you from building the wealth you desire, you can begin finding out how you can continue to respect your experience and beliefs and still make changes. Suppose you had answered as above: if you were to become more wealthy, perhaps you could set aside some of your wealth to help people in developing or underprivileged countries. Certainly, they won't be helped in any way by your staying hard-up. But while you were unaware of your values around money, those hidden values trapped you. Equally, you could continue to value your working-class heritage while becoming wealthier: there are many ways of respecting it more effectively than by remaining poor yourself.

Or perhaps you are being held back by an assumption that building wealth means you will have to forego treats, pleasures and everyday extras in order to save. Doing the maths on the one hand, and reminding yourself that building wealth is about regular conserving, not total abstinence, will help break down this particular lock-in.

If being wealthy means betraying your working-class heritage, it's going to be fraught with internal struggle around identity, loyalty and behaviour that'll make it very powerful. For someone who sees being wealthy as being able to be generous, it's going to be a much smoother ride.

So what does 'being wealthy' conjure up for you? What beliefs does this give rise to? Jot these down.

▪ *What Do You Think Will Happen If You Become Wealthy?*

Sometimes what stops us are the assumptions we make about the future – the anticipated consequences of achieving our goal. We knew someone very skilled in his profession and well able to earn several times his existing salary who we came to realise was held back by a fear that he would lose his friends if he became richer than them. While for years he wasn't aware that this was the reason, he somehow always managed to hold himself back from the outstanding achievements he was actually capable of – and the financial rewards that would have followed. His friends were more important to him. It wasn't until he answered this question that he began to realise how much he was assuming, and how untested his assumptions were. It freed him up to achieve and he found that his friends really were his friends because they stuck by him.

Complete these sentences:

- If I were wealthy it might mean that...

- If I were wealthy I'm afraid that...

Taken together with what you wrote earlier, these are your beliefs around what becoming more wealthy could mean for you. Do these support the behaviour you need to engage in to become wealthy?

▪ *Conserving Wealth Right Now*

NLP offers some very useful tools at this stage of the process, too. One is chunking down (see page 32). Once you have clarified your long-term goal, it's helpful to chunk it down into smaller, manageable stages. If your aim is to be earning x-thousand in ten years' time, or to have so much invested by the time you retire, what would be a reasonable amount to aim for in five years? in two years? What might you aim for by the end of this year? And of course this leads to another kind of chunking: what are you going to need to do that will achieve these increments? You can chunk again: if you need to find a new job, or increase your skills, what can you do this week, or today, that will in some way lead towards it? You could make a list of things that would help, and relate each to a place on your time frame.

Another NLP skill that comes into its own here is that of creating a compelling future (see page 33). The richer, more detailed, more exciting, more attractive, more real your imagined future is for you whenever you think of it, the more it will help you do whatever you need do to make it a reality. It's this attractiveness that will help you say no to tempting expenditure when it's not really in line with your aims, or give you courage to make a risky phone-call, try for a job that's a little out of your expected reach, commit yourself to long-terms plans and so on. If you tend to have an away-from motivation, try creating a compelling future of poverty in old age – and use that to help you take appropriate action now!

Becoming clear about what you want, identifying the obstacles that may currently be holding you up, and ensuring that your goal is both achievable and sufficiently attractive to keep you on track are the essential processes that will help you build your wealth. The principle of conserving means that building wealth needn't mean depriving yourself: instead, the power of choice which you acquire will become a reward in itself, and the habits of saving and prioritising will enable you to make the changes you need effortlessly. Perhaps most transforming of all, wealth won't be something you acquire only at some distant time in the future: NLP helps it become an experience which you can have in an ongoing way, just as soon as you start doing what's required.

How to Be Happy

Happiness is a highly individual state, a complex combination of physiological, mental and emotional elements. For some people, it's being totally relaxed on holiday without a care in the world. For others, it's being really stretched intellectually. For still others, it's the moment after they've completed the marathon. It can last a moment. It can last months – or even, depending on how someone defines it, for a lifetime.

Happiness is not necessarily dependent on events or achievements. In fact, NLP shows us that it results from how we process our experience rather than what our experience actually is.

Jenny was a second-year student at Oxford University. She lived in an attractive college building, had settled in well and seemed to have made friends. Her academic work was excellent. Yet she was phoning home to say how miserable she was. Her parents simply couldn't understand it. 'Why can't you just be happy?' Jenny's father asked with exasperation. 'You've got everything you wanted.' Across the landing Ted was struggling with his work, which he found much harder than he had expected. His essays were often late, and he had had to resit his first major exams. On the social and sporting front, though, things were better. He had been selected as a member of the college's rugby team, and he had plenty of friends both in college and outside it. He was a happy man.

Happiness doesn't correlate in obvious ways with external circumstances, nor with wealth or success – in fact, many wealthy and successful people are miserable. One succinct way of describing the how-to of happiness is offered by the authors of *Know-How*, Leslie Cameron-Bandler, David Gordon and Michael Lebeau, who say, 'The art in having [happiness] is in wanting what you get.'(Real People Press, 1985).

Being happy is a process. It requires us to engage in a particular activity because it involves *selecting*: out of all the information and experience that is available to you, you pay full attention to what gives you most rather than what gives you least.

Let's look at two people with very different ways of dealing with the events of their lives.

Arthur had worked as an accountant in the same city firm for many years. He was the longest-serving member of his department and very good at what he did. Not an ambitious man, he had stayed at the same level of responsibility where he felt comfortable, and had seen many colleagues, and many managers, come and go. He had a long memory, which helped the detailed procedural work he did. But it also worked against him, for whenever Arthur talked about his workplace the things he seemed to remember most clearly were times when he'd been let down, or undervalued, or exploited. His friends and family had been subjected to many such anecdotes. Arthur grumbled and felt cheated; but he never said anything directly or took any action when he felt wrongly used.

Alice had had a hard life in external terms. She brought up seven children on her husband's small and irregular income as a labourer. Only now, in old age, were they able to relax, though they had nothing saved and only a state pension to live on. When one of her granddaughters asked her about her life, Alice said without hesitation that she had been very lucky: she had had the best kind of husband a woman could, wonderful children, a roof over her head and friends all around her. Yes, it had been hard sometimes, but she wouldn't have changed it.

Arthur and Alice had very different ways of processing their experiences. Arthur had been relatively successful at work, but somehow what stuck with him was not the fact that he had been a valued member of the firm for forty years, but the incidents in which he had felt powerless or taken advantage of. Out of all the incidents he could have remembered, those were the ones that rose to the surface. He was rarely contented, though in fact he did have many things in his life that could have made him so – if he had been attentive to them. Alice had plenty of memories which could have made her feel that life had used her poorly; she could have felt hard done by very easily; but she naturally focused on the things that had made her feel valued, supported and content. She was someone who had the knack of being happy.

▪ *Choosing to be Happy – or Not*

These two people clearly processed their experience quite differently. As coaches, we see a number of key issues emerge repeatedly with people we work with:

1. How you respond to things which are not how you'd like them to be.

2. How in tune you are with yourself.

3. How you interpret your experience, and how autonomous you feel.

4. What you notice on a daily basis, and how you construct your memories.

5. How you feel about the people around you.

6. Whether you ensure that there are enough things in your life that give you meaning and pleasure.

And underlying all these are the two themes we have been highlighting throughout this book: awareness and choice.

Responses to difficult situations

When Arthur felt exploited or neglected, he kept his feelings to himself, bottled up anger and resentment, and allowed it to fester – for years, in some cases, as his anecdotes showed. And from his experiences, he developed a generalised belief that 'you're only noticed if you're flashy'. Alice could have felt resentful too: life had dealt her poverty and hard work, but she believed there was no point in just complaining about that. She'd speak her mind if she felt angry, but she didn't hang on to such feelings. She had made a very different generalisation about life: she thought it was good on the whole, believed that things could be sorted out if you tried, and that there wasn't any point in getting worked up about things you couldn't change.

> **TIP** Act on things that bother or annoy you. If there is nothing you can do, don't go over and over the events in your mind or tell others endlessly about them. Every time you repeat something you ingrain it. Choose to ingrain good experiences. Where a person, a role or a situation continues to make you unhappy, angry or uncomfortable, find a way to change it. We have known people leave jobs – and relationships – that made them unhappy, even if they weren't sure where they were going next. Closing a door on experiences that limit you – and becoming clearer about what you want – is sometimes a first step to opening up a better future.

Being in tune with yourself

Being in tune with yourself is the root of owning yourself and your life. This is what creates the experience of congruence, where you are all of a piece. And it entails being aware of your experience, and respecting it. It means giving yourself the right to own your experience and then acting on it.

Arthur didn't own his experience. He suppressed his negative feelings and so became incongruent. These unacknowledged feelings then fired his internal dialogue which went on commenting and complaining long, long afterwards. Nor had he learnt to give full value to the things that did go right in his life. Alice spoke her mind and then got on with life. She focused on the present and the future, where she had power to influence things, rather than on the past, which had already gone.

> **TIP** Acknowledge your feelings, and ask yourself what action, if any, you need to take. By committing to action you channel the feelings and this changes them. In this way you become increasingly congruent.

Interpreting your experience

NLP has been described as 'the study of the structure of subjective experience', because it shows us exactly how we construct our internal 'realities'. One way of dealing with the overload of information that comes to us from external and internal experience is to simplify and generalise: where Alice's generalisation about life was an enabling one, Arthur's added to his resentment and bitterness. He believed people cheated and undervalued him: that was what he expected, so he noticed what made him miserable instead of making the most of what might have given him confidence and pleasure.

Alice, on the other hand, believed there were some things she couldn't change about her life – she was not trying to fool herself that hard work, poverty and an irregular income were fun – but she was able to gain enjoyment and meaning out of the choices she could make. She was proud of being a 'good manager', of always having a meal on the table for her family, of clothing her children adequately. Her home was welcoming. She was loyal, and received loyalty from friends and family in return.

> **TIP** Notice what generalisations you're making about people, life and the universe. Notice how what you believe tends to 'come true'. What other information might you be overlooking? In particular, listen to your internal dialogue, since this both reflects and confirms your generalisations. 'That's typical...' Ask yourself of what? of whom? How is it typical? If what you're noticing is negative, look for exceptions. The way you think now sets the frame for how you will feel and behave in the future.

> **TIP** Make room to notice evidence that may run against any negative generalisations. Get into the habit of breaking them down by adding 'and' – and then something which is also true but neutral or positive. For example: 'This has been a lousy day. And the dog is still pleased to see me' or 'No one had time for my feelings today. And I shall make time for myself this evening'. Using 'and' in this way both allows you to say what you feel and helps you deconstruct your generalisation.

What you notice day by day

Arthur and Alice went through life noticing very different things, like people viewing the world through differently coloured spectacles. When Arthur noticed something upsetting, he immediately linked it to other things that had upset him, so reinforcing them. Alice was really good at noticing small things and made the most of small delights like a bush flowering in the autumn rain, or a joke at the bus stop. She always noticed humour and kindness in other people. When something upset her, she treated it as an exception to her view about the world, rather than as confirming a negative view. That way, it was easier to let it go.

> **TIP** Practise looking for what's enjoyable, what you can do, what you like, and what's fun, or rewarding, about yourself and other people. Model people who are contented or optimistic. Ask them how they do it. What do they pay attention to? Often, it's easier to find something small to relish, so when you are overwhelmed it's a good idea to chunk down and really focus in. At the end of the day, spend a few minutes 'panning for gold' by making a list of all the good and just pleasant things that happened. Even if it was only a smile from a sales assistant, recover and re-experience it. That way, you end your day on a good note, and at the same time build your new habit of noticing what's good.

How you feel about others

Where Arthur complained that the trains were getting more and more unreliable nowadays, Alice told her husband how a young man in the waiting queue had shared his umbrella with her – and how, when his bus came, another passenger had offered a share of hers in turn. She was often delighted by things like this. Arthur's sense of letdown meant that he would notice, instead, how someone pushed ahead of him to grab a taxi.

> **TIP** Retell good stories, not bad ones – to yourself as well as others. Make a habit of provoking pleasant behaviour in others instead of waiting passively to discover if they will offer it voluntarily. Someone we know has 'smile days' when she makes a point of smiling at people she passes. Many (not all) smile back.

Meaning and pleasure in your life

Though Arthur owned his house and his car and took his annual holidays abroad, was a fully paid up member of the golf club and had his pension fund, he really didn't own his life. Alice owned, and enjoyed, hers.

> **TIP** Make a list of things in your life that you could feel satisfied with. Read it through to yourself. If you still feel discontented, ask yourself what you really want. Take your answer seriously. Does it – could it – meet the well-formedness conditions for outcomes (see page 63)? What could you do next?

▪ *Happiness and Health*

Our personal quota of happiness has other implications, too. Happiness has a lot to do with our well-being. Arthur's discontent was reflected in, or perhaps expressed by, a stomach ulcer and poor sleeping patterns. Alice's body had been subjected to far harder physical stress – but even in her eighties she was active and fit, helping her husband on their allotment and managing to fit in regular visits to an infirm 'old lady' down the road who was actually just two years older than herself.

Learning how to be happier can help us at the same time as we learn how to be healthier. What's going on in your brain affects what's going on in your body – for good or ill. As we've seen elsewhere in this book, there's now a whole field of study – psycho-neuro-immunology – devoted to how these mind-body connections affect the workings of the immune system, both positively and negatively. When you feel good in yourself, you have a better chance of remaining healthy. When you're depressed, your immune system may be too.

Are you, like Arthur, less than happy, or even unhappy, often? Would you like to change this? Before you do so it's probably going to help to know more about how you structure your experience. One useful NLP way is to start getting clear about how you personally do 'happy' and 'unhappy'. This is where contrastive analysis can be really useful (for a full discussion, see page 35). Take two pieces of paper: on one, jot down as much information as you can about the last time you were happy, and on the other, information about the last time you were unhappy. For each, consider the following questions. We're going to give you an example to show you how.

Positive experiences

► What was it like?
  – *When I was happy I felt really light.*

► How specifically did you know you were happy? What did you see, hear, feel, taste and smell?
  – *I felt myself humming. Colours seemed bright.*

► Did you know almost immediately, or later, that you were happy? What were the sub-modalities associated with how you felt?
  – *I knew almost at once. Everything seemed to move quickly and effortlessly. Visually, there were sharp visual contrasts and details.*

► What made you happy?
  – *Being praised at work.*

► What was going on around you?
  – *Ordinary office activities. Typing, phones, people talking and moving about.*

► What was going on inside you?
  – *Bubbling and bouncing.*

► Was there any internal dialogue? If so, what was it?
  – *Not that I remember.*

► How did you feel about yourself? other people? your life? the world?
  – *I felt good about myself. A bit surprised that they'd chosen to praise my work. The world was a good place.*

► Did the experience connect you more, or less, strongly with other people?
  – *More strongly.*

Negative experiences

► What was it like?
  – *When I was miserable I felt heavy and cold.*

▶ How specifically did you know you were unhappy? What did you see, hear, feel, taste and smell?
- *Things seemed to become treacly and slow. Everything was an effort.*

▶ Did you know almost immediately, or later, that you were unhappy? What were the sub-modalities associated with how you felt?
- *It took me several hours before I realised something was wrong – as though it had crept up on me. Like things were solidifying or freezing.*

▶ What made you unhappy?
- *A row with my partner.*

▶ What was going on around you?
- *We ended up spending the evening in separate rooms. We put off going to bed because we didn't know how to face each other without making up, and we didn't want to do that yet.*

▶ What was going on inside you?
- *I thought how stupid I was for letting something so small escalate like this.*

▶ Was there any internal dialogue – if so, what was it?
- *Yes, I was telling myself off.*

▶ How did you feel about yourself? other people? your life? the world?
- *I felt bad about myself. I was angry with him. All the life and warmth had gone out of things.*

▶ Did the experience connect you more, or less, strongly with other people?
- *I felt sort of on my own.*

Look at the patterning of your answers. The person in our example process-es a lot visually and kinesthetically. Misery is particularly kinesthetic, and when she's miserable, she adds in critical internal dialogue too. Knowing this won't change what happens in terms of external events, but it can help her do something different. She could, for instance, modify the tone of her internal dialogue and make the content more encouraging (for example, by reminding herself of how she and her partner have solved arguments before). She could train herself to access visually by using the eye-accessing cues outlined on page 43 to shift away from the negative kinesthetic experience. She might choose to remind herself of good memories of the relationship drawn from the past. There are no standard right answers, but there are lots of possible options – please think of a couple right now.

Boiled down to its simplest ingredients, to be happy you need to:

1. Refuse to put up with what makes you unhappy – do something about it.

2. Find out what makes you happy, and do more of it.

3. Train yourself to filter experience so that you pay full attention to everything that enriches you.

▪ *Summary*

► Happiness is not mindless optimism: it's a way of processing experience and a consequence of what we pay attention to.

► It's an everyday state, not an altered state. Furthermore, it's an easy-to-produce state, not an artificially induced one.

► It's a complex state, which relates very specifically to you as a unique individual. Finding out about what happiness means for you is an essential step to bringing it within your control. So if you're thinking: 'I just want to be happy', ask yourself these questions:
  – What does happiness mean as far as I am concerned?
  – How specifically would I know if I was happy – what would I see, hear and feel?

► Happiness is something you can actively create and manage, because you can create the context and the attitude of mind which encourage it.

► At the same time, it's a by-product of how you are going about managing your life and the way you perceive things in general, rather than a state you can set out to achieve on specific occasions or overall.

► It involves body, mind and often spirit.

► It usually involves sensory acuity.

► It often involves making a positive generalisation from a specific experience. It's marked by contentment rather than ecstasy, calmness rather than agitation, or being hyped-up or even 'high'.

▶ Though happiness is highly individual, you are not limited to your own brand of it. Think about people you know who are happy – how do they do it? Watch people who seem to be happy – what do you notice about them? Model them to broaden your own repertoire.

▶ If you do these things you will be happy more of the time.

CHAPTER 16

Making Work Rewarding

Whether you're a social worker, company CEO, teacher, dustman or airline pilot, work takes up a huge chunk of your life, so it's really worthwhile to ensure that it's as rewarding as possible in every way. Work means different things to different people, however, so a good beginning is to ask yourself what place work has in your life. Is it:

- Something that you begrudge doing because it takes up too much of your time or your life?

- Something you just do without thinking about?

- Primarily a means to pay the rent or the mortgage?

- A way to fund hobbies that are important to you?

- Pocket money – you don't rely on it to fund daily living?

- A challenge that excites you?

- A means of self-realisation and self-expression?

- A vocation?

None of these are better or worse in themselves – but they may be better or worse *for you*. If you're bored, if you grudge every moment, if you feel frightened by your responsibilities, if you fear being 'found out', if you feel you are a slave to the company ethic or a demanding boss or can't see any way to do what you really want because it wouldn't earn you enough to meet your commitments, your work may be making you stressed, unhappy or even ill. Even if you aren't, but still have a sneaking feeling you have more in you than this, or dread doing the same old thing until you retire, this may be a good moment to review the relationship between yourself, your goals in life and your work. It may help at this point to look back at your balance wheel (see page 132). How did you rate work in relation to the other things in your life? If the slice of your time work takes up is significantly larger than the satisfaction it gives you, this tells you it's time to think about making changes.

In this chapter we're going to explore four key skills which can help you get a better fit between yourself, your goals and your work. There are a number of points we'd like to make at the outset.

1. Over time, work can be more or less rewarding, and the same is true of specific jobs you may have.

2. It's important to get a good fit between you and your job. This can involve looking at the relationship between what's important to you and any promotion prospects. Sometimes people can be seduced by the prospect of promotion, and start climbing a ladder which isn't really right for them.

3. You don't have to be defeated if you feel like a square peg in a round hole. NLP coaching helps you become really curious about this kind of issue. Realising that there is a mismatch can allow you to stop blaming yourself or the job, and can become useful feedback to help you start planning some changes.

You can use logical levels (see page 48) to help you find out just where your job does, or doesn't, fit you. Sometimes it's great at certain levels but just doesn't work for you at others. When you know this, you can start to make some informed choices. Maybe there are some easy environmental adjustments which will do it for you. But sometimes, you'll realise you've been seduced by the package but are ill at ease, at an identity level, with what you're doing. That's when coaching can be vital if life is not to be wasted.

▶ **Environment** Think of the physical setting of your work, but also think of it as a social environment. What kind of facilities, and what kind of social patterning, suits you? There are a thousand questions you could ask. Is there somewhere to park your car? Does your office have a window? Does it have a view? Do you have your own space – or do you just find a free workstation and log on? Do you work on your own, or in a large room with other people? Do people go out together after work? Are there social activities and clubs? Whatever the specifics are for you, what's most important is how what you've got matches up with what you like.

► **Behaviour** What specific activities are you engaged in? Is the mix right for you? Are there things you'd like to be doing in a work context but are unable to in your present job? Are you doing what you enjoy doing? Or are you having to adapt in ways that make you feel uncomfortable?

► **Capabilities** Are you able to play to your strengths and do what you're really good at? Are you able to develop new skills as part of this job?

► **Beliefs and values** When colleagues don't share your beliefs, you can feel very isolated or undermined. You can even begin to wonder about the validity of your beliefs. Or you can begin to despise your colleagues and become cynical. The higher up the logical levels you go, the higher the potential cost of the mismatch.

So is this job and this organisation in tune with your beliefs and values? Do you feel able to say what's important to you in this environment – or do you feel you have to sanitise what you say? Do you feel your skills are valued?

► **Identity** If a job is in conflict with your sense of identity, you're going to feel very uneasy. You'll feel you're being asked to do things that aren't really you. If it's in keeping with your sense of self, it's enormously affirming and can be very energising. You'll naturally have a lot of enthusiasm. So how enthusiastic do you feel? Are you comfortable with the role you have? Do you feel able to be yourself – or are you living under deep cover in this organisation? Discovering where the areas of match and mismatch are between you and your job is a good basis for deciding the way forward. In the rest of this chapter we're going to look at four ways in which you can make your work more rewarding in every sense. Bearing in mind what you've just discovered about your personal fit with your job can help you pick and choose among the elements of this chapter, and identify where you can use NLP strategies to help you.

Though NLP approaches and tools will certainly help your career progress and support your financial advancement, they can also do much more. In our view as coaches, work should be worthwhile, give you a sense of purpose, enable you to develop more of your potential and enhance your experience of being alive. We would wish that your work be spiritually nourishing. At the very least, if you are to get the most out of work, it needs to give you more in exchange for your time and your skills than just a salary. You are giving your work a substantial slice of your life: this section will show you how NLP can help you find it a rewarding process in every sense.

How to Manage Yourself and Others

▪ *Managing Yourself*

The first step in managing yourself at work is to know who you are managing. You need to become aware of the kind of person you are, as well as your *modus operandi* and your goals. That's why it may be helpful now to revisit our discussion of meta programmes on page **54**: ask yourself what implications they have for you if you are to ensure the right match between you and your work. Some examples from people we've coached may help clarify how this can happen.

Finding the best fit between you and your job

Aran was a bright teenager who loved animals. His family had always had cats and dogs, and Aran became interested in dog training when he was ten and the family got a boisterous new puppy. As the puppy matured, Aran started to take her to agility training and competitions, which they both enjoyed. At school, Aran was doing well across a range of subjects, but with a particular bias towards the sciences. One day he overheard a family friend saying to his mother: 'Aran's so good with animals, and so good at science – he really ought to become a vet.' Later Aran said angrily to his mother: 'I don't want to work with sick animals. Just because I can do something doesn't mean I have to.' Aran's mother's friend had been sorting for similarities, which led her to think that Aran's love of animals would match well with being a vet

– a job involving animals. But this left out a very important element: he liked well animals, not sick ones; and he liked training, not fixing. His careers teacher at school, who was an NLP practitioner, asked Aran, 'What do you want?' Aran decided to take an Open University degree in the sciences, so that he could study while living at home and be able to keep up his agility training and competing.

Kelly was good at maths when she was at school, and went on to college to train in bookkeeping. She found it easy and enjoyable, and soon got a job in a smallish local firm. They were really glad to get her, because their previous bookkeeper had not been very reliable. Kelly soon got the books sorted out again, and everyone was pleased. But after a while Kelly found she was getting bored. She thought it was because the firm was small, so she applied for another job in a larger organisation with a busy staff social life. But once again, after a few months Kelly got bored. After she had changed jobs a few more times she started to worry that prospective employers might think she was unreliable. She thought that a coach might help her.

When her coach asked her what she really enjoyed most about work, Kelly realised that it was the first few months in a job, when she was getting to know and master the systems. It was only once things were running smoothly that boredom set in. Kelly's coach helped her to recognise that she loved installing, updating and streamlining systems. Her personality was inventive and her motivation was a towards one and very options orientated (see page **56**). This fitted better with a short-term, crisis-managing work structure than with a long-term, regular job in the same organisation.

With her coach's help, Kelly decided to create her own tailor-made job: she would offer small firms a bookkeeping rescue package. She could step in when they were in trouble and set up the systems they needed, and she could fill in while their bookkeepers were off sick, or on holiday. She went back to college to update herself and broaden her skills base, and started to spread the word locally about what she was offering. Within a short time, she had created a job which gave her all the challenge, variety and stimulus she wanted. And because the need was always there, she was rarely short of work. In addition, where many people with similar skills would have enjoyed working within their 'comfort zone' in a regular job, Kelly liked to spend much more time in her 'stretch zone', and by inventing her own business she was able to create a job which satisfied her customers' needs while also satisfying herself.

Knowing what's important to you

What's an ideal recipe for work? For most people it would probably involve some or all of the following: pleasant surroundings, interesting tasks and processes, socially compatible people, a sense of purpose and achievement, appropriate reward. If you chunk up (see page **31**), you find larger issues like comfort, meaningfulness and acknowledgement. If you chunk down, you can begin to add the specifics which you want for your own version of satisfaction at work. And these will differ from person to person. To clarify any possible position, ask yourself the following questions:

Chunking up:

- What qualities, values and beliefs does this job embody?

- How do these fit with the beliefs and values that matter to me?

- Will this job make me a bigger person?

- Will this job satisfy me?

Chunking down:

- What *precisely* would be my ideal environment, task, organisation, role?

- What *specific* details would I be wanting in my best-fit job?

- What would let me know that it matched?

- How does this compare?

In drawing up this specification, remember that you can always compromise with any item if you choose: but if you compromise without choosing, it's you that usually ends up being compromised! Awareness is the platform upon which you can build wise choices, design effective strategies, and discover what you can achieve. One manager whom we knew had a job which involved a great deal of travel. His office base, where he spent rather less than half his work-time, had no natural light. For some people, such an environment would have been unacceptable, perhaps to the point of distress or even illness; but to him it didn't matter.

For him, the office was just a place for making phone calls and dictating letters: his workspace really didn't matter to him so long as it had the facilities he wanted. Another office-worker had a well-equipped office in a modern building with a pleasant view – but found the work boring and the office itself isolating. She would rather have been located in a bustling open-plan office with plenty of people and activity around her. For her, her empty silent office was the difference that made a difference – and so she left.

If you wouldn't be prepared to spend eight hours a day at home in discomfort, why allow yourself to do so at the office? Life doesn't stop when you arrive at work, so make sure that it has the qualities that work for you at every level. And be prepared to consider the relationship between high-level values or identity issues and environmental or behavioural specifics. If your office, or your department, is located in a basement, or in an old hut on the outskirts of a large complex of buildings, how easy is it for you to feel your work is central to the organisation's values? If your office equipment is dilapidated and the decorations faded, do you feel cared for? There are always 'good reasons' for things like these – but what is the effect? Our surroundings convey messages to us which may not be intended – but has anyone realised what these messages might be, or done anything to correct them or compensate for them? And how does it make you feel if you have to explain them away or deaden yourself to them? We knew one head-teacher whose first decision on taking over a run-down urban school was to redecorate the staff room and improve its facilities. He wisely recognised that taking care of his staff at an environmental level through small chunk details would help improve their morale at a belief or identity level – and that this, in turn, would improve their effectiveness in a difficult situation.

Checking out your direction

People take jobs for all kinds of reasons, and stay in them for reasons both positive and negative. Taking stock from time to time of what your job means to you, and how it relates to your sense of direction in life, is one useful way to own your work experience. Perhaps you took the job some time ago because it was the next stage on a career ladder. Is this a ladder you still want to climb? Perhaps you took the job to supplement the family income: you know what the family is getting out of it – but what are you getting out of it? Perhaps you have begun to feel uneasy, or your old sense of conviction is waning, or you're really more interested in what you do outside work: does that tell you it's time for a change – even perhaps a radical change?

What you do with your working life is essentially a decision about your life as a whole. Answering these questions for yourself will also tell you more, of course, about good fit between you and your job. This can be helpful not only because it feels confirming but because it lets you know just what makes for that good fit. If changes are proposed, you'll know what you want to retain or defend, and what matters less to you.

Gut feelings are there for a reason, and we urge you to pay attention to the information from them: consider how this relates to your skills, potential and comfort; and examine how your here-and-now experience at work connects to what you want for your life as a whole. This is an act of self-leadership.

So take a few minutes to think about yourself and your job. Does it still help you go where you want to? What are the matches and mismatches? Start to become curious about them, and about any uncertainties you have. Often in coaching, uncertainty is the beginning of learning and discovery, if you take the time to explore it. You may find it helpful to refer back to the notes you made about fit at the different logical levels, and to build a profile you can use in evaluating how your work fits you now and what you might want to do in the future.

Managing your state

Recognising and understanding states (see page 77) is an essential part of managing your life at work as much as outside it. NLP has helped us understand the complex interrelationship of many mind-body processes that go to make up a state; but even more importantly, it has shown us that states can be recognised, managed, created and changed. This is enormously empowering.

For example, what happens when you have slaved away to finish something, only to have your boss tell you he really wanted something else done first – or that you should have done it differently? Your first reaction may well be one of exasperation, hurt or defiance. Your feelings may have been 'caused' by the way he told you – but so long as you blame them on him you remain a victim, and relatively powerless.

As soon as you recognise the state you are in, you have stepped – even if it's only momentarily – from first position into third (see page 69). Taking third position offers you a kind of 'time out', and a different perspective for assessing the situation.

Recognising the state you are in, when the state feels negative or inappropriate, can be a very helpful way to begin regaining your power to influence the situation. Getting curious about how you do this is equally valuable. Both will help you change your state for a while. And this will allow you to gain a distance from the feelings involved, to re-establish equilibrium and to make some choices about what would be a more effective state from which to operate. Recognising states in others, too, can be very helpful. For example, you might remind yourself that your boss is always tetchy in the late afternoons (low blood sugar? too many meetings? *his* boss getting to him?) and that he's actually the one in an inappropriate state. You could then decide to button your lip and get on with what he wants, knowing that tomorrow morning he will be apologetic and only too ready to appreciate your hard work. Or you might decide that he has changed his priorities yet again, that this is one time too many and you need to tell him you are not prepared to work like this. Other kinds of state management can be helpful at work, too. So far, we've talked about changing an unpleasant or ineffective state. But what about using your knowledge of states to ensure that you are prepared in advance to be in the *right* state for something? Perhaps you already know that your concentration is best in the morning: why not ensure that this is the time you book your most important meetings? Or perhaps you know that it takes you a lot of time to gear yourself up to do things: how could you use this knowledge to ensure that you were in the right state at the right time? Do you, like Kierkegaard, do your best thinking as you walk – and, if so, is there space and time for you to do this? What kind of states are most helpful for working on your own? as part of a team? for making a presentation? If you aren't sure that any one of these states is within your existing repertoire, who do you know who seems to use it naturally? How can you model them?

What sort of a state are you in at work?

Think about your most effective work states. What characterises them? You may identify several. Can you build up a profile of each, and what triggers them or helps anchor them? Some people, for example, find they are more creative if they are physically active, for example pacing about.

Others prefer to have a quiet and reflective space into which ideas can come. Do you think best with a cup of coffee or tea at your elbow? Do you like charts and coloured pens, are you best bouncing ideas off others? Environment and behaviour both contribute to creating and maintaining states: find out how they contribute to yours, so that you can make the most of what supports you and minimise or change what interferes. Does your internal dialogue contribute to your resourceful states? Do you encourage yourself, or 'talk yourself through' things? Do you hear the voice of a friend or mentor advising or supporting you? Once you know what you do 'naturally' in resourceful states, you can choose to do it deliberately to ensure resourceful states when you need them.

Think about your least effective states – the ones that get in the way or tend to sabotage your effectiveness and sense of control. What characterises them? Can you trace any of them back to where and when you first experienced them? What are the triggers that activate them? Do you find it difficult to work well if there is noise – or if you have to keep stopping what you're doing to answer the phone? Do you hear that little nagging voice that questions your ability, or compares you with others? Once you have identified the patterns, you can begin to find ways to change things and help you stay in an effective state for what you are doing. You might make some environmental changes – installing an answering machine, for example – or some changes to your internal dialogue. By now, you will have encountered a number of different NLP strategies which you can use to intervene favourably in your habitual patterns – once you know what they are.

▪ *Managing Other People*

The issue of influence

Some people assume that thinking about how to manage other people is in some way 'manipulative'. Premeditation, according to this view, means that your actions are somehow less authentic than if you just did whatever came into your head. There's an undertone of sneakiness and cheating about shaping your behaviour according to what you want. Or is there? Well, there could be – if you didn't care about what the other people in the situation wanted or felt.

However, it's inevitable that you'll end up influencing people, one way or another. The person who brags and alienates everyone is enormously influential, for instance, but in a quite unintended fashion. And since we can't help but affect others, recognising this and putting it to good use is a lot more responsible than just acting off the top of our heads.

From modelling people who are excellent communicators and managers, it has become clear that they use their influence in a very particular way. They always seek to produce a win-win situation, whether they are using their influence to manage downwards in a hierarchy, sideways as part of a same-status team, or upwards to pass information and ideas to people who manage them.

Seeking a win-win outcome for everyone involved is known in NLP as 'dovetailing outcomes', a concept we've already encountered in Chapter 13, on building good relationships. To dovetail outcomes, you'll need to:

▶ Know what your outcome is.

▶ Be clear how you'd know if you'd got it – what you would see, hear and feel.

▶ Check what the other person's outcome is.

▶ Clarify what they'll see, hear and feel when they've achieved it.

▶ Find out how the current point at issue fits with your outcomes and with those of the other parties.

▶ If there is disagreement, look at the logical levels and check at which one there is a fit, and at where there seems not to be one. Often, the fit will be on a higher level than the point at issue. For example, you and your boss may both agree that the customer's needs come first, but disagree on just how to achieve this.

▶ Reaffirm that there is agreement between you, and on what level, to re-establish that you have a basis to build on.

▶ Ensure you have an agreed evidence procedure that will demonstrate to the satisfaction of both of you that you have achieved this outcome.

The how-tos of managing downwards

If you are a manager, you have extra licence for your influence on other people. And you have an additional responsibility for making sure that you exercise that influence in a win-win way. NLP can help here in a number of ways. The checklist below includes seven different activities that will be particularly useful. If you're looking to become a more effective manager, just take each in turn and treat it as a project for some days. One manager we coached turned these into a seven-week programme, with great results.

1. You can develop your sensory acuity to really see and really hear what is going on around you. Do this by giving yourself manageable tasks in those systems you feel could be strengthened.

2. You can develop the habit of taking second position (see page **68**), so that you check out what other people are likely to be experiencing – particularly as a result of your actions.

3. You can remind yourself that, whatever intentions you have in communicating with them, *the real meaning of your communication is the message received.* How people respond to you tells you what message you have actually given them. So how did they respond? And what does that suggest is needed next?

4. Pay attention to your staff's meta programmes and representational systems (see pages **54** and **73**) to help you understand where they're coming from.

5. You can model people you have encountered who are really effective managers. How do they do it? What happens if you do the same? You can also model anyone, at whatever level in the organisation, who is effective at what they do, or at getting on with the people around them. What can you learn from them?

6. Being a good manager often means being a good learner. And learning is much easier if you are mentally flexible. Increase your flexibility by making a habit of viewing things from different perceptual positions (see page **68**), so you have more information when you make decisions. How would this look from outside? from the customer's point of view? if you were a fly on the wall?

7. Play to your people's strengths. Ask yourself what can you learn from them. How can this help you achieve your goals more easily? One really good manager we know commented that the art of good managing was to adjust the job. What's your view on this? How might trying on this view help you make changes that work for you and your staff? And what would the limits be?

Managing upwards

How can you manage someone above you? You don't have authority. You can't tell them what to do, or set their priorities or their targets. You may not have their experience and their skills, or be able to take the kind of overview of many organisational roles and processes that they are used to. But remember: you *do* have influence over anyone you come into contact with. The question is what kind of influence will you create and how will you use it?

Wendy's first job after graduation was as a university administrator. This involved acting as personal assistant to the dean of a university school, managing six secretaries who worked for the academic staff and setting their work priorities; liaising with subject departments and arranging all the teaching needed for the students in the school each term. Because of the range of tasks involved, she had a half-time secretary, Amanda, to work for her. Amanda was about the same age, but she had had much more work experience. She was quick and conscientious and very personable. Quiet and unassuming, she did what was asked of her rapidly and efficiently. After a while, Wendy began to notice that Amanda was also doing something else: she was anticipating what needed to be done. She would come in and say things like: 'I wondered if we should be beginning to prepare for...'; 'I've started getting the letters ready for...; 'Would you like me to phone and ask...?' In effect, she had begun to shadow parts of Wendy's job, so that she was already doing what was needed before being asked. This made both their lives easier – and it made the school administration much faster. Wendy has always been grateful not only for the practical help she had from Amanda, but also for what Amanda taught her about being an efficient administrator. Amanda was managing upwards.

In fact, managing upwards effectively involves many of the same elements as managing downwards. Indeed, if you took the seven activities we outlined above and worked your way through them you'd be far more effective at managing upwards. However, we would also add:

▶ Dovetail with your superiors' outcomes to produce a win-win situation. To do this, take second position to understand where they are coming from.

▶ Check their outcomes – and yours – against the well-formedness conditions (see page **63**).

▶ Chunk up (see page **31**), if necessary, to find a belief or value in common.

▶ Plan and work to future needs without waiting to be told what to do, by:
  – Laying out a through-time time-line – perhaps in a commonly understood form like a year planner, diary or flowchart – to make different stages in a process visible (see page **58**).
  – Checking viability, dovetailing and flow of the processes involved in your natural processing.

▶ Take time on a regular basis to relate each stage of your involvement to the through-time structure, especially if you or others are more in-time.
  – Take these qualities on at an identity level.
  – Use time-line awareness to vet your promises before you make them, so that you don't promise what you can't deliver.

▶ Be sure to deliver. Keep promises and deadlines and maintain quality. To do this:
  – Check out your own feelings and needs, and respect them – and then make your commitment.

Once you have done these things, you have done your best to ensure that your promise is well-formed. And if for any reason you can't keep it, you will be able to explain why rather than making excuses for a failure you really knew was on the cards all along.

For more information on managing upwards – and indeed on applying NLP at work – see *NLP and the New Manager,* by Ian McDermott and Ian Shircore (Texere, 1998). For now, though, we would only suggest that you give comfort and become an ally. You know how wonderful it is when you can rely on someone, and if that person also brings you things you wouldn't otherwise have access to – like information or new ideas – they're even more valuable. Become that person to your boss! Ask yourself what you can bring to the party. How can you make your boss's life easier?

How to Increase Your Influence

Becoming more influential is about making the influence you already have deliberate, purposeful and enabling rather than accidental, random and hit-and-miss. It's about control – not of others, but of yourself, your resources and what you do with them. It relates to achieving your desired outcomes, but through an alignment with those of the other people involved.

▪ *Why Bother to Influence Others?*

Influence is about empowerment – and not just your empowerment. Many people feel disempowered and disengaged at work because they lack influence. When someone says to you, 'I can't do anything about it: it's not my job,' or 'I'd like to help, but you see the decision isn't mine – it rests with headquarters,' they may be expressing disempowerment. Suppose instead that they'd said, 'I quite understand how you feel. What you need to do is to take that complaint to x...,' or 'Let me tell you the person at headquarters you'll need to route that through.' You'd feel different, and so would they. To that extent, they would have been influential.

A useful criterion by which you can measure your influence and that of others is to ask to what extent it contributes to the achievement of your, or others', outcomes. In coaching we talk about *forwarding the action*. Does your influence forward the action?

Anyone can be influential, not just people in positions of power or responsibility. And anyone can help someone forward the action that matters to them, at any of the logical levels. You might help someone feel more confident, so that they were able to take on a challenging task; you might help them clarify an issue of values that was blocking them; you might remind them of their existing capabilities, or teach them a new skill; you might do something with them or for them, or help them do something for themselves; you might make a difference at an environmental level. They might do the same for you. All these acts are acts of influence.

Remember: you spend a lifetime at work, so it's worth ensuring that it is meaningful, purposeful and satisfying. And one strand of bringing this about is to develop your skills for influencing people and situations in a win-win way. What you do at work, and how you do it, helps define your sense of self. In other words, it has an impact on you, day by day, at a very high of the logical levels.

Negative influence

Without the power to influence your surroundings, you are likely to experience one or more of these feelings:

- Anger

- Disappointment

- Frustration

- Helplessness

- Withdrawal and disengagement

- Demoralisation.

Take a few minutes to think about situations you have experienced that involved influence or the lack of it. Think about a time when you felt disempowered. What logical level was involved? How could you, or anyone involved in that situation with you, have forwarded the action? Now, by contrast, think about a time when you experienced influence in a really useful way. How did that happen? What logical levels were involved? How was the action forwarded?

Bosses whose response to what their subordinates do is a version of 'Yes, fine, whatever...' are extremely influential: they are actively contributing to a state of disengagement and apathy in their workforce by ensuring an absence of useful feedback. Feedback can be a major source of influence. Clear, specific feedback – 'That was quickly and efficiently done'; 'That paper has all the right ideas but the wording needs tightening up'; 'That's a good idea but now we need to look at detailed costings' – delivers both praise and an awareness of what is limited or lacking in a form the receiver can both understand and work with.

Becoming aware of the many possibilities you have for influencing others on a day-to-day basis will also help you become more aware of your own value. Influence in this sense is about offering others something they will be glad to receive in a manner that helps them receive it: whether it's practical help, emotional support, ideas, comments, suggestions or con-structive criticism. And we all have the power to do these things, whatever our roles or positions in the hierarchy. Influence in this sense is valuable currency, which can be shared and spread around and which increases the overall value of the organisation and everyone in it.

How can you influence others?

Influence involves interaction and is an act of leadership. However, you need to pace and only then should you attempt to lead (for a discussion of pacing and leading, see page 66). Words are one of the prime tools of influence because they enable you to pace and lead. Imagine how differ-ently you'd feel about someone who said, 'No, that's not the way to do it,' and someone who said, 'Well, I can see where you're coming from, and that you've found that this works, but I'd like you to think about this approach as well.' Words have power, and the way we use them can make all the difference to how others feel, and how they respond – and thus how influential we can be.

Pacing can be done at many levels, both verbal and nonverbal. You can pace someone else's rate of speech, their body posture, their language, their ideas. Pacing is an important way of creating and maintaining rap-port, and because actions speak louder than words, pacing will often carry a more emphatic message than words where the two are at variance. If you pace someone else's speech patterns, you are talking their language – even if you are disagreeing with the content of what they are saying. If you are matching their kind of body language and rhythms, you are conveying understanding and respect even if your aim is to help someone change them. If someone is agitated, for example, you will influence them more easily to become calm if you first match their speed of speech and move-ment, rather than just urging them to 'calm down'.

You can also increase your influence by setting some useful anchors (see page 24). A doctor we know, fully aware that he only has a maximum of five minutes for each patient in his surgery, makes a point of looking up and pushing his chair back from his desk whenever a patient comes in and sits down: the message he conveys is that he has time for them and is giv-ing them his full attention. He wants them to feel at ease and unhurried, so that they can tell him what they want to say and he wants to know. Pushing his chair back is his way of changing his own internal state as well as signalling to them that he's available.

Once we have established rapport, we are in a position to begin influencing. Changing gradually from a rapid manner to a calm one shows someone who is agitated that you know what it feels like – and also models to them that this can change. The doctor made space for his patients by pushing his chair back; but he stayed upright and focused for a few moments to pace his patients as they went through their rehearsed accounts of what was wrong. Only then did he lean back, encouraging them to experience a greater sense of space and relaxation themselves. A naturally empathic man, he had begun doing this naturally – but being also a reflective person, he became aware of what he was doing and its effects and was then able to do the same thing deliberately.

It's also possible to influence people by *mismatching* them.

When she was at junior school, Wendy's daughter Charlotte commented that one of the teachers often seemed cross, and some of the children were afraid of her. She decided that she would see what happened if she made a point of smiling at this teacher whenever she came across her – even though she did not really know her and was not taught by her. Charlotte reported after a week or two that the teacher was now smiling at her every time they encountered one another. Influence rests upon sensory acuity. Charlotte's influence was based on her initial observations of the teacher's sour, hurried behaviour and expression and upon the fact that these made children fear her. She was curious about what would happen if she behaved in a way that would be likely to elicit a different kind of response.

What responses would you like to elicit from people around you, and how might you seek them nonverbally?

Noticing patterns is an important step on the way to becoming influential. Patterns of behaviour, patterns of speech, patterns of reaction, patterns of approach to situations or problems, patterns of thought and attitude all provide invaluable information when it comes to using your influence to create win-win situations whatever the context. And noticing people's individual patterns is one way of respecting their individuality.

Influence is part of being genuine

When you show someone through your actions that you have noticed and respected how the world is for them, and when you act on that basis to help create a win-win situation for you both, you convey in the clearest possible way that you genuinely respect them, however much you may disagree.

Influence is not the same as trying to change other people. If influence isn't based on the kind of respect we are talking about, people can feel like they've been had. This is what gets labelled manipulation, and it can be fatally undermining if you wish to be influential.

Equally undermining can be any sense of a discrepancy between what someone says and what they do. This is just as true in an organisation. An underlying issue in some of the caring professions, for example, is that while the explicit values of the profession are about caring and support for the individual, all too often these values aren't applied between colleagues within the organisation. The result is a discrepancy between the 'espoused theory' of the organisation or the profession, and its actual practice. And such discrepancies can call the genuineness of the organisation, and of individuals within it, into question. In NLP terms, the organisation lacks congruency. In order to be truly influential with other people, you act in accordance with your espoused beliefs. Again, in NLP terms you need to walk your talk.

How can influence benefit others?

When we think of influence, we are often thinking, initially at least, about achieving what we want. But influence is frequently something that other people want from us, too. People can want to be influenced, not just to influence. For example, have you ever been in an organisation where good leadership was lacking? A lack of leadership is a lack of influence – and people are very aware of this lack.

Equally, you can be seeking influence when trying to decide between differing pieces of competing electrical or computer equipment. Often it is more than just information we're after. We want to know, 'Well, what would you do?'

We all look for influence when we have run out of ideas, or need information or support. At these times we're willing to place ourselves in someone else's hands. There is a degree of vulnerability here, which also makes us very angry when we feel we have been taken advantage of, or not heard, in some way. But where we have signalled our willingness to be influenced and have been so respectfully, it can be a thoroughly useful and welcome experience.

The same is true of others – so there will probably be times when they're looking to you for influence. Responding appropriately is much easier if you're clear about the differences. So we're going to finish by asking you to get clear about these by considering the following scenarios:

▶ Think about a time when you wanted advice or expert help, and when you were influenced in a way that respected you. How did that person go about it? How was that for you?

▶ Think about a time when you wanted help, advice or information, and when you didn't get it as you'd hoped to. How was that for you?

▶ Think about a time when someone tried to influence you without first building rapport or seeking to match your needs. How was that for you?

Given your responses, how do you think it is for others when you're seeking to influence them?

How to Get On at Work

What does 'getting on' at work mean to you? It might include:

- Promotion

- A bigger salary

- More responsibility

- More interesting work

- Being liked

- Becoming more influential

- Minimising stress and hassle.

Look through this list and tick the items you consider to be important.

Look again, and notice which logical levels are involved. Which are the ones that motivate you? Does the job need to enhance your identity? Must it fit with your values? Is it important that it uses, or stretches, or teaches you new skills? Do you want it to match up to your financial needs or offer you good facilities – or in other ways take care of you behaviourally or environmentally?

Now we would invite you to consider:

1. How would you know if you had 'got on' in the ways you have ticked? What specifically would demonstrate this to you? (If you said more responsibility, for instance, what kinds of things would constitute that, as far as you are concerned?) What specifically do you have in mind? (If you ticked bigger salary, exactly how much more would a 'bigger' salary need to be?))
2. If you didn't tick every single item – why? Are some of these really not important to you or are you just resigned to not getting them?

As coaches, we have often found that people limit their own ambitions, either quite unconsciously or because they don't actually believe it's possible to have so much. And because people act upon their beliefs as if they were fact, the beliefs become facts – for them. If you believe, for example, that managers can either be effective and disliked, or one of the lads and useless, you have a choice to make – and you won't explore ways in which you could be liked *and* still be effective. If you believe that work can only be hassle-free if you have a low-level, routine job without major responsibility, and that the power to take initiatives and make decisions inevitably involves stress, then you have another kind of choice to make. And you won't go on to explore ways of minimising or alleviating stress, ways of leaving work at the office, or ways of interacting that promote hassle-free relationships.

Take another look at your list. Become your own coach by asking yourself which items you would *really* like to include? And what beliefs were operating that stopped you from including them the first time? How do these relate to your personal beliefs about success and failure? Now are there any other items you would like to include?

This might also be a good time to ask yourself those two useful NLP questions – *What stops me?* and *What would happen if I did?* to help elicit the assumptions and personal meanings that may be buried in your choices about getting on. You may have dreamed, at the beginning of your working life, of getting to the top of the ladder, or of having your own business, yet here you are now, somewhere in the middle still. Asking yourself *What stops me from getting promoted?* or *What would happen if I did get promoted?* may help you discover obstacles in the 'reality' of your thinking and assumptions. Getting this information may help you recognise that being where you are *is* just what you really want – in which case, why not own it and enjoy it? Or it will show you where limitations arose in your thinking and behaviour which have effectively blocked your progression. Knowing more about those and about what you do really want is the first step to moving forward again.

Knowing yourself and what fits for you

Getting on at work involves, first of all, having a good fit between you and the job. And you can use NLP tools to help you build profiles of both to check the degree of fit.

Building a profile of yourself and your job/organisation using the logical levels is one way to establish the degree of match between you from issues of environment to issues of identity. And as NLP shows, the higher up the levels you go, the more important any discrepancies are likely to be. That said, never underestimate the importance of environment. In one organisation we were involved with, the productivity of two different departments varied considerably in ways that were difficult to account for. So did the absentee rates and staff turnover. What was going on? One important factor that no one had previously noticed was that in one department, all their staff had to be located in neighbouring offices on the same floor; there was a handy coffee machine in the corridor, too, where they tended to meet and chat. By contrast, staff in the other department had offices on different floors, and no focal social point. You've probably guessed that it was this, the second department, that had the lower productivity and higher absence rates.

Use the information on meta programmes in Chapter 3 to check how your personal profile fits with that of your job. What kinds of skills are needed for your job? What kinds of tasks are involved? Do they suit your meta programmes? The degree of match between you and your job at a meta programme level can be a source of great satisfaction, or friction. One manager in a large organisation we knew was looking for a really efficient PA. His last one had been super-efficient, but even so, somehow he wanted a bit more than the people he was interviewing seemed able to offer. Just what this was became clear when he wrote out a weekly timetable for her that included a half-day each week labelled 'initiative time'. His previous PA's strengths were procedural ones, but what he really wanted was someone able to generate options too.

It's also important to think about how the context of your work – as opposed to its content – suits you. Do you like to be part of a team? Do you enjoy working alone? Do you prefer to have close support and supervision, or to be given a task and left to get on with it? If you are managing others, can you and your department tolerate someone who, for example, is a poor team player on the strength of their go-getting drive and sales skills? If you recognise the potential conflict between someone who is self-referenced and highly competitive in meta programme terms, and a group which is cooperative and other-referenced, you can begin to find ways to manage the situation. Or you may, on the other hand, support your staff member when they move to a workplace or job where their skills will be valued without the possibility of friction.

▪ *Getting on*

Share your secret skills

Once you have checked that the fit between you and your job is good enough, what can you do to help you get on? In our experience, it's a mixture of asking and showing. In other words, it's about how, and what, you communicate to whom.

Who knows about the skills you have? Many people have 'secret skills' – ones which are not known about at work. One of the ways in which we limit ourselves is by thinking of *what* we can do rather than *how* we go about it. We concentrate on the content, not the process. Think about your life outside work. What hobbies do you have? What social and recreational groups are you involved in? Your secret skills may be one way you can get on at work – provided you first recognise that they are skills, and that you let other people know about them.

Angela was a mother of young children, who had only worked briefly before her marriage. As her children grew up, she became very involved in school activities. She helped with the milk delivery; she ran jumble sales; she became a founder member of the PTA. She didn't think about going to work again until her husband was unexpectedly made redundant. Talking their problems over with a friend who was a coach, Angela lamented the fact that she didn't have a marketable skill. The coach pointed out that in fact she did: she had plenty of experience as an administrator and manager and speaker: it just happened to have been involved with school. He helped her make a list of what her marketable skills actually were, and a CV which demonstrated how effective they had been. Angela's friend reframed what Angela had thought of as hobbies, or just things she did, as skills.

With a new confidence in herself, Angela applied for a job as an office manager in a small but expanding firm. The company knew it was taking something of a risk in making the appointment, but the boss was convinced by Angela's quiet confidence as well as by her CV. Six months later, he told her how glad he was that they'd taken her on, and how well he felt his risk had paid off.

What secret skills have you got – and how could you make more use of them? How might you reframe them so that you could get more mileage out of them? Who needs to know about them? How are you going to ensure that they do?

Pay attention

If you are in a senior position and managing others, you can turn this around. When you ask someone to do something, watch their immediate body language and facial expressions. If they seem to hesitate, or if their body language, words or voice-tone seems hesitant or in any way negative, check it out, whatever they are saying verbally. Reflect back what you have seen or heard: 'You seem rather doubtful. Is there a problem?'; 'You're saying "Yes" but I sense a reservation of some kind. Can you tell me about that?' Give their hesitations your respect, invite them to elucidate further – and then you won't be let down by their broken promises later.

Go the extra mile – if it's worth it

People who get on are those who value their time, their energies and their skills and invest them wisely. So should you. They are among the most precious things you have to offer. The best reason for calculating how much of any of these you are going to invest is what it's worth – and that may mean many things. It may be worth it to you to go the extra mile if it helps finish an important job on time, helps someone out, shows your boss what you can do, supports colleagues you value. There are all kinds of valid reasons for doing more than expected – so long as you know what's expected and you make the choice. But if you end up feeling exploited or taken advantage of, your resentment will tarnish something in the end, and you will have given your power away. Few rewards are worth disempowerment in the long run.

Invest your time profitably

Apart from your skills, your energy and time are your major assets at work. Investing these wisely is the next key to getting on. Sometimes this means choosing *not* to do something, perhaps because it would devalue your ability to invest in something more important; sometimes this involves deciding just how much time and energy is enough to perform an *acceptable* job, instead of the most perfect. Try asking yourself if this task is one that calls for the very best that you can do, which will use more time and energy – or if it is one where 70 or 80 per cent will do? This is a legitimate question, and it helps you recognise that a 'good enough' job is not always the same. It's another issue of matching – this time, of matching the resources you expend to the goal you are aiming for.

> Sally, a student friend, was going to a ball and didn't have any spare cash, so she decided to make a dress rather than buy one. She liked sewing, and she knew that she wouldn't need to wear a grand dress very often. When she came to finishing off the hem, she did it with sticky tape rather than sewing it by hand. 'I'm only going to wear it once,' she said. 'And I can write half my essay in the time I'll save.' Though she would have insisted she knew nothing about economics, Sally understood very well the opportunity costs of sewing that hem.

How to Have a Life as Well

You may, like many people, have trouble balancing the demands of work and home. Perhaps you work long hours or find yourself 'taking work home' mentally if not physically. In our experience, these sorts of problems are one of the commonest sources of stress and of stress-related symptoms such as headaches, difficulties in sleeping, back and shoulder pain, sometimes even susceptibility to flu and viral infections.

This is a good time to revisit the balance wheel you filled out earlier, and to remind yourself of how the different components of your life relate to each other – especially work- and non-work activities. Invariably, where there are conflicts of interest or time, issues of beliefs and values are involved. There may also be buried 'oughts', 'shoulds' and 'musts' – these again tell you there are values around. Whose oughts are they?

Organisations and professions have expectations of people who belong to them, which relate to behaviour as well as to values or capability. Often, these get tangled up with each other. Does being a junior doctor necessarily mean that you have to work impossibly long hours in difficult conditions? Older and more senior doctors may well say yes because that's how it was for them. But in some countries (New Zealand, for example) doctors' unions have successfully fought for limits to the hours that can be required of junior professionals. So what it means in terms of behaviour to be a junior doctor can vary considerably.

Perhaps you are a partner, or a parent. What actual behaviours would mean you were being a 'good partner' or a 'good parent'? Do these fit comfortably, uneasily or not at all well with the expectations of your work self and your employer, your private self and your partner?

In framing what kind of balance you want between these different demands for your attention and your time, you can also usefully bear in mind the well-formedness conditions for outcomes. Begin by getting your desired outcome into a positive form. If you naturally start with an away-from (I wish it wasn't like this... I'd like to stop doing that...) think about what you do want instead. And then check how far what you do want is actually within your control. Identifying whether the blocks to achieving your desired state are actual, out-there constraints that are truly built in, or whether they are the result of assumptions you or others are making, can be an important step towards regaining control.

Sam had a partner, Jenny, a small child and another on the way. He had a new flat, a new mortgage, and a demanding but relatively well-paid job. He and his partner were not really happy together, and in fact he'd thought about leaving before discovering she was pregnant for the second time. He wasn't very happy in the job, either, because it involved managing more people than he had expected and he lacked confidence in this area.

Sam felt trapped. He couldn't leave the relationship because of the children. He couldn't leave his job because it brought in the kind of income they needed. Everything seemed dependent on something else. Fortunately, Sam's employer provided professional coaching for its managers; and Sam's coach helped him disentangle these different wants and needs. He realised that staying with his partner and sorting out their problems was something he did really want to do – because he really wanted to be a parent to his children and make a good home life for them. On the other hand, he also realised that he wanted to find a different job as soon as he could, because he wasn't really interested in developing his personnel management skills. In the end, he and Jenny decided that they would both work part-time. This gave her a chance to use her professional skills again; it allowed Sam to take a job which fitted his aptitudes and interests more and actually paid almost as much. Between them they generated enough extra salary to provide some additional child-care when their working hours overlapped.

▪ *Coming Back to Yourself*

The advent of new technologies was accompanied by much talk about the work revolution: remember how we were all going to have to get used to huge amounts of free time? In fact, the reverse happened. It's as if having more household appliances has created the expectation that homes should be cleaner; having answer phones, fax machines, photocopiers and e-mail has created the expectation that demands can be met instantly. Firms are factoring in shorter turnaround times, and e-mails seem to demand an instant response. Companies are down-sizing, you can't rely on a job for life, and that career ladder needs to be one of your own making. The promotion is great – but get ready to relocate.

Having a life as well in these kind of circumstances can be very challenging. Some people try to buy security by giving their life to the company in return. In NLP terms, your reasons for going along with it may be away-from rather than towards. In other words, your actions may be driven by a fear of what will happen if you say 'No' or 'Enough' or 'I can't'. So you end up trying to contain all of the conflicting expectations and demands yourself, trying to juggle as best you can, and frequently suffering as a result. One finance manager we worked with had tried to convince himself, and his family, that they were all better off because his work meant he could provide them with a better and more secure standard of living. But when we first met him, Jim was suffering from irritable bowel syndrome and having frequent arguments with his wife. Neither his wife nor his kids actually felt better off. What Jim needed to do was to come back to himself and decide what was important to him. We used the wheel of life to begin this process.

You can too. Refer back to the wheel of life and ask yourself how much of your life and energy you really want to invest in each slice. How much of these are invested in your work? Is the proportion acceptable to you? Is it what you want? If it isn't, take time to ask yourself just where the fit is wrong. Note down any physical or emotional signs that tell you so.

In our work with Jim, we next compiled a complete list of all the things he wanted to do in a given week and how many hours he wished to spend doing them. We find this is always an interesting exercise. There are 168 hours in any given week. Every time we do this we find that when we add up all the activities they come to well in excess of 168. Jim's came to 243! Now he understood why he was feeling so stressed and why his body was flagging this up.

Again, we suggest you do this for yourself. The figure you arrive at will tell you a lot. Remember, though, that if you're to get a decent amount of sleep you can deduct 56 hours from your weekly total. So what you're really looking at is 112 hours per week. It doesn't matter how 'smart' you work: there will be a limit to the number of activities you can actually factor in to this amount of time. That's why it's essential you decide what's most important to you.

As NLP coaches, we believe that it is possible to work, to be engaged at work, and to have a life as well. And we believe that this can start from the moment that you begin to engage with what's most important to you. You can do this right now. Just ask yourself:

- What's the most important thing in my life right now?

Jot your answer down – the one that first came into your head. And then ask yourself:

- Now, what's *really* the most important thing in my life?

Often, the first answer is coloured by beliefs, by traces of other people's agendas and the drama of the day. If your second answer was just the same as your first, you are fortunate – but you're also probably in the minority!

Your second answer is your benchmark for testing and judging how congruent your actual life experience is with what matters to you. Getting these two in sync is an ongoing dynamic process which will involve your continuing attention. Physically keeping your balance means you have to keep rebalancing. You are forever correcting for imbalance. And psychically, the same is true. Balancing your work and non-work activities doesn't begin at a specified time, and it isn't something that can be completed or finished: it's an ongoing process of managing the different strands of your life in a way that satisfies and fulfils you with the least possible stress.

Modelling people who get on at work, who are fulfilled at work, who are influential and who have a life shows us that it's done by becoming aware of your own wants and your own responses, and by responding to them. It shows us that just as taking care of yourself is actually a good basis for taking care of others, working well with yourself is the essential foundation for working well with anyone else.

CHAPTER 17

Being Spiritually Alive

MANAGING KEY AREAS of your life with more ease and effectiveness involves developing your awareness and expanding your range of choices at all of the logical levels: environment, behaviour, capability, beliefs and values and identity. Related to all these levels is a condition we call being spiritually alive; but it also goes beyond them.

What does it mean to be alive in spirit, and how can NLP help? You have probably met people who have many things going for them in life, yet seem somehow dead inside. Things may seem fine for them on all of the logical levels, yet something is still lacking. The extra dimension is a sense of purpose and perhaps a *vision*. Ideally, it's these that inform and drive us at all logical levels, and which can permeate our existence in all the systems of which we are a part. Your sense of purpose and vision is what gives meaning to everything else, whether it's consciously articulated or more intangible, something around which your life is unconsciously organised. They underpin small daily actions and larger purposes: they link small and large chunks together through the things you do and the choices you make. Such purpose and vision has nothing to do with external measures of your importance, or value, or status: it's something much more personal. You don't have to be Mother Theresa or Abraham Lincoln to have it – though they undoubtedly did. You don't have to be engaged in activities which involve many people or take place on a wide social stage. Purpose and vision is what makes meaning of your life, for you.

Just as each of the logical levels gives you information that relates to a question (who, what, why, etc.), so this extra dimension gives you information that helps answer the question 'Who (or What) else?' It may involve you in wondering 'What's it all for?' or 'What's life about?' or 'How does my life fit into the grand scheme of things?' At times, it may evoke a sense of curiosity, wonder and awe.

Being spiritually alive in this way is a quality of experience that may include being spiritual in the commonly accepted religious or metaphysical sense, but this is only one manifestation of this form of awareness. There are plenty of people who are alive in spirit, who have a sense of the vision and purpose informing their lives and who have no religious affiliation.

What they have in common is a sense of something that includes yet goes beyond themselves. Words like 'purpose', 'meaning', 'value', 'significance' indicate that they feel there's a link between the daily events of their life and a wider meaning. There's a coherence at a really high level. And what these people also seem to have in common are the qualities that get variously labelled as 'being grounded', 'centred', 'purposeful', 'engaged', 'energetic' and 'concerned'. We could say that there is a sense of connectedness which may link us to others, or to nature, or to God, and which informs our life at every level.

Being spiritually alive is not directly measurable in terms of the 'importance' of what you do as far as the outside world is concerned. It doesn't correlate with education, social class, wealth or age. But as NLP shows, it doesn't have to be an accidental gift either. If you model people who are alive in this way, you can identify certain things they have in common. If we were to sum these up we could offer you the following four pointers to being spiritually alive:

1. Stop trying.

2. Be present.

3. Create a more spacious awareness.

4. Allow an attitude of gratitude.

How to Stop Trying

On the surface, 'trying' can sometimes yield positive results. It involves effort, intention and application, and these can be positive values. So why should halting all that be a way towards becoming more spiritually alive?

The downside of trying is that it involves conscious effort, as opposed to unconscious elegance. Too often, it involves tension, even anxiety, which inhibit ease, creativity and flow. Frequently it is goal-focused at the expense of curiosity and experimentation. Too much trying can limit your awareness and your resourcefulness. In short, trying is often very trying, being accompanied by oughts, musts and shoulds, which can narrow your awareness and even lower self-esteem.

The American sports coach Timothy Gallwey, who we encountered in Part One and who developed his Inner Game techniques around the time NLP began, said that trying interferes with the realisation of our true potential. He pointed out that trying involves *doubt.* So in his coaching work he encouraged people to bypass these pitfalls by concentrating simply on awareness and experimentation. He helped them to build trust in their ability to process and direct effective action at an unconscious level.

In stressing the value of unconscious understanding and control, Gallwey wanted to redress a balance that he felt had previously been all in favour of consciousness. Yet clearly, conscious processing has real value – in the right place. Let's explore how you can make a fuller use of both parts of your brain, and develop a sense of greater trust and harmony between them.

The unconscious part of your mind is really good at:

- Making connections and links (working by analogy)

- Being creative, going beyond the known

- Working with emotions

- Connecting with your physiology and organising its behaviour.

When you allow yourself to pay attention to the details of your experience, it's easier to develop a state of relaxed concentration, in which your mind and body can work freely at a number of levels, harmoniously and without interference.

When you stop trying, you are able to use more of your mind to connect more easily and more effectively with your body, and to be more sensitive to feedback and able to respond to it. And as we've shown, your body gives you information all the time about what you unconsciously 'know'. Stopping trying is a real benefit, both because it removes tensions and because it allows you to be more involved in your experience. Instead of being preoccupied with what *ought* to be, you notice instead what *is*. This in turn means that you get more feedback, can process it faster, and relate to what's going on inside yourself and in the world outside with greater speed, accuracy and flexibility.

So where does the conscious part of your mind come into this? The conscious part of your mind is really good at:

- Analysing

- Sorting information

- Prioritising and ordering

- Working in a linear order

- Learning and using procedures, rules and categories.

Consciousness is needed to formulate questions, to help you decide what to notice, or to validate enquiring more closely into a 'gut feeling' or an intuition (both indicating unconscious processing). If you consciously encourage yourself to become more aware in a non-judgemental way, you will gather more information, and be less likely to distort its meanings through assumptions and prejudices. You can train your conscious mind to become more self-aware, so that you notice when you are becoming judgemental, for example, or when you're criticising yourself. You can become alert to the limitations of your meta programmes, and deliberately encourage expanding your ability to sort information in less familiar ways. You can make a conscious decision to gather, and respect, information that comes to you in a range of ways through all of your senses, and to respect and utilise your unconscious processing more. All of this is the antithesis of 'trying'. In our experience, most people find it a great relief to 'try' less, and a great delight to discover that in doing so they become more, not less, effective.

In criticising, or in attempting to drive yourself, you become for a while less whole, more split. Being integrated and at the same time self-aware is an important aspect of being spiritually alive. When the

American psychologist Abraham Maslow talked with people to find out about their 'peak experiences', he found that one thing they had in common was a strong sense of being whole, alive and present in their experience. Trying gets in the way of this very effectively.

▪ *Stocktake of How Much You Try*

How much of the time would you say you're busy trying? What kinds of situations or people trigger you into trying? Do you try to finish projects, try to meet deadlines, try to be nicer to your partner, try to be more patient with your kids, try to drive less impatiently, try to relax...? How much of your internal dialogue involves oughts, musts and shoulds? And does all this trying register in your body? Where do you stiffen and tighten? Would you say you have recurring patterns of stress, anxiety or ill-health that relate to trying?

By contrast, now consider how often you let go and experience an easiness in yourself and your activity. Some people call this a flow state. You may be working hard – as in running a race – but you're not actually trying. You enter what is sometimes called 'the zone'. In its purest form you experience effortless accomplishment. You do less and accomplish more.

What kind of situations, people or activities trigger you into letting go? Do you have ways of easing into some kind of flow state – or are you relying on counterfeits like alcohol and TV? Almost anything could take you into this altered state if you engage with the activity and go beyond yourself. Yes, it could be meditating, but it could also be surfing, gardening, painting, making love or whatever.

How does this state affect your body? Does it make for an easing out of muscles, for clearer vision, for a loss of cravings, or what?

Suppose you were to start exploring what enabled you to transcend your usual limitations and to achieve a greater ease, accomplishment and joy. What might this bring into your life?

Being Present

Being present means that you are really connected with your experience and can process it without interruption or distorting filters. It means noticing what's actually going on for you, right now, this moment, rather than judging it or dismissing it. Being present can involve both processing detail and appreciating how this is part of something larger: you're taking in every colour and form in a fabulous sunset and feeling at one with nature, or feeling exquisitely yourself and at the same time lost in the other as you're making love.

Being present is something that can happen much more easily when you stop trying. Trying can take you out of your immediate experience in a number of ways. It may dissociate you from it – you become an observer, and often a critical one, of yourself. It can add other voices to your internal dialogue in the form of precepts or hectoring from influential figures, past or present. Trying can also be symptomatic of internal conflicts and arguments between different parts of yourself.

Being present is what naturally happens if you don't get in the way. That's why we've listed some of the most common ways in which you can *not* be present so that you can notice which you tend to do most. You can:

► Get distracted from what you are experiencing by imposing norms on your experience. You might tell yourself you should be enjoying something even though your heart really isn't in it.

► Leave the present and get waylaid by anticipating the future – either by being anxious about what you fear or by fantasising about what you'd like to happen. When you imagine something bad happening, your mind engages with the scenario you're creating, and since 'reality', as far as the mind is concerned, is what it's experiencing, you're likely to create the effects of a real disaster in your physiology and emotions right now. Fantasising about good futures can be one way of helping bring them about, but only when you connect those dreams to what needs to happen now, today and next week, and only when you check whether they meet the well-formedness conditions.

► Leave the present and rerun what happened in the past: go over old grudges or failures or replay again and again situations where you're unsure about the wisdom of what you did.

► Keep reminding yourself how people have taken advantage of you, or done you down. At its worse this reinforces the effects of the experience each time it is rerun, and can rapidly lead you to make distorting generalisations like: 'You can't trust anyone', 'People are all thoughtless and self-serving', etc.

► When things seem to be going well, ask yourself what the catch is or what might go wrong. While there can be a self-protective intent behind this, it's another way of undermining your trust and involvement in your present experience. Done enough, this can make you doubt the evidence of your own senses, and undermine both your confidence and your self-esteem.

Knowing which of these is most applicable to you gives you the next step if you want to be more present. Use the NLP tools you now have, first to get curious about exactly how you get in your own way, and second to start doing something different. Being present involves becoming open to your experience. Sometimes your experience – illness, doubt, uncertainty, lack of progress, frustration – will be uncomfortable. But attempting to hide or deny unpleasant experiences involves us in another form of trying, and creates another degree of removal from our experience: we run the risk of becoming less aware of our experience as a whole. In essence, what you can't be with runs your life.

When people are asked about their peak experiences, they don't just pick happy ones. Peak experiences can involve sadness, pain and death. The vision of connectedness which is so commonly a part of them may even involve a sense of mystery at the parting of the spirit from the body. Or it can include wonder at the strength of the human spirit.

What happens if you allow yourself to experience unpleasant things as fully as pleasant ones? Usually, allowing yourself to pay attention to the experience and the feelings means that you actually feel more congruent with yourself, and are able all the sooner to seek remedies or make changes to improve the situation.

Pessimism and cynicism are actually ways of attempting to avoid hurt or disappointment. They are attempts at self-protection – but when you acknowledge hurt and disappointment for what they are, you can in fact deal with them more easily.

If you are open to your experience, and develop your awareness of your own sensory processing, you will enhance your trust in yourself. You will also build your credibility with others.

Cultivating sensory acuity (see page **76**) is one way you can help yourself be present. The more you notice, the more it anchors you into your experience, whether it's observing the fine detail of a flower, or a person's expression, or hearing the different instruments in a piece of music – or noticing what's going on inside you.

To be present you will need to be able to be in-time. If you have mainly a through-time sorting style, training yourself to adopt an in-time style when you choose will give you a whole new world of felt experience. (See page **58** for a discussion of in-time and through-time.)

Being able to relate your experience to a larger perspective or dimension makes being present even richer. In fact, this is one way in which we naturally recognise the extra dimension of spirit in ourselves and others. When Princess Diana reached out and touched AIDS sufferers at a time when people feared that the disease was contagious, and when others were literally treating them as 'untouchables', her gesture of confidence and engagement with the sufferers publicly connected their present state with their unchanged identity and value as human beings. Her vision informed her actions, and was expressed through it. And this made a link not only between what she believed and what she did, but between one event and a much broader belief in human connectedness and importance.

How to Create a More Spacious Awareness

NLP and coaching both emphasise the importance of awareness as a key to enriching and managing your life. It's awareness that allows you to notice the patterns of thought and behaviour in yourself and others, and thereby to model what works and what doesn't: in this sense, it's the key to understanding and to change. Enhanced sensory awareness also makes life more enjoyable and allows you to become more subtle and more effective in your interaction with others and with yourself.

However, there is another dimension to awareness. If you think of those times when you've been stressed and harassed, one thing that seems to happen is that you become constricted, be it by physically tensing or through straining to see your way through. It's as if you begin to pull in, and your awareness does too. One client described how his way of seeing changed when under this sort of pressure. His peripheral vision became narrower 'and so does my thinking'.

By contrast, when you are at ease with yourself, you can experience an easiness which extends beyond the physical. Things don't get to you in the same way. Instead of wishing life could be nicer to you, you feel able to handle what comes your way and you can entertain new possibilities. 'It's like there is more space on the inside of me' is how one client described it. We call it a more spacious awareness.

Creating mental space in your life is a great way to foster this kind of spacious awareness. Giving yourself regular time away can be invaluable. But you don't have to travel far. For some people, simply taking time out stops them from getting into any obsessive tunnel vision.

So how can you create space in your life which gives you room just to *be*? This is a question worth coming back to regularly. In coaching, we find one of the most significant changes for people is when they feel they have the space to choose how they'll be and what they'll do.

There are many ways in which your awareness can grow over time and some of them will definitely stretch you. Having children is a case in point. Though parenting is strenuous, time-consuming, and at times exhausting and frustrating, it continually forces you to consider how your own existence relates to that of the others you care about in such a deep and intrinsic way. Parenting makes you take different positions. It often makes you vividly aware of how it is in your own first position, yet at the same time your partner or children may be clamouring for their right to understanding and acceptance, so you need to be able to go to second position in order to know what it's like for them. Sometimes you also watch events with the concerned, regretful, approving or understanding eye of third position, even though you are passionately involved in them.

Literature and the arts, exposure to other places and other cultures all make you aware of worlds outside the ones you are familiar with. In different ways these bring you into contact with different customs and different assumptions, they make you more aware of your own. Travel can broaden the mind not simply because it shows you different ways of life but because in doing so it can make you develop an anthropological awareness of your own.

For example, in Western culture, individualism is held up as a highly desirable goal. But in some Eastern cultures, the desirable goal is to belong and contribute to the culture, in family, organisational or national contexts. Encountering these differences not only gives us the opportunity of understanding the 'reality' of other people's worlds: it requires us to look afresh at our own.

Life events can also stretch your awareness. Life has a way of getting you to re-evaluate what you take for granted. One extended family we knew had been held together by the regular telephone communication of the three sisters, who kept each other informed of events, organised family gatherings and enshrined what every family member through three generations recognised as the 'family values'. Only when the sisters died one by one in their eighties did this fundamental yet unobtrusive role become clear: their children, who had always liked each other and felt close, realised that they would now have to take on their mothers' roles if they were to maintain the sense of family that was so important to them.

So far, we've looked at how external events can propel you into stretching your awareness. But it can also be done deliberately with the help of NLP techniques and approaches. Try these, referring back to Chapter 3 if you need to refresh your understanding of specific tools:

▶ **Have a look from a different position** Look at your habits: your environment, your behaviour, your skills and capabilities, your beliefs and values, your identity. Put yourself in the position of the visitor from Mars, or the interviewer seeking to build a profile of you. How has this habitual pattern of thinking, acting or being come about? What does it mean to you? Is it still valid, or is it an outmoded monument to your personal history? Do you feel comfortable explaining it to this imagined outsider, or do you now begin to wonder about its place as part of your life? When you learn something, it passes from your conscious awareness into unconscious storage: that's often very useful, as many learnt patterns don't need to be re-evaluated. But this can also mean that you maintain old ways of being even when they are no longer appropriate. Taking the curious outsider's view is one way to bring such patterns into awareness and to give yourself the opportunity of making choices about them.

▶ **Allow yourself to ask the big questions** What do I really want in my life? What's the most important thing in my life right now? What have I never done that I'd really like to do? How could I chunk that larger dream down into manageable tasks so that I could begin to make it a reality? What would be the first step? As the saying goes, life is not a rehearsal: so ask yourself if yours is the kind of performance you can be satisfied with. Encouraging your own visions, connecting with what's important to you, allows you to explore your boundaries, and to discover how to enrich your life now rather than regretting it later.

▶ **Ask yourself what you really value** What qualities or behaviours in yourself and others are important to you? Then ask yourself how closely your life matches these values. Are you living them yourself? Do you make sure you're around other people who live them? If you come up with a lot of 'No' answers, chances are that your sense of being alive in spirit is being compromised. What's the first step you could take to bring your life into closer alignment with your values?

▶ **Let your body help you** Having a more spacious awareness has its physiological dimension, too. Your body is one of your best sources of information about your state of being. Emotional patterns such as holding on to anger, resentment or disappointment will all tend to be reflected or expressed in physiology. How possible is it to be in a state of relaxed awareness, for example, if you are holding your breath, or if your shoulders are tight, or your stomach sour or bloated?

You can pay attention to your physiology and use it as a way of monitoring your spiritual aliveness. When you are feeling at your most alive and most connected with your personal sense of vision, what do you notice in your body? Is it, for example, a feeling of lightness, or swiftness of movement? Do you, as many people have described it, feel that everything is flowing? Do you feel connected? as if you have room to be and to move? Do you see clearly? By contrast, when you feel most out of sorts, do you feel heavy? lethargic? jangly? manic? stuck? slow? Is everything bright and sharp? or is it discordant? Do you feel hemmed in? Noticing what's going on will tell you if you're on track and moving in the right direction. Information like this can be used like a compass to help you pinpoint what you need to do.

When you're sluggish, depressed or off-colour, notice what's producing this. When you're as wound up as a nine-day clock, notice what's producing this. Use your state as a biofeedback mechanism to alert you to changes you need to make. And when you're feeling easy in yourself, able to see the bigger picture and more open, be sure to notice what helps you achieve this. Because this is what you want more of in your life.

EXERCISE: Monitoring the Current Situation

► Spend a few minutes paying attention to how you are feeling right now. Is your body relaxed and alert or tense and uncomfortable?

► How are you currently responding to this feedback? Are you making the most of it and letting it guide you?

► If you have not yet begun to work with the information your state is giving you, what might be the first step you could take right now?

▪ Taking Care At Every Level

When you actively seek to promote states of relaxed awareness, you are giving yourself the best chance of self-healing and of achieving that mix of being in the moment and being congruent with your deeper values which characterises being spiritually alive. Learning and practising one of a number of state-altering skills is one way to make this happen. Meditation, autogenic relaxation techniques, self-hypnosis and yoga are all ways that can help you at this body-mind level. Each produces a state which has been variously called 'focused absentmindedness' and 'restful alertness', characterised by physical calming, changing electrical activity in the brain and the production of endorphins.

So you might want to consider what physical and mental skills you would like to develop to help maintain and restore your well-being. Even if you already have a way of doing this, it's worth asking what else you might do. Often you'll find there are new pleasures you could enjoy at the same time.

Tony was a client who asked for our help in becoming less stressed. His work in a computer software company was highly pressured, and when he was off-duty he lifted weights and played squash. We pointed out that his state was much the same whether he was at work or not: it was characterised by speed, competitiveness and the drive to achieve. His mind and body were always under pressure. As a result he wasn't sleeping well and found it hard to relax. His busy diary held little time for anything spontaneous and his friendships were suffering.

Once Tony understood this, he decided to make some radical changes. He decided that he would set up as an independent consultant, so that he could have more control over the work he took on and the hours he worked; and he booked himself some piano lessons, as this was a skill he had always thought he'd like to learn. Even as a beginner, he found that playing the piano put him into a totally different state of being: one of attentiveness and calm, one which grounded him in the moment and reminded him of a whole dimension of life that he'd hardly given time to before. It wasn't long before he bought himself a piano, so that he could make this experience part of his everyday life.

How to Have an Attitude of Gratitude

Think about the really special moments in your life – your 'peak experiences'. Did you, like many other people, feel a sense of gratitude? This is a very common component of peak experiences, one which is usually linked to that sense of 'something beyond' which characterises being spiritually alive. For some people, it's directly linked to their religious beliefs – a gratitude to God. For others, they may not feel grateful to anything, they may just feel gratitude for their experience. One person described it as 'a sense of thankfulness just for being alive here, this moment, right now'. For some this can be a very prayerful experience: the Christian mystic Meister Eckhart said that the simplest prayer was the words 'Thank you'.

EXERCISE:

Think of a peak experience in your life. Often these are unique moments that stay with you for ever. For some people, it is the birth of their child. Perhaps it was a time when you completed something really important to you, a moment of sudden insight or realisation, a remarkable experience or a time when you had a great appreciation of beauty. Rerun it in your mind. How did you feel? Did you have a sense of connectedness, of wonder, thankfulness or gratitude?

Gifts require receivers. To receive a gift, you have to be open to it. Cultivating the kind of awareness we are talking about is one way to help yourself become open to receive what's on offer. You can begin to do this very simply by pausing long enough to notice and to be present in your experience. For Ian there is a moment just before each meal when this is easy to do. Some people would call this 'saying grace', but he doesn't necessarily say anything. What moments of attentiveness and openness might you create in your life on a regular basis?

The art of experiencing can be cultivated each and every day – whatever may be going on in the rest of your life – if you encourage yourself to stop and notice what the world is offering you.

Being alive in spirit is what crowns and makes meaning of life. It can make us feel that the whole complex world is one rich unity, or that this one special moment, this one particular experience, in some way stands for the whole of human experience. It is perhaps just a question of emphasis. The important thing is that in such moments you can have a most powerful sense of connectedness between yourself as one unique individual and something much larger.

In our experience, NLP shows us that we don't have to wait for these powerful experiences to happen to us: it gives us the tools to cultivate them, to become open to them and to live more fully. We very much hope you will enjoy doing so.

NLP Coaching and Training Courses

If you have found this book of interest you will almost certainly enjoy actually working with an NLP coach. You might even think about becoming one yourself eventually.

To be sure of finding someone who is thoroughly trained you will need to ascertain that they have both extensive NLP training – at both Practitioner and Master Practitioner level – and *specific training as an NLP coach.*

With coaching now the flavour of the month, we urge you to be very careful and check out people's credentials. At the present time, it is very much a case of buyer beware. For this reason, you might want to contact International Teaching Seminars (ITS), whose Director of Training is Ian McDermott. ITS has pioneered NLP coach training and maintains a directory of fully trained coaches which you can access on its website (see below).

Many people who start using some of the NLP tools realise that it would be extremely useful to them to be able to be more proficient with all that NLP has to offer. If you would like to know more about NLP there are certainly plenty of books already available and we have included some in the Bibliography. However, the best way of learning NLP is to do it. Because NLP is skill-based you can learn an awful lot very quickly in hands-on training that gives you the opportunity to practise the how-tos.

ITS is one of a handful of internationally renowned NLP training institutes worldwide. It is also the UK market leader in full-scale NLP training and focuses on the practical applications of NLP. ITS offers numerous short courses and also full-length programmes, including Practitioner, Master Practitioner and Coaching Certification training where you can be trained by Ian McDermott and the best international NLP trainers around the world.

For further information on coaching or NLP check out the ITS website, which contains many articles as well as details of all training and the ITS Coaches directory. If you would like to receive free updates you can do so by e-mail. Just go to the website and give us your e-mail address.

To reach Ian McDermott for coaching or training, or to get further information:
ITS website: www.itsnlp.com
Email: info@itsnlp.com

Alternatively, to receive a free brochure, please call ITS on:
Inside UK: 01268 777125   Fax: 01268 777976
Outside UK: +44 1268 777125   Fax: +44 1268 777976
Or write to:
International Teaching Seminars
ITS House
Webster Court
Webster's Way
Rayleigh
Essex SS6 8JQ

You can contact Wendy Jago at:
3 Wood Lane
Small Dole
Henfield BN5 9YE
England
E-mail: wendyandleo.jago@virgin.net

Bibliography

There is a growing number of books on coaching and several hundred books on NLP, so we've put together a starter bibliography. The NLP titles are drawn from Ian McDermott's books, which cover many of the key areas. We've themed these so that you can pursue particular interests.

Coaching

Coaching: Evoking Excellence in Others, James Flaherty, Butterworth, Heinemann, Boston, 1999

The Inner Game of Tennis, W.Timothy Gallwey, Random House, New York, 1974

The Inner Game of Work, W.Timothy Gallwey, Random House, New York, 2000

A Simpler Way, Margaret Wheatley and Myron Kellner-Rogers, Berret-Koehler, San Francisco, 1996

Coaching for Performance, John Whitmore, Brearley, London, 1992

Co-Active Coaching, Laura Whitworth et al, Davies-Black, Palo Alto, California, 1998

Your Inner Coach, Ian McDermott & Wendy Jago, Piatkus, London, 2003

NLP

Brief introductions to NLP:
Way of NLP, Joseph O'Connor & Ian McDermott, Thorsons, London, 2001
First Directions NLP, Joseph O'Connor & Ian McDermott, Thorsons, London, 2001

Personally applying NLP:
Manage Yourself, Manage Your Life, Ian McDermott & Ian Shircore, Piatkus, London, 1999

NLP & Business:
Practical NLP for Managers, Ian McDermott & Joseph O'Connor, Gower, London, 1996

NLP and the New Manager, Ian McDermott & Ian Shircore, Texere, London, 1998

NLP & Health:
NLP and Health, Ian McDermott & Joseph O'Connor, Thorsons, London, 1996

NLP & Therapy:
Brief NLP Therapy, Ian McDermott & Wendy Jago, Sage, London, 2001

The Systemic Dimension:
The Art of Systems Thinking, Joseph O'Connor & Ian McDermott, Thorsons, London, 1997

Index